JANKO JESENSKÝ

ON THE ROAD
TO FREEDOM
<u>AND</u> FROM CAPTIVITY

Slovak
Literary
Centre

ON THE ROAD TO FREEDOM
Followed by From Captivity

by Janko Jesenský

First published in Slovak as *Cestou k slobode:
Úryvky z denníka 1914–1918* in 1933

Translated from the Slovak and introduced
by Charles S. Kraszewski

This book was published with the financial support
of the SLOLIA Board, Slovak Literary Centre.

Proofreading by Gareth Pugh

Book cover and interior book design by Max Mendor

www.glagoslav.com

ISBN: 978-1-80484-113-6
ISBN: 978-1-80484-114-3

First published in English by Glagoslav Publications in November 2023

A catalogue record for this book is available from the British Library.

JANKO JESENSKÝ

ON THE ROAD
TO FREEDOM
AND FROM CAPTIVITY

TRANSLATED FROM THE SLOVAK AND INTRODUCED
BY CHARLES S. KRASZEWSKI

GLAGOSLAV PUBLICATIONS

CONTENTS

INTRODUCTION

On the Road to Himself: Janko Jesenský's Memoirs and Poems from Russian Captivity

Charles S. Kraszewski

The story of the Czechoslovak Legions, of which Janko Jesenský's *On the Road to Freedom* [Cestou k slobode, 1933] is one of many eyewitness accounts, is a foundational myth of the modern Czech and Slovak states. I use 'myth' here in the original sense of the word – meaning an account of a heroic truth expressing a community's core significance, intended to remain in the consciousness of that community and inform, with pride, subsequent generations of their identity, preserving in them the ideals of those enshrined in the myth. Books like *On the Road to Freedom* are important, especially since myths are no less susceptible to the whims of those in power, who often twist their meaning, eviscerating the truth they present to suit their own purposes.

For example, one of the proudest moments of the Czechoslovaks' anabasis through Russia, briefly mentioned in Jesenský's memoir, is the Battle of Zborów in Galicia (now Zboriv in Ukraine), which took place on 1–2 July 1917. The gallantry of the volunteers was so great – indeed, they were fighting for their lives[1] – that Kerensky's government au-

....

[1] In Wadowice near Kraków (the birthplace of Karol Wojtyła, later

thorised the formation of additional Legions under direct Czechoslovak command, autonomous of the Russian Army. This saw their numbers swell to between thirty and sixty thousand soldiers.[2] Following the war and the establishment of the Czechoslovak Republic, it was from here that, with the help of the officials of the Republic of Poland, a Czech Legionnaire was exhumed and transferred with honour to Prague, where his remains were laid to rest in the chapel of the Old Town Hall on the Staroměstské Náměstí as the first Tomb of the Unknown Czechoslovak Soldier.[3] I say 'first' because soon after the Nazis occupied the Czech lands in 1939, the tomb was dismantled, at night, and the remains disposed of in an unknown location. Jan Galandauer surmises that they were unceremoniously dumped into the Vltava.

Following the Second World War, another soldier was exhumed and transported to Prague, with more difficulty this time, as Zborov (the Czech name of the village) was now located within the borders of the Soviet Union, and the Soviets did not look too kindly upon the Legions in Russia, who had fought most of their battles, on their roundabout way

....

Pope St John Paul II), two Czechs who had fought in the ranks of the Russian Army were executed for treason in December 1914. Four years later, near the end of the war in June 1918, thirty-nine Czechoslovak Legionnaires captured by the Austrians on the Italian front were put to death. See Petr Jokeš, *Czesi: Przewodnik po historii narodu i państwa* [A Guide to the History of the Nation and the State] (Kraków: Avalon, 2020), p. 268.

[2] A (rather outdated) *Area Handbook for Czechoslovakia,* eds. Eugene K. Keefe, et al. (Washington: U.S. Government Printing Office, 1972), p. 38, suggests the lesser number; Jokeš (p. 267) puts their number at sixty thousand in Russia alone.

[3] This, and all information concerning the Unknown Solider and the Memorial on Vitkov, I take from Jan Galandauer, *Chrám bez boha nad Prahou. Památník na Vítkově* [A Cathedral Without God. The Memorial on Vitkov Hill] (Prague: Havran, 2014).

home, against the Bolsheviks. And anyway, the Memorial on Vitkov Hill, with its towering equestrian statue of Jan Žižka, was soon diverted from its original use – a memorial to the Czechoslovak Legions – into a rather ghoulish mausoleum for Communist dignitaries, the centrepiece of which was a glass coffin in which the poorly embalmed corpse of Klement Gottwald was displayed until nature and politics had their way and his mortal remains had to be removed and cremated.

Today, in the independent Czech Republic, the Monument on Vitkov has been returned to its original purpose. At its centre may be found the tomb of the unknown soldier and a memorial in honour of the Czechoslovak Legionnaires, including 'rings' of earth from each battlefield where they shed their blood in sacrificial devotion to a state that was just being born, with difficulty.

Monuments surround us. The memorialisation of the past is one of the things that sets us humans apart from other animals. They range from the communal to the personal, from monuments to the Slovak National Uprising of 1944, for example, of which there are at least two here in Banská Štiavnica, one of them literally metres away from where I am writing these lines, to the personal, and for most people insignificant – such as the birth certificate of my grandmother, for which I wrote just the other day to the records department in Spišské Vlachy. What they all have in common – the celebratory and the mundane – is that they are testimonies to the truth. This particular person came into the world in this particular town on this particular day; these particular people accomplished this significant achievement, and where and when.

Horace suggests that, in his poems, he has 'built a monument more durable than brass.'[4] This has certainly been

....

[4]   Horace, Ode 30, Book III: *Exegi monumentum aere perennius.*

proven true in his case, and should be true in the case of all literary monuments testifying to the truth, such as Janko Jesenský's *On the Road to Freedom.* The crucial importance of these seemingly flimsy, yet stubbornly enduring, monuments, which are books and other scraps of paper, was made evident to me today, by chance.

It was during a walk up Kalvária here in Banská Štiavnica. To the right of the path, on the slope as you approach the first church, lies a little grave. It's easy to miss, unless a wreath or some flowers have been left upon it to catch your eye. I noticed it before but never went over to have a closer look. Today, coming back down, I walked over and read, on the tasteful granite slab with the elaborate state symbol of the old Czechoslovak Republic, that this was the grave of František Brož (1897–1919), a Czech soldier of the 94th Czechoslovak regiment, 'who died defending Slovakia.' This chance meeting with the grave of a hero of the Czechoslovak Legions brought vividly to my mind a passage from the latter chapters of Jesenský's book, in which, after the establishment of the Provisional Czechoslovak Government in Prague following the end of hostilities in Western Europe, with the Russian Civil War still hanging in the balance, some of Jesenský's comrades began to grumble:

> 'All of the Allied states have acknowledged all lands occupied by Slovaks to form an integral, indivisible part of the one Czechoslovak state. This being the case, the Hungarian government had no right to declare any such armistice as would bind the Slovak regions. The borders of the Czechoslovak and Magyar states shall be determined at the peace conference.'
>
> There you go! And here we are, stuck here, instead of settling our accounts at home with the Magyars.[5] A peace

....

[5] Slovaks and Magyars (called 'Hungarians' in English, although in

conference has been called for the beginning of the new year, and here we are spilling our blood!

For the surrender of the Central Powers, whatever that meant for faraway lands such as Great Britain or the United States, was only an intermission of sorts for those old nations, becoming established as new states, carved from the empires of Prussia, Austria-Hungary, and Russia. Here, hostilities did not necessarily end, as armed forces more often than plebiscites began to determine where new borders, supposedly redrawn according to ethnic data, were to be placed.

The elaborate Catholic shrine of Kalvária, a pious goal of pilgrims in Banská Štiavnica, occupies one of the higher hills overlooking the town. It is in this context – Czechoslovak resistance to the incursions of the Magyar troops of Béla Kun's Magyar Soviet Republic – that František Brož met his death. Along with another soldier, Brož was stationed in one of the towers of the lower church on 6 June 1919 as a lookout, when a missile fired by the Magyar troops impacted the tower, killing him outright and gravely wounding his comrade.[6]

Following the successful defence of Banská Štiavnica by Czechoslovak troops under the command of Jozef Šnejdrák, the troops were soon called to Zvolen, and for this reason, perhaps, Brož was hastily buried on the slopes of the holy

....

the past this term was applied to all inhabitants of the Habsburg Kingdom of Hungary: Magyars and Slovaks, Croatians and Romanians) share a long and, since the nineteenth century at least, contentious history. For an account of this from the Slovak side, see Ľudovít Štúr, *Slavdom. A Selection of his Writings in Prose and Verse* (London: Glagoslav, 2021).

[6] Anonymous, 'Banská Štiavnica – Kalvária,' <https://kriz.epocha.sk/banska-stiavnica-kalvaria> [accessed 4 December 2021]. The name of the wounded soldier, who died later, is not recorded in any of the sources I consulted.

mountain.[7] Things became complicated in 2015 when, for reasons unclear, the former Slovak ambassador to Russia, Jozef Migaš, a left-leaning and rather controversial figure in Slovak politics, arranged for the grave – which up until then had been merely a mound of grass marked with a cross – to be covered with a simple granite slab identifying the remains below to be those of an 'Unknown Soldier of the Red Army, Our Liberator'[8] crowned by a bright red star. This, obviously, was a shock to many of the longtime residents of Banská Štiavnica, who remember quite clearly that the grave had been there long before the Red Army 'liberated' that portion of Czechoslovakia near the end of the Second World War. Valéria Bernáthová, who has lived in the town since her birth in 1927, recalled visiting the grave with her mother as a child and placing flowers on it in memory of her own uncle, who died in the war on the Yugoslav front. Ľudovít Dupal, who photographed the burial of all Red Army soldiers who fell during the battle for Banská Štiavnica in 1945, was even more vociferous in his objections to the supposition of a Russian buried in the grave on Calvary: 'I'll take poison if there's a Red Army soldier buried there.'[9] Dupal's testimony is among the most interesting offered in Daniel Vražda's article on the question of the soldier's identity:

....

[7]   Martin Macharík, cited by Daniel Vražda, 'Z neznámeho vojaka urobili Migaš s Rusmi červenoarmejca' [Migaš and the Russians Turned the Unknown Soldier into a Red Army Soldier], *Denník N* (9 July 2015), <https://dennikn.sk/182872/z-neznameho-vojaka-urobili-migas-s-rusmi-cervenoarmejca/> [accessed 4 December 2021].

[8]   *Neznámy Vojak – Červenoarmejec – Osloboditel.*

[9]   *Na to zoberiem jed, že tam neleží červenoarmejec.* This, and all other quotes from the residents of Banská Štiavnica, are taken from Daniel Vražda's article, op. cit.

JANKO JESENSKÝ

My father always said that a soldier from the First World War lay here. I remember him saying to me once, 'Look – the same thing might have happened to me' […] But you know what's interesting? All the while the Communists were in power [in Czechoslovakia] there was no such [Red Army] memorial there.

Oľga Kuchtová is another resident of the town who remembers her father speaking of the fallen soldier as a Czechoslovak killed during World War One:

I stamped my foot [when I saw it]; I was covered with a cold sweat; I couldn't believe my eyes. To change the identity of any deceased person and to disgrace such a sacred place is simply not right. They ought to take this shameful thing in hand and return the grave to its original appearance. And I also think an apology is in order.

One can only imagine what Brož himself might have thought of the desecration of his grave. He, who fought against Bolsheviks and indeed died at the hands of Communists, was now identified as a Red Army soldier! That granite slab must have lain heavy upon him indeed.

Justice was finally done in early 2017, when the false (sacrilegious, in both a religious and a historical sense) grave slab was removed, to be replaced by the present one, testifying to truth. This truth was only arrived at due to the determined labour of Daniel Vražda and his colleagues, who, by patient and dogged research at archives, military and civilian, in the Czech Republic, were able to certify that indeed, this was no Red Army soldier, but František Brož (vel Brosch), from the village of Mnichovo Hradiště, in the Mladá Boleslav region of north-west Czechia, a Czechoslovak Legionnaire who fought against the Bolsheviks in Russia and died at the hands of their Magyar Communist allies in Banská Štiavnica. His resting place is now covered by a granite slab bearing the great seal of the Czechoslovak state he helped into existence, with all of its historical regions of Bohemia, Moravia, Slovakia, Silesia, and Carpathian Rus represented.

Such an importance little slips of paper in village archives may have.

CENTRAL EUROPE AND THE IDEA OF HEROISM

The English-speaking reader who takes this book in hand is sure to contextualise it with the literature of the First World War with which he or she is familiar. These include the youthfully enthusiastic poems of Rupert Brooke – a much, much better poet than his familiar 'The Soldier' ('If I should die, think only this of me: / That there's some corner of a foreign field / That is forever England') would lead one to believe, Wilfred Owens' familiar, bitter 'Dulce et decorum est' and Robert Graves' similarly sardonic *Goodbye to All That*. The greatest American work of the World War One years is certainly E.E. Cummings' good-humoured memoir *The Enormous Room*. Every nation that participated in the great slaughter has its literary fruits, most of which, one reckons, the authors wish they never had never been given the occasion to write – to mention just one more from the 'other side,' anyone interested in the literature of that period ought certainly to look into the war poems of the great Austrian expressionist, Georg Trakl.

But what sets apart the great majority of writings from Czech and Slovak authors of the period, and this includes of course, the present book, is the unfeigned distaste of authors like Janko Jesenský and his erstwhile companion in the Czechoslovak Legions, Jaroslav Hašek, to the Habsburg regime, to which as soldiers of the Austro-Hungarian forces, they had sworn their fealty. Jesenský has no stake in the government at Budapest, to say nothing of Vienna; when he becomes separated from his unit during one of the only firefights mentioned in his book, he doesn't spend much time wondering *if* he should desert, but *when* would be the most propitious moment for doing so. In Hašek's short story 'Osudy Pana Hurta' [Pan Hurt's Destiny], published in the legionnaire journal *Čechoslovan* in 1916 before the author's *second* desertion to the ranks of the Bolsheviks, we read the account of a Czech unit of the Austrian army crossing the lines to captivity:

> Before he knew it, he intimated the sad truth. His brigade was disengaging from the enemy, and the remnant of his company was to remain and keep on firing until... He didn't finish his thought, because Cadet Holava completed it beautifully for him: 'And our job is to stick around and let them kill us.'
>
> After a long, long time had passed, and it all grew quiet again, Cadet Holava spoke up once more. 'You know what, boys? Each of us is supposed to be issued a hundred more cartridges. But if we just set them aside, and lie down, and not shoot, the Russians'll let us alone.'
>
> This was much to Pan Hurt's liking. How long he slept, he didn't know. However, when he heard the thunderous cry 'Hurrah!' from before and behind, he grabbed his gun and crawled out of his hiding place.
>
> Suddenly, he was face to face with a Russian soldier and his bayonet. To his great surprise, the smiling soldier addressed him quite good-naturedly in Czech: 'Set that popgun aside, mate, or I'll give you what for.'
>
> And whenever Pan Hurt would speak of his time in captivity, he always began with the words, 'So I set my popgun aside... and we marched off to Russia. I caught up with Cadet Holava and said, "So then, we've been

captured," and he replied, "Obviously. I've been waiting on this for three whole months.'"[10]

The account is a fictional one, and yet it is plausible, since the Czechs – at least since 1620 the nation in the empire most inimical to Vienna – and the Slovaks – who had even more reasons to disengage from Magyar-dominated Budapest – saw the war as their best chance at freeing themselves from 'foreign' oppression and establishing an independent state. They had few qualms, if any, about deserting the ranks and seeking a better lot with their Russian 'brethren.' As Slovak journalist Milan Getting put it:

> The long-awaited time had come when something was to happen. What this something would be no one dared to express in words, but in the heart of every loyal Slovak there was a feeling that this something would be done by the Russians... From the very first day of the war our sympathies were on the side of the Triple Entente Powers.[11]

The Czechs and the Slovaks, unlike their kindred nation, the Poles, traditionally looked toward Russia, the 'big Slavic brother' in the East, as a potential protector and liberator from the German and Magyar majorities that stifled their national aspirations at home. While the architect of the modern Polish state, Marshal Józef Piłsudski, aligned his volunteers with Austria against the Russians (Poles have long known what 'brotherhood' with Russia signifies), the rather naive

....

[10] Jaroslav Hašek, 'Pan Hurt's Destiny,' in *The Secret History of my Sojourn in Russia* (London: Glagoslav, 2017), p. 63.

[11] Milan Getting, cited in Blanka Ševčík Glos and George E. Glos, *Czechoslovak Troops in Russia and Siberia During the First World War* (New York: Vantage, 2000), p. 9.

traditions of Pan-Slavism were quite popular in the Czech and Slovak lands. When the morning comes, and Jesenský finally determines on crossing over to the Russians, he does so, crying out: 'Don't shoot! I'm a Slav!' – which perfectly encapsulates the attitude of most of his Pan-Slav comrades: genetics trumps politics; the Russians are better, 'righter,' because they are 'mine,' while the Austrians are to be rejected solely on the basis of their foreignness. It is, of course, one of the ironies of history that, had the successor to the Habsburg throne, Franz Ferdinand, not been murdered in Sarajevo, he, and his morganatic Czech wife, might have reformed the Empire to Jesenský's liking, as Franz Ferdinand, murdered by Slavic nationalists, was (unlike his uncle Franz Joseph) rather inimically inclined to the Magyars, and fairly pro-Slav.[12]

KDE DOMOV MÔJ? WHERE (INDEED) IS MY HOMELAND?

Speaking of the Staroměstské Náměstí, or Old Town Square, in Prague, the tourist standing at the Prague Meridian and gazing up at the Mariánský Sloup, or Marian Column, that acts as a gnomon casting the shadow whereby 'Prague time' was measured by astronomers since 1652, might suppose that it has always stood where it soars today: between the bastion of mediaeval Catholicism which is the Church of our Lady Before Týn and its contradiction; Vladislav Šaloun's over-

....

[12] For this, see David Fromkin, *Europe's Last Summer: Who Started the Great War in 1917?* (New York: Vintage, 2007): 'According to [...] informants, it was the belief of the conspirators that Franz Ferdinand advocated 'trialism': he intended to make the Slavs full partners in government along with Austro-Germans and Hungarians [*i.e. Magyars*.... And yet the Serb Gavrilo] Princip, who killed Franz Ferdinand, did so for a muddle of misinformed reasons. Although the Archduke was the most pro-Slav member of the Habsburg hierarchy, the youth believed that he was anti-Slav.' (pp. 122, 261.)

large monument to Jan Hus across the way. And yet what we see there today is but a fairly exact modern replica of the original Baroque image set up and consecrated on 15 August 2020 to replace the original, which had been torn down on 3 November 1918 by a mob led by Franta Sauer (1882–1947), an anarchist from Žižkov with a moustache unfortunately similar to that made infamous by Adolf Hitler. In her *Prague Panoramas*, Cynthia Paces describes Sauer's motivations in this way:

> The destruction of the Marian Column was nonetheless a creative act. Sauer-Kysela wanted to make Prague a truly new capital city, free from the icons of the former regime [...] New life also involves death. The peaceful, even anticlimactic Czechoslovak independence movement lacked the cathartic bloodshed Sauer-Kysela admired from his French and Russian revolutionary heroes; thus, he symbolically invented the destruction and rebirth of Prague [...] Sauer-Kysela gave no address in Old Town Square, but let the monuments send his message. Fallen and shattered, the Marian Column said that political Catholicism would no longer be tolerated; it was of the old world, and its fragments belonged in a museum. Towering now over the square alone, the Jan Hus Memorial, emblem of the Hussite movement long admired by Czech socialists for its tolerance and egalitarianism, proclaimed the message of the social revolutionaries.[13]

Whether or not bloodshed can ever be 'cathartic,' or the iconoclasm of any group of ideologues 'admirable;' whether or not 'new life' necessarily demands 'death'– these are questions

[13] Cynthia Paces, *Prague Panoramas. National Memory and Sacred Space in the Twentieth Century* (Pittsburgh: University of Pittsburgh Press, 2009), p. 94.

we needn't go into now, as they are beyond the scope of our present essay. But despite the academic Newspeak so familiar from the most recent outbursts of righteous indignation directed at granite and bronze,[14] Paces' comments succinctly reveal the motivations behind the Czechs' destruction of the Marian Column in particular, and their distaste of all things Austrian and Catholic in general. Although the Czech lands had formed a part of the Holy Roman Empire since the Middle Ages, and for a short time in the fourteenth century Prague had even been the seat of Emperor Charles IV, tensions between Czechs and Germans, Hussites and Catholics, local nobility and the emperor, had been seething since long before the decisive battle of White Mountain in 1620, which cemented Habsburg rule in Bohemia and Moravia until the fateful year of 1918 and the establishment of the independent First Czechoslovak Republic. People's memories are both long and selective. It is just such ancient grudges that animated Jaroslav Hašek – Jesenský's Legionary comrade and

....

[14] Of course, every generation and every ideology has a tendency to take a hammer to the monuments of their predecessors. In my own beloved Kraków, from my student years I remember well the monument to the Red Army that used to stand near St Florian's Gate and the plaque set in the wall of a building along Szewska Street, indicating where Lenin had rented a room once when passing through the city. No trace of these remain today. Contemporary discussions concerning such things basically revolve around how the removal of memorials from the public square will skew how history is taught in the future. A more interesting quandary is posed by the reestablishment of statues once toppled, and the effect their reappearance may have on art and history created in the interim of their absence. For example, since the Marian Column is again standing in the Old Town Square, will any future readers catch the allusion to its absence in the long poem *Půdorys města* [City Plan, 1968] by the Czech Catholic poet Rio Preisner? 'Ale jestli ztrácíš rovnováhu, Mařenko, / z té výškové stavby beznaděje…' [But if you lose your balance, Mařenka, / atop that soaring structure of hopelessness…]

Sauer's drinking buddy – to construct the initial thrust of his comic masterpiece *The Good Soldier Švejk* as a literary battering ram directed at the two 'foreign' pillars of Austrianism and Catholicism, and Sauer himself to literally knock down an actual column that – unlike the definition he gave it – had nothing to do with Austrian Counter-Reformational triumphalism over Slavic, Czech Hussitism, but was rather a votive offering set up in thanksgiving for Prague being spared an invasion of the Swedes during the 'deluge' of the mid-seventeenth century. Although modern migration patterns and the overexuberant multiculturalism of the European Union is challenging the idea of the European nation-state, we have grown so used to the Wilsonian map of the continent as to be startled at the freshness of Petr Jokeš' assessment of the situation of the Czech nation in the Empire at the outset of the war:

> The Czechs weren't quite in love with the monarchy, but at the outset of the war, no one in the Czech lands seriously considered separation from it. Austria-Hungary was a state in which the Czechs were well capable of functioning. Czech politics at the time sought to improve the nation's situation within the framework of the existing state, not to shatter it. This attitude was made all the easier by virtue of the fact that, practically speaking, the entire Czech nation was found within the borders of the monarchy, and so the Czechs – in contrast to the Poles, (and Romanians and Serbs for that matter) – were not faced with solving the problem of reuniting a nation divided between several powers.[15]

....

[15] Jokeš, p. 262.

Why, indeed, were the Czechs so eager to punch out of Austria? It's a question well worth asking. Histories both old and new suggest that the breakup of Austria-Hungary in 1918 was far from predetermined. 'The Austrian Emperor [Blessed Karl I Habsburg], in an effort to stabilize conditions [...] declared Austria a federal state in which the Czechs and Slovaks, as well as other minority groups, were granted autonomy. Revolutionary action, however, had progressed too rapidly and too far to accept anything less than full independence from Austrian control.' Thus the authors of that 1972 *Area Handbook*.[16] Nearly half a century later, the Czech author Petr Jokeš writes in a similar vein:

> Right after assuming the throne, Karl committed a faux pas in regard to the Czechs. Under pressure from István Tisza, the prime minister of Hungary, he had himself quite swiftly crowned King of Hungary, while never accepting the Crown of Bohemia. The Czechs read this as a clear signal: the monarchy is going to continue to give preference to the Magyars. If at the beginning of the war practically no one gave serious thought to separation from Austria-Hungary, as the war progressed such ideas began to appear with ever greater frequency in the Czech lands. Karl I had a chance to change this – but he did not take advantage of it.[17]

Once the centripetal force was set spinning, it was impossible for the centre to hold. And so, in the words of that (so anomalous a phenomenon!) Austrophile Czech poet Rio Preisner: 'Throughout its entire existence the Austrian monarchy was bound to the preservation of the cultural and political integ-

....

[16] Keefe, et al., p. 38.

[17] Jokeš, p. 266.

rity of Central Europe, in opposition to Germany and Russia. Its tragedy was that both the Germans and the Russians understood, and to a certain extent respected, this task of hers, whereas the nations that constituted Austria did not.'[18]

It would be unforgivably flippant, and supremely ignorant, to suggest that early twentieth-century Czech tendencies for independence from Vienna were based on hurt feelings. But although one can draw up a balance sheet of sorts, setting advantages versus disadvantages, and pose Jokeš' insightful *cui bono?* and even *quantum bonum?* in regard to Czech independence, in the case of Janko Jesenský's Slovakia, the matter is more clear-cut. That Hungarian crown worn by the Habsburg emperors signified an ethnic mix even more complicated than that of the Germans, Poles, Czechs, and Slovenes in Austria. Here, Slovaks, Serbs, Romanians and Croats co-existed with Magyars, the dominant ethnic group even more determined than the Germans in Austria to impose their language and their culture on the state.

The Magyars had arrived in Central Europe in the early Middle Ages, around the ninth and tenth centuries, from Central Asia. The Magyar language – like Turkish and Finnish – is not related to the Indo-European group. Assimilation with the Slavs and other European peoples came about quickly; the Magyars converted to Christianity, and an early king, Stephen I (c. 975–1038) is a national saint especially venerated in both Hungary and Slovakia. Although the Magyar language was greatly influenced by Slavic loan words (especially in the areas of agriculture and terms associated with permanent settlement), the language itself continued to be cultivated, and by the nineteenth century had become the distinctive determinant of ethnic identity. At the risk of

....

[18] Rio Preisner, *Až na konec Česka* [Unto the Very End of Czechia] (London: Rozmluvy, 1987), p. 238.

over-simplifying matters, one might say that, given centuries of living side-by-side, worshipping the same God and engaging in common political and cultural activities, a certain amalgamation of peoples occurred in the Hungarian Kingdom, and adherence to the Magyar language and other cultural distinctions became a matter of choice, if not to say opportunism, for many. For example, the architect of the modern Hungarian nation-state, Lajos Kossuth (1802–1894) came of Slovak Lutheran stock and, while he himself was inveterately opposed to Slovak tradition and nationality, his uncle Juraj Košút (1776–1849) was a Slovak patriot.

By Jesenský's time, Magyar demands had grown to an oppressive head. Not only was the Magyar tongue forced through in mid-century as the administrative language of the Kingdom,[19] replacing the earlier compromise of Latin, but a series of restrictive policies were enacted throughout Hungary tending towards the Magyarisation of the entire population. And whereas Kossuth made some concessions toward the Romanians and Croats, he refused to even recognise the Slovaks, among whom the policies of Magyarisation were most fiercely directed, in both civic and ecclesiastical spheres, in an attempt to stamp out Slovak language and culture. As Ľudovít Štúr argues in his 1843 article 'Jazykový boj v Uhorsku' [The Language Battle in Hungary]:

> The Slavs do not complain that the Magyar language was elevated to the administrative language, replacing Latin; they are sorely pained only at the arbitrary results that arise from this, such as the officials of the administration using Magyar also in their relations with the Slavs who

....

[19] In effect, the imposition of the Magyar tongue, spoken by 2,000,000 citizens, on the 5,000,000 non-Magyar population of the Kingdom. See Ioan Lupaş, 'The Hungarian Policy of Magyarization,' *Bulletin of the Center for Transylvanian Studies*, Vol. 1, No. 1 (1991), p. 7.

know no other language save their mother tongue, and how the courts and all matters related to legal issues are executed only in Magyar even in regions that are entirely inhabited by Slavs. The result of this – as anyone can easily understand – will be absurd, awkward, and messy for the Slavs. In a country where there are many millions of Slavs, they wish to completely ignore the Slavic tongue in courts, and accept no petitions composed in Slavic![20]

Paranoid Magyar policy[21] went so far as even to ban a popular children's periodical, the *Noviny pre naše dietky* [Newspaper for Our Children] as a 'harmful' publication that 'tries to nip in the bud love and loyalty towards the Hungarian homeland.'[22] Behind this rather comic absurdity lies the chilling reality of policies which, however 'gentle,' can only be described in categories of ethnic cleansing. In 1874, the very year of Janko Jesenský's birth, the government of Hungary enacted an official policy of forcibly relocating orphans and children deemed impoverished from their families to 'pure Magyar districts.'[23] It is no wonder that, in the fateful year of 1848, during that 'Spring of the Peoples' when the Magyars sought

....

[20] Ľudovít Štúr, 'Jazykový boj v Uhorsku,' in his *Diela* [Works], ed. Rudolf Chmel (Bratislava: Kalligram / Ústav Slovenskej Literatúry SAV, 2007), p. 45.

[21] Raymond Pearson speaks of a 'psychological disposition' among the Magyars 'towards what might be tritely called "insecurity-based aggression."' Seamus Dunn and T.G. Fraser (eds.), *Europe and Ethnicity: The First World War and Contemporary Ethnic Conflict* (London: Routledge, 2005), p. 89.

[22] Eleonóra Babejová, *Fin-de-siècle Pressburg: Conflict and Cultural Coexistence in Bratislava 1897–1914* (New York: Columbia University Press, 2003), p. 202.

[23] Gilbert L. Oddo, *Slovakia and its People* (New York: Robert Speller and Sons, 1960), p. 145.

to establish their own independence from Vienna, Slovak volunteers rushed to the (Austrian) colours in the hopes that their loyalty to the crown would result in autonomy from a Budapest that sought to re-engineer their souls out of their native ethnicity; it is no wonder that the Slovaks of the early twentieth century held fast to the ideals of the *národné obrodenie* [national revival] movement of the previous century, which bade them turn their eyes both to the west – toward political unity with their close kin, the Czechs – and to the east – to the great 'Slavic' empire of Russia, as possible rescue. The former of these tendencies was to result in success; as to the latter – Jesenský's *On the Road to Freedom* and the poems from the volume *Zo zajatia* [From Captivity] provide a record of his hopes and disenchantment.

This Magyar-Slovak tension is what we should keep in mind when we read the entertaining account of Jesenský's 'first case,' sparked by the furore he gave rise to at his ultra-Slavic appearance in Bánovce:

> What the?! What's with the Pan-Slav! Instead of saying *kissaszonka* for 'little miss,' he says *slečna!* For 'I kiss your hands' he pops off with *ruky bozkávam* instead of *kezítcsókolom*; calls himself *služobník* for 'your humble servant' and not *alászolgája*, and when you say 'Praise the Lord,' *dicsértesék*, he comes back at you with *naveky ameň*, 'for ever and ever,' just as he should, but... in Slovak!

Humorous, for sure. A good sense of humour is characteristic of the tone of *On the Road to Freedom*. But this is much more than a funny story. Jesenský causes a fluster not on account of *what* he says, which is all right and proper – and which should be the only important thing, – but *how* he says it, in Slovak, and not in Magyar. That's what gets him into trouble. It's senseless – just as senseless as the division of people into separate communities (which is probably inevitable) and mutually inimical ones (which should never happen) on the basis of a different ethnolect. It is an irony of history that the first printing of *On the Road to Freedom* took place in the fateful year of 1933 – when the Nazis came to power in Germany; men who were about to precipitate the worst continent-wide slaughter in modern history on the basis of this very faulty syllogism: You do not speak the same language I do, therefore, you are different from me, and thus we are enemies.

The same concentration on the folk – given great impetus in the early romantic period by the Slavophile German author Herder, which resulted in the preservation of so many indigenous cultures in a Europe dominated by great empires – was weaponised in the twentieth century, by men of the same nation (and others, too) as elements in 'racial' warfare.

Despite the fact that certain initial symptoms of the coming conflagration were already perceptible during the period covered by Jesenský's narrative – the fledgling Polish state was fighting successful border wars on an ethnic basis in both the west (the Great Polish Uprising) and the east (the Polish-Ukrainian War), and armed conflicts between Slovaks and Hungarians, such as the aforementioned battle of Banská Štiavnica were underway – the great bloodbath was still far in the future. So far, as a matter of fact, that – again, irony of history! – one of the Hungarians in the group of notables at Bánovce who 'distanced himself from the local attorney Dr. Janko Jesenský, later a famous Slovak writer, known in those times as "a public Pan-Slav"' was none other than the local priest – later Monsignor – Josef Tiso (1887–1947), head of the collaborationist Slovak Republic following the collapse of Czechoslovakia in 1939.[24]

....

[24]   Aliaksandr Piahanau, 'A Priest at the Front. Jozef Tiso Changing Social Identities in the First World War,' *Revue des études slaves*, Vol. 88, Issue 4, p. 737.

That said – and this is a point I believe worth dwelling on, later – there is very little ethnic animosity to be found in Jesenský's writing. Although he notes down a conversation with his Magyar fellow-POW Geréb to exemplify the basic intransigence of Magyars toward the very idea of Slovak autonomy, the conversation is recorded in measured, friendly terms, and Jesenský himself does not cease to fraternise with Magyars – even, after some hesitation (because of his own sense of inexpertise), teaching them Russian. When 'racial' expressions raise their head in Jesenský's narrative, they do not arise from any pseudo-scientific prejudice or hatred, but rather descriptively:

> I was pinched by an inner discord. There was this kind of general grumbling inside me – like Jews at prayer in a synagogue. This one bellows, that one bellows back, and again the grumbling. The noise grows. The voices increase, and the gesticulations are ever more numerous, ever faster, until you think they're going to start tearing at each other's hair...

We, who live after Auschwitz (and after Monsignor Tiso, whose collaborationist regime sent so many thousands of Slovak Jews to their deaths there), wince when coming across passages such as these, of which there are several in *On the Road to Freedom*. But Jesenský is not indulging in what we might term racist speech here; he is reaching for a metaphor – one that may seem to us as inappropriate as it is vivid – but nothing more. It may be difficult for us to process such speech today, but it was widespread at the time – 'Such a village-market Jew he is,' the Russian Timofei Ivanich exclaims to Jesenský in reference to another Russian, in reference to his stinginess – and as unpleasant as it may be to some readers, we cannot bowdlerise texts in the same way as we tear down (and put back up again) the monuments that decorate, or befoul, our public squares. Although our times are more sensitive to any sort of speech that stereotypes other groups of people and we strive to eschew it ourselves, we should not judge the thoughts or speech patterns of people who predate our sensitivities by the measure of our own times. Likewise, in reference to another identifiable minority in the Slovakia (or Hungary) of his days, the Roma, or 'Gypsies,' Jesenský employs another stereotype as he twists and turns on his prison cot wondering how he might make some extra money in the camp: 'What good is a lawyer's education here? If only I were a cobbler or a tailor, or at least a Gypsy musician. There's a pass to the good life, with boots... A fee for sewing trousers – and music for the sobbing soul is always in demand.' The reference to 'Gypsy musicians' is a stereotype, and perhaps again, one such as the more sensitive among us in the third decade of the twenty-first century might wish to avoid. But it must be admitted that it is not a denigrating stereotype, and Jesenský would probably be surprised at anyone taking offence at it. After all, on the ocean passage from Siberia, he too is the object of a similar stereotype, when an Italian officer is 'miffed' at the Czechoslovaks, suggesting that 'we should be ashamed of ourselves that none of us savages played any instrument, and we from a nation so famed for its musicians!'[25]

It is often said that books are windows onto other worlds. The truth of this statement becomes vividly apparent when we consider writings such as Jesenský's memoirs, which predate, almost by a hundred years, our rapidly expanding multicultural society. If we keep in mind the explosion of access to information from all over the world that has resulted (for

....

[25]   This is not just a reference to Dvořák and Janaček. There is a (stereotypical) saying: 'Co Čech to muzikant' [Every Czech's a musician], which is similar in meaning to the (stereotypical) Polish saying: 'Wherever two Poles gather, there are three opinions.'

good and not so good) from the technological revolution of the late twentieth century, the immediacy with which we can access, not just words, but images – sounds and moving pictures – from all over the world, and add to that the frequency with which so many of us travel the globe, I reckon that we can muster some understanding for a man in 1918 travelling beyond the immediate borders of his country for the first time – and because of a war – gaping at sights he never dreamed that he would see. Consider his description of the pier at Yokohama, as the Italian liner Roma drops anchor:

> Until they let us disembark, we walked around, gazing at these [people] and at the shore. The port was a model of cleanliness. Rows of delivery vans constantly rolled up. Japanese with some sort of loops on their backs, in blue caftans, unloaded the goods with a fantastic alacrity. Japanese women stood near the sacks with needle and thread in hand to stitch up any that had been torn. Others, dressed in brighter colours, with high hair-dos, in wooden clogs, most of them carrying children, strolled about the shore. They kept their hands plunged into their broad sleeves and seemed unapproachable. But they looked at us, and we looked at them, both with curiosity.

This is description, not evaluation. Before we wag our heads at Jesenský for indulging in exoticism, it is good to remind ourselves of the fact that this *was* exotic to him; for concentrating on the differences between people – that these differences exist, and were even more striking back then than they are now, due to the context in which the writer found himself. Before we shake our finger at the (now) dead white European male for gazing at the Japanese as if he were visiting a zoo, we ought to remind ourselves of the fact that cage bars are transparent both ways: *they looked at us, and we looked at them, both with curiosity.*

In short, considering the particular cultural context of Slovak-Magyar antagonism that we describe above, Janko Jesenský's *On the Road to Freedom* is remarkable for how little (anachronistically speaking) 'racist' speech is to be found in it. That there are, however, hints of the coming age of catastrophe, and that he senses them, is obvious. Two of the most blood-curdling examples of this occur during the so-called anabasis of the Czechoslovak Legions, when, freed of both POW camps and Russian oversight, they are on their way to Vladivostok along the trans-Siberian railways. The first:

> Some of our echelons were at the station in Chelyabinsk. They were supposed to head east. There were also some trains there with Austro-Hungarian POWs, the majority of whom were Magyars and Germans; these were heading west. One of these POW trains was already speeding away, when one of the POWs threw a piece of iron at one of our volunteers and hit him right in the head, as a result of which he fell down, stunned. Our men stopped that train and made the POWs hand over the guilty party – whom they killed on the spot in their anger.

This episode is so fraught with horror, and sorrow, that it's difficult to say anything that would rise above the risibly gratuitous comment. What was the intent of the Austro-Hungarian who threw that piece of iron? Was he intending to hit the Czech volunteer he 'stunned?' Was it tossed blindly, or with premeditation to harm? Did he mean to kill, or was it a – admittedly horrid and stupid – joke? Was the volunteer merely 'stunned,' i.e. did he come back to his senses, injured as he was, and heal, or was he killed? And so, did the punishment – if a lynching can be called punishment – fit the crime (if the result of a bad, split-second decision, perhaps taken out of anger, perhaps not, can be called a crime?) It's hard for me to express the feelings I experience when dwelling on this passage. If I (as a reader) suspend my disbelief and insert myself into the scene on the platform, of course I feel sorry for the lad who was struck by the metal, especially if he was badly injured. But what horror, what sorrow I feel for the guilty party. What must he have felt when he realised that the train was being stopped, people were searching for him, people were handing him over, and he was made to march – helpless, whatever he deserved for the stupid thing he did – to face the angry mob that was about to tear him limb from limb?

If I am not mistaken, this is the only example of racial, or ethnic, violence in the book. Again, whatever we think about right and wrong and justice, this is a lynching, and the lynching occurs because one of 'them' – undefined 'Austro-Hungarians' – hurt one of 'ours.' Here the coming age of Nuremberg Laws and Hans F. K. Günther begins to tint the horizon.

Now, I am not equating the Czech Legionnaires here with Nazis. What I am seeing is anger exacerbated by tribal sensitivities, something that also plays a role in the second example I offer below:

One day, an echelon of German prisoners was passing through the station. Our boys threw themselves upon them, stripping them of their money, their clothes, their bedclothes and coverings, their underclothes, packages and crates – whatever they had – all the way down to shaving mirrors and leather straps. There was a haggard, bony officer in command of our echelon. He himself strutted about with a pouch slung round his neck and urged on the looting. Some of the Germans tore their banknotes to pieces before his eyes; if they weren't to keep them, he wouldn't get them either. He had these men taken away and shot, not far from the station. I saw their bodies and was ashamed of this bestiality. But I said nothing; I didn't dare get mixed up in that, or they would have shot me, too.

Once more, there is a lot that happens here, but one recoils from commenting out of a fear of treating so horrendous a scene in what can be nothing but an offhand, trite manner. Again, two groups, and mob behaviour in which national identity plays a significant role. 'Our boys' have at the 'German prisoners,' egged on by the 'haggard, boney officer.' The fact that Jesenský offers the 'save my own skin' excuse for non-involvement (before we blame him, let us reflect on how we might have acted in his place) says something important, not only about human nature, but about how the entire experience of the war, of captivity, and the return home, with all its shining aureoles and all its deep darknesses, as here, shaped him. For what Jesenský sees here is not the triumph of one nation, or ethnicity, or race, over another, but the even more frightening realisation of the corruptive nature of power. The behaviour of the officer in the face of the actions of the German soldiers destroying the banknotes of which they were being pillaged, is, one imagines, not something that he would necessarily engage, in the 'normal' world. But here he finds himself in a situation where *he* makes the rules, and as is the case with most people, due to our corrupt, postlapsarian nature, those rules will be savage. But let us move on. What more can be said?

LAND OF PUSHKIN, LAND OF LERMONTOV

The point of this sonnet, written in the first days of his Russian captivity, is the disconnect, the alienation, that Jesenský suddenly felt upon finding himself in the land he had always admired from the descriptions found in the writings of his favourite poets. The discrepancy between his old daydreams, back reading 'in his cosy room' and the 'cold flagstones' he now reclines upon is jarring. One of the main themes of *On the Road to Freedom* is the abyss that yawns between the rosy ideal – the beautiful language of Russia's greatest Romantics – and the prosaic reality – the 'bellows' of the prison guards. Can this be the same language? Jesenský's *On the Road to Freedom* can be read as a record of the author's successive loss of illusions, which will pare him down to that inner, real core of humanity that we reference above. One of the first illusions that disappears is one of the most important: that of 'mother Russia,' so dear to the hearts of the innocent Pan-Slavists, whether Czechoslovak or not.

The closest that Jesenský comes to racial, or ethnic-attitudinal speech occurs during the first period of his captivity, on a prison train, in a wagon with a group of bitching and moaning Magyars, cursing everyone and everything for their present fate, including their progenitors:

> Their endless swearing offended me, but I let them carry on, in the assumption that our fate is in God's hands, and if it weren't for fathers and mothers, we'd be seeing neither war nor Russia. But when they started berating the Russians and making fun of them, the blood in my Slavic heart began to boil. And it was thus that I learned that my ardour for Russia hadn't completely cooled.

It would cool quickly enough – as witnessed to by the sonnet 'Russia,' one of the first penned during his captivity in Kharkiv. The poem ends with this pained address to the country he once dreamed about:

> Then, my feet trod your dusty roads, it's true;
> passing through mountains, woods of birch and larch,
> with madly beating heart I rushed to You,
> my fetters burst, smashed through the prison bars –
> I shall be free!...

> In a quaint barracks yard,
> For you...
> greet me with prison fetters too.

It is no different after liberation. As he begins to fill various roles in the nascent bureaucracy of the Czechoslovak National Council Branch in Russia, he is called to Petersburg. And there:

> We went off to Liteiny Prospekt. Nevsky flashed, intersecting it: a straight, broad, big-city street, but naked, without any trees. I had been expecting something awesome, wide, beautiful, with side-paths shaded by trees and pavements of devil knows what sort of material; sparkle, flamboyance, luxury, and here – nothing of the sort. No different from a hundred other big-city streets. A so-so effect. But Pushkin himself strolled about here! Gogol writes about the Nevsky Prospekt! Here Lermontov strutted... Has my heart grown so hard?

In the very first line of his biographical sketch of Janko Jesenský, Józef Magnuszewski presents him as a Romantic epigone.[26] That may be true, but if there is any Romanticism to Jesenský, it is that of Krasiński's Count Henryk, when the scales finally fall from his eyes and he beholds the 'maiden of poetry' to be what she actually is – the rotting corpse of a whore the devils have been using to draw him away from the real world and his responsibility to his wife and child,[27] or that of Jesenský's beloved Tatyana, when she ponders the

....

[26] Józef Magnuszewski, 'Literatura Słowacka' [Slovak Literature], in Władysław Floryan (ed.), *Dzieje Literatur Europejskich* [The History of European Literatures] (Warsaw: PWN, 1989), Vol. 3/1, p. 854.

[27] See Zygmunt Krasiński, *The Undivine Comedy*, in his *Dramatic Works* (London: Glagoslav, 2019).

library of the absent Onegin to discover in him a fraud – Harold in Muscovite dress.[28] And what an interesting context for Yokohama! The rapture he was expecting in the northern city is proven to be a figment of his imagination, while contact with the real world of the exotic east fires him with enthusiasm.

But it is neither the reality of what loping across no-man's-land to the arms of his Slavic 'brethren' turned out to be, or the deflation of the Romantic dream-world of Pushkin and Lermontov to the grey embankments of the frigid Tsarist capital that cause his beautiful Russian illusion to fall away as much as it is his experience with the Bolshevik revolution. Not freedom is the result, but anarchy:

> Instead of dispersing the screaming, 150-headed hydra of a mob, the militia cautioned the citizenry not to irritate the demonstrators.
>
> Kronstadt declared itself an independent republic, defying the provisional government, arresting its officials and holding them in dungeons, sending off a cheekily defiant ultimatum to the council of ministers.
>
> The army was an 'undemocratic establishment.' Nothing but superior officers, chiefs, commandants, differentiations, and ranks, ranks, ranks. One star, two, three, and the rest were just to heed what they say. Where do you have equality amongst people here? Equality is a laughing stock in the army, just like fraternity, just like democracy.
>
> And now one began seeing the gentleman officers themselves walking about with mess tins in search of rations. Standing, waiting in line along with all the other soldiers until their turn came. And the common

....

[28] Cf. Pushkin's *Eugene Onegin*, which Jesenský translated into Slovak in 1942.

soldiers would laugh at them, making them the butt of
their jokes.

At the front, there were even murders. The soldiers
there had started killing their own superior officers.

For the reader interested in history, perhaps just as intriguing as the account of the Czechoslovak anabasis is Jesenský's
eyewitness account to the Russian revolution. Citation after
realistic citation could be piled up here to counter the most
effusive propaganda of any *Ten Days that Shook the World*. We
will offer just one more, about a practical matter, that can
lead to an absurd, but no less real, imprisonment:

> There was money; you might stock up, but what was it all
> worth since bread was not to be had, a hunk of cheerful
> bread was even out of one's reach. You couldn't eat your
> ham or your sausage without bread, and if you couldn't
> eat, why, there was no sense in drinking, either. The
> bread they gave us made your whiskers stand on end –
> black it was and as hard as a frozen clod. Only furtively,
> somewhere at a tram stop or a train station, could you
> perhaps get some real bread for 100–200 roubles, but you
> had to be careful lest they grab you and toss you in the
> slammer along with the peddler.

The unspoken truth here is contained in that last sentence.
Communism didn't *become* totalitarian under Stalin. Any system that sees speculation in the selling of bread, and is willing
to toss both baker and consumer into the can for trading on
the staff of life, is totalitarian from the get-go.

Jesenský has little love for the Bolshevik government, but
Russia is another story. Whether or not it was painful or
disappointing to see his idealistic dreams of the great 'Slavic
empire' vanish into thin air, his respect for, and later longing
after, the Russian people is a strong current that runs through

the book. One of the more touching scenes concerns his former landlady, her daughter, and a boarder friend seeing him off at the train station as he is leaving Voronezh for points west:

> It was then that I was summoned to the office of the regional military commandant, where I was informed that, at last, the *bumaga*[29] had arrived, according to which I was to be transferred to Kiev.[30]
>
> Madame Nagurskaya boiled some eggs for me to take on my journey; she also gave me compote, rolls and salt. Then, along with Mmlle Marusya and the teacher Pustovalov, she escorted me on my way.
>
> Not only death separates us from others forever – life can, too.
>
> 'We'll hardly see each other again, however long we live, O my dear Russian souls!' I thought, and even said something like that when I thanked them for taking such care of me. 'Come see us, when the war is over!' I called out to them at parting.
>
> 'And you come back here!' they replied.

A lot is to be found in that one sentence, 'Not only death separates us from others forever,' – so much understated love, regret, and fondness. And once more we see a peeling away of the layers of human veneer to draw closer to a core lesson that will only intensify as the story continues: nations, politics, religions – all of these are mere accidentia – the only thing that is really important, the only thing that, in the end,

....

[29] Russian: Document.

[30] Spelling according to the accepted transliteration current at the time of the composition of the Slovak original.

is real, is the individual person; the only true faith that which is preserved by one human being in regards to another.

In an early review of Jesenský's novel *Democrati,* Andrew Valuchek says that 'he does not spare the representatives of democracy, the great and small office-holders, and indicates that systems do not change men basically, but only give them something different to growl about.'[31] This insightful statement can probably be used to sum up the reduction to the human core that is the main thrust of *On the Road to Freedom.* For as we have already stated, *Cestou k slobode* is a record of the successive loss of illusions: in the multinational Austro-Hungarian Empire, through Russia, through – not independence or the Czecho-Slovak idea itself – but Czechoslovakia as an ideal. Jesenský's time spent in the rarefied atmosphere in proximity to the founding fathers of the state, such as Tomáš Masaryk and Milan Štefánik, does not knock them off their pedestal (we can't seem to free ourselves from that leitmotiv of monuments and their destruction!) but they are de-bronzified. As great as Štefánik may be, he can also be calculating, petty, and vindictive; Masaryk is a jolly old grandfather, benign, but also, if not obtuse, at least harbouring a pooh-pooh-ish attitude towards individual squabbles that get in the way of great politics. Both Štefánik and Polák he treats as boys engaging in a 'soldiers-will-be-griping-soldiers' quarrel, and he seems to see the Legions in Russia not as individual men longing to get home to their families, but rather as pawns that he can move about at will on the chessboard of the Versailles negotiations.

Now, Jesenský embarks on his long journey home in the company of several other men gathered together as a 'dele-

....

[31]   Andrew Valuchek, '*Demokrati* by Janko Jesenský,' *Books Abroad,* Vol. 11, No. 4 (Autumn, 1937), p. 500.

gation,' including Josef Patejdl and František Polák. Like all groups of friends, no matter how close, quarrels will erupt when nerves are frayed by constant commerce with one another, especially in the cramped quarters of a ship sailing halfway around the world. Petty squabbles and sniping erupt time and again in the last chapter of the book, as the patience of the 'delegates' begins to wear thin. But as soon as they drop anchor in Italy and learn that Štefaník is aiming to extract a humiliating pound of flesh from Polák for a (perceived or real) slight received of him, all of the irritation and petty animosity in the little group disappears, and they gather around their friend. Summoned into Masaryk's presence upon their return to the new capital of their state, Prague:

> We had an audience with the President.
>   Smiling and gracious, he had us sit down. Patejdl began with the memorandum we'd composed on the ship and had all signed, concerning Polák.
>   'Is this your work, Doctor?'
>   Patejdl nodded in agreement.

The very first order of their business is an act of opposition to Štefaník, the national hero of Slovakia, in defence of their friend. The fact that it is Patejdl who takes the initiative here, and affirms that this is 'his work,' is telling indeed – for Patejdl, as the leader of the group, had himself been the target of most of their ire and disappointment as the seemingly endless trip kept dragging on. And although the chapter, and the book, ends with Jesenský leaving Prague for Slovakia, with our knowledge of the career in government service he was to shortly assume, this scene does not have the feeling of an ending, but rather a beginning. And a hopeful beginning at that, because there is no firmer foundation upon which a state can be built than simple human solidarity – and that, indeed, is the lesson that Janko Jesenský comes away with here. It is the individual person, not the faceless state, or the still more faceless system, that is important. Period.

As an engaging and valuable testimony to a dramatic period in the history of Europe and the world – World War One, the chaos of post-Revolutionary Russia – *On the Road to Freedom* is an important addition to the political history of East and Central Europe, and a foundational text of the Czechoslovak state. The same can be said for many other eyewitness accounts of the Czechoslovak Legionary epic, including the much different texts of Jaroslav Hašek. It is also the work of a talented writer with an eye for striking detail. His description of the Siberian winter betrays a real writer's enthusiasm for his subject, which is powerful enough to overcome the harshness of a biting cold that few of us have experienced:

> The bright, starry Siberian nights once more began to gladden my eyes with their huge moons, as did the pleasant winter mornings – green at dawn, then grey, becoming still and sunny days with the temperature hovering between 12 and 15 below; and the surrounding hills, grey with frost like Russian *papakha* [...] At the start of December the winter turned sharper. The temperature dropped to 27–30 degrees below zero. The dawns could be magnificent, for they glowed with a rose-coloured light, and the mountain summits were as white as if coated with lime.

If there is anything to the theory of poetic inspiration, the notion that real writing is not just a craft perfected by creative muscle memory, as it were, but an almost material inter-melding of the artist's soul with nature, there is no better place to look for proof of it than in such passages. To speak of one's eyes being 'gladdened' when the temperature 'hovers between 12 and 15' degrees *below zero*, to be able to use the term 'magnificent' when the mercury drops a full fifteen degrees south of that, is as good an indicator of true poetic rapture as you are likely to find.

We will speak of the poems that Jesenský wrote in a moment. Here I would just like to say that, while some of them are quite stirring and even beautiful, Jesenský's poetic approach is more philosophical than painterly. In the best of his poems – at least those in *From Captivity* – a selection of which we offer here, he engages the reader with ideas, rather than presenting him with plastic, sensual images such as one finds in the descriptive sonnets of Joachim du Bellay or Adam Mickiewicz. Curiously enough, he reserves the photosensitive paper of his metaphorical stock for his prose. For example, his description of the four sculptural groups on the Anichkin Bridge:

> Four bronze horses and a bronze man at each of the four corners of the bridge. The horses are rearing and the men are trying to control them. They depict a process of pulling them under control from the very start, and the struggle gets more and more heated. The man is struggling more and more strenuously, until he's straining with all he's got.
>
> Involuntarily, the battle with the Bolsheviks came to my mind.

Another writer, another poet, would have taken those four sculptures and arranged them in verse in such a way that the battle with the Bolsheviks would have come to the *reader's* mind under the gentle direction of the poet's words. But we cannot blame Jesenský for not being something he simply isn't. This is not to say that Jesenský is unable to suggest larger themes through subtle, direct poetic descriptions framed in a short paragraph. Consider, for example, another prison train, in a cold season, and Jesenský lacking a proper mantle and boots:

> Then one of the POWs, Eliáš Kováč, died on the cot below us. It struck me that he had some nice boots and an overcoat that was almost new.
>
> 'It wouldn't be out of order to slip them off him,' I thought. 'What good are they to a dead man? They'll bury them along with him, and a beautiful mantle and pair of good boots will just rot along with him. And they would come in so handy to me! How my mood would improve – how much warmer I'd be!'
>
> But I chased the ghoulish thought from my mind.

It's harder to think of a more effectively framed statement – only seven sentences in length – that says so much about the struggle of a man in challenging circumstances to retain his human dignity. While he is quite right in his logic: Eliáš Kováč no longer has need of mantle and boots, which will go to waste once he's lain to rest, even more important than one's own comfort is the respect owed to the departed, who even in death retains his human dignity and does not become an object from which spare parts can be harvested. It is also important – and a masterful bit of subtle writing – that Jesenský records the dead man's name. Not only would this be the sort of detail that grieving families in such situations crave – where did death come upon my brother, my husband? What were the details of his burial? – but it underscores the very human dignity we have just pointed out. This is Eliáš Kováč here, not some clothes-horse, or anonymous, unimportant stiff.

Jesenský's talent for dramatic dialogue is also apparent in a story from the beginning of the memoirs. A regiment is called to attention on the parade ground, and a beetle is seen frantically racing among the rows of boots:

Soldiers get very sentimental. Sentimentalism doesn't have to be mute. You can find it in mockery, irony, clamour and din. When we were carrying on the loudest, it was a sure sign that we wanted to stifle the scream that was welling up inside. When we were cynical and coarse, we were merely dressing up our own sorrow in flashy clothes. When we were laughing and gibing, even this was just a mask for our concealed sadness.

One couldn't say anything against the war. But how many silent protests did I witness!

You could see this among nearly everyone who had already been to the front, and had undergone the baptism of fire and blood. I once saw one of these fellows express pity for some beetles that had been knocked from tree-leaves:

'Don't step on them!'

'Why not? They're harmful pests,' came the reply.

'They only want to live,' said their protector.

'And you – you've never done any harm?' spoke up another soldier, in support of the beetle-protector, '... We've killed people, so crush us too while you're at it.'

And the beetles scuttled away safely.

So much for sentimentality. Although one would be hard put to call Jesenský a humorist, there are flashes of great comedy in *On the Road to Freedom*. For it is a realistic story, and real life tends to be funny at times. The character of the old teacher, from whom Jesenský rented a room, very briefly, in Russia, is so startlingly, absurdly tautological that he must have been just as the author describes him. Such an obtuse chap would be entirely unbelievable in a work of fiction:

'This here is a washbasin,' he went on. 'You pour water into it like this... This jug here is for water, and water is what we wash ourselves with...'

'What do you know!' I interrupted him. 'Back home, we wash ourselves in grain alcohol.'

He had no idea that I was joking.

'Here they use grain alcohol to make vodka,' he explained in serious tones. And all of a sudden, he asked: 'Have you ever tasted vodka?'

'Nope.'

He brought some over and poured me a shot. If not for the vodka, I'd've figured he took me for an idiot.

Likewise, the description of the statue of Peter the Great in the park at Voronezh has a disarming absurdity to it that can only be compared to Hašek's description of the painting of the martyrdom on the wall of Otto Katz's sacristy, in which the martyred saint seems to be asking his torturers, 'Gentlemen! Why on earth are you doing this to me?'[32]

Farther on was the statue of Peter the Great in the park named for him, wearing a snowy *papakha* on his head; thick whiskers, grim brows, and an anchor in his right hand. He was pointing somewhere with his left. History can tell us where, but it seemed to me that he was pointing at a park bench, of which only the backrest was protruding from the snow. It was as if he were saying:

'In Germany they clear away the snow and cart it out of the city to give the sun a little hand. So that spring might come along a little more quickly, along with dry pavements. But you lot do nothing? Your main street, Dvoryanskaya, is still covered in ice and the cobbles are

....

[32] *Jakpak jsem vlastně k tomuhle přišel, copak to, pánové, se mnou děláte?* [How did I arrive at this pass? Gentlemen, what are you doing to me?]. Jaroslav Hašek, *Osudy dobrého vojáka Švejka za světové války* [The Adventures of the Good Soldier Švejk in the World War] (Prague: Baronet, 1996), p. 88.

JANKO JESENSKÝ

already dry beneath! In Germany, they'd break up that ice and cart it off! They'd have a nice dry road. But you? You even let this *papakha* of snow here on my head. That's how you honour me?'

Hašek himself makes an appearance in *On the Road to Freedom*, as he and Jesenský briefly met in Kiev, an episode narrated in the anecdotal style of Josef Švejk himself. And just as when in Hašek's novel, his dog-thieving hero turns to his affronted prey and commiserates with him on the similarity of their situations – just like the dog, the soldier is also stolen from his home, and has nothing to say about it,[33] so Jesenský draws a similar conclusion from the songbirds held captive by Doctor Kazakov:

> Kazakov was a great lover of birds. Some twenty different songbirds chattered, leapt about, and sang in ten of those cages. There was a clatter of chirping there just like in the woods, especially in the morning. I would gaze at these little creatures: each one of them sent forth one sound or another. Only the famous lark kept quiet. The first few days of his captivity, he kept hopping about, batting himself against the bars, wanting out. Then he just kept impatiently pacing back and forth in the cage, never uttering a sound. The poor thing!

But even Jesenský nods, and, unless he is being incredibly subtle with his minimalist descriptions of a whorehouse in the red-light district in Tokyo, it is dumbfounding that he does not see the connection between the girls on display and the prison-camp from which he has just recently emerged:

....

[33] *Když se to vezme kolem a kolem, je vlastně každej voják taky ukradenej ze svýho domova* [When you consider it closely, every soldier is also stolen from his home]. Hašek, *Švejk*, p. 179.

In the evening we went off to Yoshiwara. This is the red-light district. Two streets fully lined with shotgun barracks filled with Japanese girls. You enter through the gate and there, behind a lattice, just like in a shopwindow, crouch Japanese girls, undressed for all the world to see, keeping themselves warm around coal stoves. If you're not afraid, you can pick one out for yourself from among them. Although we were soldiers, we satisfied ourselves with just a look.

As much as I'd like to give him the benefit of the doubt, I actually do think that Jesenský just doesn't get it here. Another thread that runs through the book, although not an ever-present one, is his tendency to think of himself before others. In Voronezh, for example, he refers to the generosity of a certain Czech named Čižek: 'From time to time he would be seized by a fit of gallantry. Once he invited us out for wine. The wine was old, sweet, red, and dear. It was a real shame that no one reciprocated, and thus we remained, so to speak, at just one bottle.' Again, unless this is the subtlest auto-irony, we have to wonder: it didn't occur to *him* to reciprocate? After all, at the time, he wasn't penniless. He had received some money wired to him by his wife back at home. And yet again:

Freedom in poverty is like licking honey through a glass pane. Yet another might say: a roof over your head, a full stomach, a cigarette, and, yes, just such a table and lamp in a warm, quiet room with a cup of hot tea and a good book... But is any of that possible without money? No. For that sort of peace you need the same thing you need to make war: money, money, money.

Back home, my wife had no income to speak of. With those hundred roubles that she sent me in Siberia, her well had run dry. It is true that Professor Kvačal wrote me in Voronezh that he was sending me an additional ten roubles; Messrs Hunčík and Kutošík sent me twenty more, but that was all too little. Petrograd wasn't responding to my plea for a job there. Kiev was silent, Moscow deaf.

'Back home, my wife had no income to speak of.' And he can refer to her sending one hundred roubles to him, at which 'her well runs dry,' so flippantly? And leave it at that, while moving on in his story to an enumeration of other wire transfers he's counting on? It may have been a natural attitude, and perhaps even a necessary one, for a prisoner of war, thrown back on the mere need to survive, to think about himself before all others, including his wife. But still it is not pretty.

Yet perhaps this too is part and parcel of the naturalism (rather than Romanticism) that we find in Janko Jesenský's writings. He has, above all, a practical attitude to the world, as evinced by his comment concerning Tolstoy's pacifism, delivered to the enthusiastic son of the doctor who translated the Russian great into Slovak:

> Tolstoy rejects war. He goes to such an extreme that leads him to the position that Russia means nothing to him; all he wants is for people to sit at home, sow and reap and pray just as Christ commanded them. He would be ready to sell the whole great Slavic empire for one devout Our Father.
>
> 'This philosopher of yours won't suit us,' I said to Makovický. 'At least not now. It's beautiful what he says, really, but only on paper. Practical reality is a different matter altogether and has been such since the beginning of the world – and so it shall be until the end.'

It is a natural practicality shared even by the Socialist mates of his, who make up a portion of the delegation he's travelling home with, under the direction of Patejdl:

In Singapore and Colombo we paraded around so that the invalids who were travelling with us under the care of brother Major Jirásek began to get envious, and griped that we were travelling like barons: we had nice clothes and boots, we ate in the dining room and slept in private berths. They didn't give a thought to who we were once, who we were now, and who we might become. They wanted equality. The brother Socialists began to scratch their heads. All this didn't quite fit their Socialist programme. The invalids were right. But instead of giving up their berths to them, they said that even democracy has bitter pills and these must be swallowed…

No, it's not pretty at all.

JESENSKÝ THE POET

At the breakout of the war, Janko Jesenský already had one volume of poetry in print: *Verše* [Verses, 1905], a collection of short stories, *Malomestské rozprávky* [Small Town Narratives, 1913] and two plays that remained in manuscript. At the risk of stating the obvious, writing was important to him. At his entrance into Russian captivity, the only possession he begs to retain is his notebook (which also contained letters from his wife) – probably the same 'notepad' he was proud of being able to conceal on his person when thrown into gaol in Hungary for insubordination. It was in this notepad that he wrote one of the poems contained in *On the Road to Freedom*, the sonnet beginning with the line 'In bitter brawl the whole world grapples, sweats…' Although, as for all writers, written expression was a compulsion for Jesenský, and he would go on to bring out eight more volumes of verse, nine volumes of prose, translations from Pushkin (*Eugene Onegin*) and Sergei Yesenin, as well as a history of Slovak literature and a work on Slovak orthography, the future county governor of Nitra and Vice President of the Slovak Regional Government was one of those people who, in the words of a modern American poet, did not consider himself 'placed on this earth to express himself.' And so, when called in front of Milan Štefaník towards the end of his saga in Russia and appointed to the delegation that was to travel home, during which roles and responsibilities were handed round, his jaw drops to hear:

> 'And you'll write a little poem for us, when we come back to Slovakia,' Brother Minister said to me.
>
> Now, I always put the writing of verse on the back burner, when there was other work to do, as a plaything of sorts, as a good cup of wine in pleasant company. Žďársky used to say that the writing of poetry was a luxury, especially when you can say the same thing in prose, and that in a more understandable and natural way.
>
> 'What?' I thought. 'Am I not good for anything else, except the writing of "little poems"?'

Whatever other significance Janko Jesenský has for his country, this is what he is known for.[34] Just as, according to its subtitle, *On the Road to Freedom* arises from 'Fragments of a Journal 1914–1918,' so the poems eventually collected in the volume *Zo zajatia* [From Captivity, 1918][35] were gathered

....

[34] The great Polish Bohemist Józef Magnuszewski calls him a poet especially noted for 'an elegance of form [which] compromises a wealthy and intricate complex of expressions of the emotional relationship between man and woman. Criticism of bourgeois morality is also found in his poetry, nor does the life of his nation remain without an echo in the poetry of Jesenský written in these years.' Magnuszewski, p. 854.

[35] The volume was originally printed in 1918 in Slovakia under the title *Z veršov Janka Jesenského* [From the Verses of Janko Jesenský]. *Zo zajatia* [From Captivity] is the title of an American edition of the poems published by the Slovak League in America in the same year in

from poems written during his time in Russian captivity. In his notes from his stay in Kharkiv, where his literary talents were put to service by the Russians as a translator and he was given the privilege of sleeping in the wider spaces of the office, he provides a short description of how the verses came to be:

> In the evenings, the Russians went off to town. I remained in the office alone. I swept the floor, collected the fag-ends of discarded cigarettes, and rolled myself smokes with some rough toilet paper. When it got dark, I lit the office lamp, drew down the shades over the windows, mended holes with needle and thread, crushed lice and wrote poems.

Whether this is false modesty or not, the listing of poetic composition in the same cross-row as 'mending holes with needle and thread' and 'crushing lice' seems to confirm the truth of Jesenský's statement quoted earlier concerning poetry as a pastime, rather than a vocation. More than that, however, these words provide a vivid context for the poems from his Russian captivity, which underscores their uniqueness as World War One literature. For although Štefan Krčméry describes Jesenský's 'scant' poetic output from these years as providing a voice to the griefs and hopes of 'fighting men,'[36] this statement can be somewhat misleading. For there is precious little, if any, fighting to be found in the

....

Pittsburgh. It is unclear who was behind the choice of title.

[36] Štefan Krčméry, 'A Survey of Modern Slovak Literature,' *The Slavonic and East European Review*, Vol. 7, No. 19 (June 1928), p. 163. 'Jan Jesenský, who had served as legionary in the Czechoslovak Army in the limitless steppes of Russia and Siberia, voiced the griefs and hopes of the fighting men in his poems, scanty in number, but powerful.'

poems *Zo zajatia* – logically, as Jesenský's direct experience with battling was limited, and he entered upon the relatively peaceful boredom of captivity at the very outset of the war. The 'griefs and hopes' expressed in the poems are less those of men in the intense context of trenches, never knowing if the next moment will be their last, but those of men set in the indeterminate hiatus of captivity, who never know when the seemingly eternal moment of their being shunted to the side, cut off from home and family, will come to an end. This is the great value of *From Captivity*, as it provides us with a different, real and expressive, perspective on a soldier's life so different from the trench-reflections of a Wilfred Owen, the horror of sensual overload in the midst of slaughter of a Georg Trakl, or even the aspirational patriotism of a Rupert Brooke. The poems of Janko Jesenský's *Zo zajatia* are not poems of man fighting against man, struggling against death, or battling a hated foreign ideology, but man grappling with endless hours of solitude, where insistent reflections on one's past treatment of a beloved wife (see the poems on the wedding anniversary, and that on his selling of his wedding band) can be just as tormenting as a wound of the flesh, if not more. As a record of a man alone with his thoughts – few of them comforting, even in the midst of hundreds of other individuals in the same excruciating circumstances – it might not be too far-fetched to see the poems of Janko Jesenský, not in the context of war literature, but rather that of a sort of secular mysticism, a POW's dark night of the soul, and his compositional context not that of Siegfried Sassoon, but rather St John of the Cross.

This approach to poetic composition is one of the most engaging aspects of the collection *From Captivity*. Whether it was consciously intended, or arose naturally from the circumstances of the poems' composition, to read Jesenský's verse journal of his captivity is to experience, vicariously, the interminable, indeterminate duration of prison life, with the monotonous hum of the void always ringing in one's ears. The prisoner can do nothing but think, and we find ourselves immersed in those thoughts of his as we follow him from prison yard to prison yard, and from city to city after his liberation from the prison camp of Beryozovka... into the larger prison of the continental mass of Russia itself. The poetic themes moved in these poems are endlessly repeated, as the prisoner's thoughts swirl about in his mind, like an eddy, constantly bringing back to the surface images and objects, memories and emotions that had been pulled down into the whirlpool, only to be lifted back into the light again.

Zo zajatia is made up of seventy-three poems, divided into two portions. There are forty-six sonnets, followed by twenty-seven *Piesne a iné* [Songs and Others], which differ from the former not so much in theme as they do in form, taking on balladic stanzas or couplets, generally four trochaic or dactylic feet per line. We offer the reader a selection of just under half of these works, twenty-nine poems culled from both groups, and arranged according to date of composition. In this way, the reader can follow the progression of the poet's thought from his initial entrance into captivity through the beginning of the legionary 'anabasis.'

When we say 'progression,' we must keep in mind the repetitive formulation of the poetic process which is *Zo zajatia.* Jesenský scrupulously dates each of his poems, and so we do have a linear progression in time. But as the poet moves from 1915 into 1916, from there into 1917 and so on, his thoughts circle back, again and again, to previous themes and memories from his past life before his enlistment – to the happy (and sad) years of his peaceful existence alongside his young wife. St Augustine's conception of linear time as an arrow progressing from one origin point (say, the creation of the world) to a final point (the end of the world), but circling back on itself again and again in 'eddies,' so that it looks like a long string with a succession of loops interspersed with straight stretches, is a fairly good image of the thematic progression of Jesenský's work.

In our selection of the poems, we have striven to include all of the themes broached by the poet. Personal, reflective lyrics dominate, but there is also more than one programmatic work, verse propaganda for the Czechoslovak Legions, to be found in the poems of *Zo zajatia*. These latter include the poems 'To Janissary Set a Janissary,' 'Throw off those Rags,' and 'On the Run-Down,' all of which are composed with the express purpose of convincing Czech and Slovak prisoners of war to take advantage of the opportunity presented by the Legions, abjure fealty to the moribund Austro-Hungarian Empire, and swell the ranks of the Czechoslovak forces, whose one and only aim is the liberation of their homelands from the 'captivity' of the multinational Habsburg state.

A separate and engaging group of the poems is constituted by comic and satiric verses. Chief among these is 'Tea,' which pokes gentle fun at the Russian obsession with the beverage, that takes precedence over even the most important obligations, and the bitter infantryman's complaint 'To the Generals,' which gives voice to the military truism that it is the rank-and-file soldier who takes all the risk and endures all the suffering, while it is the chief to the rear who reaps all the glory. These works, especially 'Tea,' have the incisive, yet light and entertaining touch of a clever Vaudeville ballad by Harry Castling, and display the same sort of witty humour with which *On the Road to Freedom* often sparkles.

The theme of the vanishing of illusions, of scales falling from the narrator's eyes, familiar from *Cestou k slobode* are found in poems describing Jesenský's swift and bumpy landing from the ethereal ideal of literature to the hard reality of life in Russia in poems like 'Russia,' 'Land of Pushkin, Land of Lermontov,' 'Parting of the Ways,' and 'Beneath the Red Banner.' This last poem, written as a reflection on the first days of revolution in Kiev, expresses both a sadness at the passing of the Pan-Slavic ideal, replaced now by a different sort of internationalism – the Marxist vision of history as a class struggle, and a sense of foreboding at how the dictatorship of the proletariat will work out in practice. Here we see in Janko Jesenský not only a sharp-eyed poetic witness to his present surroundings, but the insightful, engaged patriot, whose (naive?) devotion to the ideal of constructing a better world sets his political antennae tingling – perceptively, as it unfortunately was to turn out. Very similar to this is the poem 'The Vista Spreads.' Standing at a window and gazing out over the city, the sunset suddenly becomes a conflagration in the poet's eyes, and Kiev – Russia – the world – appears to burst into flames. It is an uncharacteristically apocalyptic moment for the poet, who generally shies from any themes even approaching the spiritual or religious, and once more makes forcefully clear to our eyes his uncanny sense of foreboding, arising from a subconscious assessment of the present political data he processes as he moves through his life, reading the papers voraciously, following military and political development from his place of enforced retirement. It is all the more chilling for it being so rare in the poems of Jesenský's captivity. Scholars of literature and art-history often speak of the 'catastrophism' present in early twentieth-century artistic expression. Around this same time, back in Prague, Franz Kafka is writing his prophetic *Metamorphosis*, a harrowing allegory of the dehumanisation of the human person that was to come about some fifteen years later, which he, mercifully perhaps, was not to experience on his own skin. In 'The Vista Spreads,' Jesenský taps into this same fore-sensed horror.

Understandably, this horror leads at times to great anger. A group of the poems in *From Captivity* are poems of rebellion against the injustice unleashed upon the world by the seemingly senseless wartime slaughter. Most powerful among these is the poem 'Resurrection,' in which the Jesenský, generally ambivalent towards religion, shakes his fist at God. Formally speaking, the poem is built around the familiar joyful Easter acclamation 'Pan Ježíš Kristus vstal z mrtvých! Aleluja!' shockingly negated, again and again: 'Christ is *not* risen!' as long as death continues to reign on earth, and the poet's nation is still 'pinned to its cross.' In 'For the New Year,' 'Will There Never Be an End to This?' and 'Who Shall Restitch the Roads that Warring Shreds' are all redolent of the frustration of a man helpless in the face of an overwhelming catastrophe – something that most Europeans of the time certainly felt.

The last thematic group is also the most characteristic: poems in which Janko Jesenský 'lends his voice to the griefs and hopes' of the prisoner of war. These range from the idea of the soldier as a slave, deprived of his individuality, found in one of the earliest, pre-captivity poems in the collection ('What Can I Give to You?') through those of the camps, where through nights of loneliness ('The Evening Chill,' 'On my Cot') the narrator expresses his agonised longing for his wife ('Go with God,' '30.VII.1909,' 'Morning and Afternoon,' '31.VII.1915,' 'The Little Picture…,' 'When the Night Falls…' and 'Open, Gate') and his sorrow at being separated from home ('Supper,' 'Yuletide,' 'One Prayer…').

All of the longing, all of the desires swelling in the lonely captive's breast, find their ultimate expression in 'A Sigh,' in which the height of felicity imaginable is to be in one's home, along with one's spouse and among one's friends, the crowning happiness of which is the thought of being buried beneath the soil of one's homeland, and the tears that will be shed by those left behind.

Thus, we see that the poems of *Zo zajatia* follow the same general curve of ideas as the sister volume *Cestou k slobode*: the narrator, Janko Jesenský the poet, is reduced to his real core – what really matters: not ideas or even nations, but the real, individual, human person one loves.

*

I will not disguise the fact that, given the repetitive nature of the poems found in *From Captivity*, I opted for a representative selection of the poems rather than a translation of the entire collection – which, I fear, might have tried the reader's patience and thus negated whatever advantage might have been derived from the (intended, I believe) oppressive experience of the collection taken as a whole. As with all of my translations, I look upon these English versions of *From Captivity* and *On the Road to Freedom* as signposts pointing at the originals, and will be gratified indeed if they motivate at least one reader to engage with Janko Jesenský in the original Slovak, where he or she can do so most fully. That said, captivated as I am myself with this multi-sided, talented writer, it is my great hope that I will return to translating more of his works in the future. My eyes are set right now on *Čierne dni* [Black Days, 1945] his poems of resistance to the Fascist government of his country during the Second World War, many of which were broadcast over the airwaves from London during that second conflict that shattered Europe in the last century – which many historians see as merely the continuation of the first, following the illusory peace of the twenties.

These translations were made possible by the Slovak Literary Information Centre (Literárne informačné centrum), which provided both financial support and a generous residency, for both of which I am deeply grateful.

I would also like to express my sincere thanks to Glagoslav Publications, for their continued willingness to support Slovak literature in the English-speaking world.

***

JANKO JESENSKÝ

The use of foreign words in the text of the book is not uniform. Russian words are transliterated into Latin script according to modern usage. Where Jesenský inserts a foreign text (Magyar, German, Russian) and does not provide a translation into Slovak (imagining, I suppose, that the reader would understand them), I gave the English translation in a footnote; in other places where he does provide one, I honoured his usage.

Historical and biographical notes can be found in the Glossary. Textual footnotes are reserved for linguistic items.

Banská Štiavnica
4 December 2021

ON THE PATH
TO FREEDOM

Fragments from a Journal 1914–1918

I. MY FIRST CASE

Instead of a prologue, I'd rather tell you the story of my first law case. Why? You'll see.

I'd set myself up as a barrister in Bánovce near Trenčín. I'm not going to describe the place. If you're curious, you can go see it for yourself. Today it's called Bánovce nad Bebravou. I was lured there by the late Dr Jozef Minárik.

'You've got a bank waiting for you there, and people, and cases...'

At Trenčín I switched to the little local line. The evening was getting on. As the last light faded, I took my place in an empty compartment, gazed out into the darkness and listened.

'Into-the-darkness – Into-the-darkness – Into-the-darkness – Into-the-darkness –' kept rattling in my ears.

When I arrived, it was only nine o'clock at night, and to my great misfortune, the local firemen were having a ball. It's understood that I simply had to be there, and as I was, it is equally understood that there was no question of my not dancing. Now, to go to a ball and dance there is quite an understandable thing. What was strange, on the other hand, was that I should lead the quadrille – in Slovak.

'Ladies! Gentlemen!... Couples here!... Simple chain... Double chain!... Change your partners to the right, lads!...'

What the?! What's with the Pan-Slav! Instead of saying *kissaszonka* for 'little miss,' he says *slečna!*

For 'I kiss your hands' he pops off with *ruky bozkávam* instead of *kezítcsókolom*; calls himself *služobník* for 'your humble servant' and not *alászolgája*, and when you say 'Praise the Lord,' *dicsértesék*, he comes back at you with *naveky ameň*, 'for ever and ever,' just as he should, but… in Slovak!… He uses the plural in formal address… And did you see how his name is spelt on his shingle? With an *S*, not *SZ*!… Pan-Slav… He takes his dinner and supper at Heindl's, where he orders in Slovak… And the other day when he was having some wine, he had the Gypsy play him 'Hey Hey, black-eyed Janko / Where've you been gadding about?' He taught the first fiddle some 'Clock struck one, clock struck two'[1] or other – a Pan-Slav as the day is long! Now, lawyers like him, and the chief bailiff, and the circuit judge, and the chemist, the parish priest and all other such gentlemen go to Baron's, while he goes round with Lapán and Minárik and other Bánovce townies… That's propaganda, that is – agitation!

Accordingly, it so happened that when I paid a visit to my fellow advocates to introduce myself, none of them returned the visit. Rather, they sent me a registered letter with these contents, written in Magyar:

'It has come to the notice of the undersigned that you, sir, are an enemy of the Magyar homeland. As long as this will be the case, we shall be avoiding all contact with you.'

Signed: Dr Wronovich Béla, Dr Wagner Ede, Dr Lakos Adolf, Dohnány Gustav, and two clerks, both of them Jews, whose names I no longer remember.

'Well, there you are!' I thought to myself: 'A magyar haza ellensége.'[2] All sorts of things might come of this. There might be a defamation suit, according to § 258. Or a duel. Or I could just take down my shingle and go back where I came

....

[1] Slovak tunes: *Aj, kaj sa ty túlaš, černooký Janku* and *Uderila jedna, uderila druhá*. They also complain that he has his last name spelt in Slovak orthography, not according to Magyar usage (according to which the 's' sound would be represented by 'sz').

[2] Magyar: 'An enemy of the Magyar homeland.'

from. I can fleer haughtily at the Bánovce tin gods and do without the camaraderie. I can go over to Baron's and give each one of them a slap across the chops, one after another.

But I'd need two seconds, at least, for a duel, and that's if there were only one duel in the offing... But six!... No, I won't be challenging them to a duel... Go back, then?... But that's just what they want – so I wouldn't be taking any bread off their table. They'd win if I left... So, what about those slaps across the chops? There's six of them and one of me, although I'm pretty well built if I do say so myself... muscular, even... But as the saying goes, 'Even geese and swine are dangerous in groups.' You never know how a brawl's going to turn out... No, I won't go over there... So, I'll laugh at them from my elevated position and proceed along 'the proper legal paths.'

And indeed I went. Yet the disciplinary judge, Dr Hocman, toed the majority line. It's true that he set a term for my deposition, but when I arrived at court, thirty minutes before the hour of nine, he looked up at me from beneath the crucifix and smiled:

'You're late, counsel.'

I pulled out my watch. 8:30.

'It's only 8:30,' I said, showing him.

'It's 9:30,' he said glancing at his own.

At which he pointed behind him with his pen at the office clock.

'But my watch keeps perfect time!' I said. 'It's a Schaffhausen.'

'And mine's an Omega.'

'Out on the church tower it's only quarter of!' I protested, pointing out the window.

'That's church time. We have our own time here.'

So I went out to check my watch against those of the other clerks. In the filing department it was 10:00. The chancellor had 10:00; the scribe in the chancery had 10:00; the other judge also had 10:00. Only my watch, and that on the church tower, showed that it was not yet 9:00. I ran down to the person in charge of the land registry in the hopes of not falling victim to an intrigue, but in vain: Here too it was 10:00. It was a perfect conspiracy: perfectly conceived and executed.

'Well, you'll be waiting long on dinner, today, Your Honour... Having set all the timepieces here an hour ahead.'

'You'll speak to me like that?' the judge huffed, rising from his chair.

'I'd quite like to file a report on you,' I growled bitterly, slamming the door behind me.

All day long I went around comparing my Schaffhausen to the watches of all the citizens of Bánovce. All of them kept perfect time with mine.

On the morrow, the office clock and the judge's Omega were also back to normal. But it was too late now. All that remained me was to file a so-called 'explanation' of why I failed to show up on time to my deposition, through no fault of my own.

But what sort of 'explanation' could I give? It wasn't my watch that was slow, but my head that was fast; it wasn't the office clocks that were fast, it was the Bánovce 'heads' that were slow.

II. WAR

'A magyar haza ellensége,' 'Pan-Slavist,' 'p.v.'[3] – these stuck to
me. Rightly or wrongly: a brand of opprobrium in government circles, an *epiteton ornans* among the Slovaks, and my
duty before my own conscience, as was my devotion to the
truth during that first case of mine.

Both the civil and military offices listed me as 'politically
untrustworthy.' Now, when you once make your way onto
a list like that, there's no rubber in the world that can 'erase'
it. It follows you around like your shadow.

The clan of Horné Jaseno have individual names added
to each their surnames, in order to distinguish themselves
one from another. There's Ďurké, and Petrošé, and there's
Gašparé. There might even be one of them with attribute
'enemy of the fatherland.' He wouldn't be the first. There was
already one rebel amongst us, the recipient of so much mercy
from Ferdinand II in that, before he was beheaded and quar-
tered, only the tip of his tongue was hacked off – the whole
thing wasn't ripped out – presumably, so that he would still
be able to stick it out at his Imperial masters, assembled there
to watch the spectacle.

Compared to the fame and 'shame' of the rector of the
colleges in Prague, my 'fame' was like a candle in the sunlight
and my shame just a fly-speck. But the fact remains that I carried on in the 'aureole' of an enemy of the Magyar homeland

....

[3] German: *politisch verdächtig* – 'politically untrustworthy.'

until that Magyar homeland found another, more important enemy to concern itself with.

War with Serbia erupted in August, 1914. States began to declare war on one another as if they were making hotel reservations.

We were informed of this on 2 August by large posters bearing the autograph of Franz Josef I. I too was scooped up in the general mobilisation. I reported to Trenčín on the morning of 4 August.

I hadn't even finished sewing a corporal's stars on the military tunic I'd 'drawn' than I was ordered to Trstená in the Orava region to guard trains and railway bridges. With one hundred twenty rounds and a carbine slung over my shoulder, a heavy cutlass at my side (the sort infantrymen carried), leather pack on my back and huge cap on my head, I sweated my way on a warm day from the Trenčín barracks to the station, where I asked if I might be permitted to purchase something to quench my thirst, that is, speaking in civilian, to down a mug of beer. There was time enough, and a tavern at arm's length, right next to the station, in the park.

The *hadnagy*[4] who led us to the station said yes. But in the army, it's like it is in the Holy Scriptures: the right hand knoweth not what the left hand doth. In the army, one general is oblivious to the actions of another, and in this particular case, one *hadnagy* was unconscious of the doings of his brother in rank. As I was on my way to my beer, a tall fellow with gold stars on his epaulettes barred my way and asked:

'Where are you off to?'

'To get a drink.'

'Mars vissza!'[5]

'Beg to report, I have permission.'

....

[4] Magyar: Second Lieutenant.

[5] Magyar: 'Back you go!'

'Shut your gob and be off, I say!'

'But,' I went on, 'my *hadnagy* permitted me...'

That did it. He was already roaring and pulling his sword from its scabbard.

I knew that fellow from somewhere. It seemed to me that he was this Nemák from the orphanage counsel, but I couldn't swear to it. He was a person I didn't take much note of in civilian life, but I would see him around somewhere. Most likely, he knew all about me and my 'suspect' history, and that's what was behind his sweetness and light. I thought to myself:

I'm not gonna tussle with you, pal. You're stronger than I am, and what's more, the military glory has gone to your head. A little fast off the mark, it's true, this is only the Trenčín train station, but all the same... You want to show everybody how you can order people about, throw your weight around a little, at least here; it's a little premature, of course, and I'm only a helpless corporal, whose elevated rank you can't see, anyway, since I've left my stars back home, but if I'm to perish from that tin blade of yours, well, I'd rather do it, if I must, on the field of 'glory,' or in the role of a *Wachter*[6] at the railroad in Trstená.

So I turned around. And that evening, they loaded me onto a wagon along with thirty six other chaps.

We rolled on all night long. On the morning of 5 August we arrived at Žilina. While we were waiting there, I heard someone call my name. I stood up.

'Come on out,' someone called, 'and bring everything you have with you.'

'This don't look good,' passed through my head, and as I strapped on my sabre, slung my carbine over my shoulder, and grabbed my small bag, I knew with near certainty that something extraordinary was about to happen to me.

....

[6] German: Guard.

JANKO JESENSKÝ

I wasn't mistaken. The same tall, bellowing *hadnagy* greeted me with a smile, and, in gracious tones, informed me of the fact that I was going back to Trenčín. 'Nothing' supposedly 'is going to happen to me.' At the station itself, he handed me over to the gendarmes. These rummaged through my bag, took away my sabre, and led me off to the military police headquarters in Žilina. Here I had a long wait. Then I was led back to the station, and finally, in the company of one gendarme, I returned to Trenčín by train.

In Trenčín I was a little worried about being made to walk in front of the gendarme, like some kind of murderer, but he was a kind enough chap to walk on the other pavement, carrying my sabre and my bag. He himself was ashamed of it all.

Then, handing me over along with some sort of papers to a captain, he reported something, but that captain just laid into him about how dare he allow me to carry a rifle!

I wanted to interpose and suggest that a carbine without bullets is little better than a shovel (and anyway, the bullets were for a Mannlicher, so the carbine in question might only succeed in firing off a round by the grace of God), but the words died, somehow, in my throat. Then the captain turned his strict and wrinkled face upon me, looked me over from tip to toe, and then, with slow, feline tread, approached me and shouted:

'In twenty-four hours, I'll be handing you over to be shot!'

The thing that struck me about this was – why only after the passage of twenty-four hours? I risked posing a question as to why I was to pay such a drastic penalty, and expressed a hope that at least I'd be given a little time to rest before the execution.

'That's no concern of mine!' he growled, and then, turning to the gendarme, he pointed at me like some kind of tragic actor on stage: 'Take him away!'

And so we left. He took me to the Honvéd Garrison, but not entirely – right at the garrison gates there was a 'magazine' of sorts, and it was here that they shut me up.

As a curiosum, I remember that I was received by the Honvéd officer Ján Drobný, who, at that time, certainly hadn't the foggiest notion that, in the future, he was to become the regional president of Slovakia.

Ceaselessly, someone was peering into the cell through the little window. The majority were Honvéd officers. Some of them – certainly, in an attempt to provoke me, but perhaps they were also animated by a sense of patriotic duty – tossed into me through the doors: 'Gazember! Hazaáruló![7] Swine!' Some of the bolder ones even had the door opened for them and engaged me with questions:

'You that lawyer from Bánovce?'

'That's me.'

'Swine! Gazember! They're gonna shoot you like a dog!'

A third one came by, and a fourth.

'You from Bánovce?'

'The very same.'

'They're hanging you tomorrow. Traitor!'

And so it went on. I clenched my fists, but my teeth as well. I thought: 'No, I'm not going to let you provoke me, you heroes you. How I'd like to smash those crooked mugs of yours! How sweet that'd be! It'd be a tonic for me, it would, but I'm not gonna dance to your fiddle.'

Even the regimental adjutant came by: Dr Lajos Dohnány. Once, he'd been a good chum of mine, back at the law school in Prešov. He acted decently, merely casting a glance at me and then turning away without a word. I reckon that he merely wanted to find out if I was that same Jesenský he once knew.

But the devils in the regimental chancellery were in need of new provocations for new, compelling evidence and grounds to proceed against me. Instead of this, though, they

....

[7]   Magyar: 'Villain! Traitor!'

did have handcuffs, and they sufficed. They led me out of the cell. 'Hands behind the back, handcuffs, and off you go' – I was dragged about the streets of Trenčín so as to put the fear of God into the citizenry, especially the Slovaks of Trenčín. This is how I happened to meet up with my brother Vlad. Walking, we bade each other farewell as if we were never to meet again on this earth. He asked me what the charges against me were, and I just shrugged in reply.

Handcuffed thus, they led me to the railway station. Sweat was pouring down my face, and I couldn't even wipe it away. Here we waited for the express for Prešporok,[8] which I believe passed through here at 4:30 p.m. There were quite a few people on the platform who knew me, including some from Bánovce. This is what chilled me the most, as I knew that their words would terrify my wife, who remained in Bánovce by herself. And that's exactly what happened. As I learned later, a certain eager-to-serve fellow named Zsámborkéthy had nothing more pressing to do with his time than to pass on the news to my wife that I was about to be shot.

So they transported me to Prešporok and tossed me into the *fogház*[9] of the IV *honvédkerületi*,[10] cell nr. 13. There they took off my handcuffs. Just how tight they had been may be shown by the fact that my wrists were swollen like balloons. The cell was a small one. There was a cot, a small table, a stool, and a coat hanger. A half-window, the pane of which was criss-crossed with thick wire, and bars. Only towards evening would a few stains of sunlight pierce the gloom. I'd watch them, often, as they wandered slowly towards the corner where the little stove was, before disappearing. Government rations, wretched. Mouldy bread, bacon (which I had

....

[8]   Bratislava.

[9]   Magyar: Prison.

[10]   Magyar: Homeland Defence District.

to pay for out of my own pocket), and which the *fogházőr*[11] had to slice for me, as everything had been taken away from me, especially everything sharp – so that I wouldn't do any harm to myself. The clowns! That way, they'd have so much less trouble in not having to shoot me. I was, however, crafty enough to conceal a pencil and a little notepad on my person, which they didn't discover when patting me down. It's from this notepad that I copy out the following poem:

> In bitter brawl the whole world grapples, sweats...
> The clash of arms has swept up even me.
> But of all these heroes, I know only three:
> Two rusty flintlocks, two dull bayonets.
> The one keeps watch, lest I smoke a cigarette
> Or plait a noose, that way to set me free;
> The other paces back and forth, to see
> That I've not filed my way through the bars, yet...
> Horseshoes ring out upon the cobblestones;
> Below my window, something's spilt or thrown;
> Keys rattle when my cell-door is slammed closed,
> Or when the thick metal is screeched ajar.
> Such is the symphony of this my war...
> *Elő́re*! *Rajta*![12]
>
> I hiss ... other words than those...

With the sort of food I was getting, even poems turn out worthless. Sometime later they offered me their own food, but even that wasn't much better, although it cost me a lot. One comfort was that now I was allowed to smoke, which before I really missed. The cigarettes calmed me. There was one other advantage I achieved too. Earlier, I had been al-

....

[11] Magyar: Guard.

[12] Magyar: 'Forward! Let's go!'

lowed out for exercise, but only walking in a circle, along the walls, alone. When I began to purchase my own food, I was permitted to pause and do some gymnastics at the partitions and railings that stood in the yard. The explanation for this loosening of restrictions I found to be the fact that the person who cooked my expensive, yet particularly bad meals, was the *foglár*'s[13] wife.

I sat here, or rather paced my cell and the yard outside, a full fourteen days. The military examining judge interviewed me, and the captain, who visited the prison, told me that the files concerning me still hadn't arrived from Trenčín somehow, and so they had no way of proceeding in my case.

It was then that I met up with Dr Milan Hodža. He was standing near the dark entranceway, leaning against the wall, as still as a statue, with a serious expression on his motionless face.

'You're here too? What for?'

'For insubordination,' he told me, quietly.

But the *foglár* had now caught on to us, and forbade us to speak, since, supposedly, 'nem szabad beszélni.'[14]

Not far from us stood some eight other natives of Trenčín, who had also been hauled here to prison for 'insubordination.'

Hodža didn't remain there long. As a matter of fact, he didn't even make it to a cell – the gate of the prison is as far as he got. Later, the *foglár* mentioned to me:

'You turned around and he was gone – like he'd never been here at all.'

One day in the WC I came across the late Dr Miloš Šimek, who at that time was an advocate in Frašták. I was very glad to see him, but he was sad, somehow, and didn't have any

....

13 Magyar: Warden.

14 Magyar: 'No talking allowed.'

new jokes to tell me – such as used to pour out of him whenever he would come up to Martin and held court there in the casino, where he'd have an audience until the break of day, storing up laughs for a whole two weeks, as his jokes passed from mouth to mouth.

I also caught sight there of a teller from the People's Bank in Frašták. He was suspected of passing Russian roubles, or corresponding with the Russian Tsar. Both of these gentlemen were in prison only for a short while. On the other hand, I frequently saw Father Kovárčik on my strolls around the courtyard, and he introduced himself to me before too long. Bielik from Sučany was also there when I arrived, and remained behind when I left.

They let me out on 19 August. The captain read me my *végzés*,[15] according to which 'fegyelemsértést követett el, mert a parancsnak csak vonakodva tett eleget' (you have committed an offence against discipline for heeding a command carelessly).[16] He told me that my papers had still not arrived from Trenčín, even though, supposedly, he had telegraphed for them three times.

'Your case has not yet been closed; investigations will continue,' he said. 'Keep out of trouble,' and he offered me his hand.

I reckon that I would have sat there longer if it wasn't for Dr Zoltán Pazár taking an interest in me. At the time, he was a judge in Bratislava (today he is a curial judge in Budapest). As he was my wife's cousin, she turned to him in her search for me through all the prisons in Bratislava.

At the *ezredparancsnokság* (the regimental command) in Trenčín, where I reported following my release from prison, one of the *hadnagys* still claimed:

....

[15]   Magyar: Warrant, writ.

[16]   Here and further the translations were provided in the brackets in the 1936 edition.

'Az nem volt fegyelemsértés, de *lázítás* a háború ellen.'
(That wasn't any offence against discipline; that was insubordination in time of war.)

Major Balloghy received me kindly. He said:

'Nothing is going to happen to you. Just watch your tongue. I'm telling you.'

He also advised me to put in for a transfer to a Magyar regiment. He assigned me to the First *Pótszázad* (Reserve Century) commanded by Dr Keller – a professor and director of a Trenčín lyceum in civilian life. A splendid man, humane. He always watched out for me, as much as was in his power, and shielded me from persecution for a long while. He even worked it so that, on account of the troubles I'd already suffered, I was advanced in rank from *tizedes* (corporal) to *szakaszvezetőr* (Zugsführer, sergeant).

This sort of elevation, of course, was much better than being elevated on a gallows, and six little stars on one's collar a lot prettier than six bullets in one's breast. I saluted upon reporting to Dr Keller, ramrod straight, fixing my eyes unwaveringly upon his pince-nez until I was dismissed.

With this, my progress along the war-path in Austria-Hungary came to an end. For I came within a whisker of seeing those rubber stars of mine fall off my collar once again.

The close shave happened on New Year's Eve. A gypsy band was playing at Café Elite. The first violin was an acquaintance of mine; he saw me there and played a Slovak tune. I sang along. Soon after that, someone requested 'Hazádnak rendületlenül.'[17]

....

[17]   The first words of the 'Szózat' ['The Appeal'], a Magyar patriotic song beginning with the lines 'Hazádnak rendületlenül / Légy hive, oh Magyar' ['To your homeland be steadfastly faithful, o Magzar']. The text is by the poet Mihály Vörösmarty (1800–1855) and the music by Béni Egresssy (1814–1851).

I didn't stand. After this came 'Gott erhalte,'[18] and again I remained seated. I don't know what devil it was kept my backside glued to that chair.

'Hats off!' cried some Jewish reserve master sergeants from a table nearby.

'Hats off?' I said, 'Why? I'm bearing arms. According to regulations, my hat must be on my head. The most I might do is raise my hand to the bill in salute. That's what the code of conduct says,' I explained.

Well, code or no code, next morning I was summoned to Dr Keller. With anguish in his voice, he asked, 'What have you been up to now?'

'I don't consider the anthem the Anthem when it's sung in a tavern,' I replied in my own defence. 'Am I supposed to come to attention every time some old ragpicker whistles it?'

'The Anthem is always the Anthem!' the captain shouted at me.

I wanted to respond that what he said wasn't strictly true, but I'd learned my lesson by then that, the greater the rank, the greater the truth. So I kept silent.

'You were singing Slovak songs,' he continued with his inquisition, his eyes blazing through the metal frames of his pince-nez.

'Military songs, Captain, sir. "Neďaleko lesa u vody. Štrnky, brnky. Trhala tam milá jahody. Štrnky, brnky."'[19] There's nothing sinister about that.'

'You are to report to Major Balloghy at 11:00.'

....

[18] 'Gott erhalte, Gott beschütze / Unsern Kaiser, unser Land!' ['God preserve, God protect / Our Emperor, our land'], the Imperial hymn ['Kaiserhymne'] by Joseph Haydn (1732–1809) with words by Lorenz Haschka (1749–1827).

[19] 'Near the wood's edge, by the water, Derry-down-derry; / There I saw the farmer's daughter, Plucking raspberries...'

The major was foaming at the mouth. Seated at his desk, he blustered that according to some act or other the Hymn sanctifies even the most remote and insignificant place, and that it is quite a different matter when someone sings Slovak songs and when it's me that's singing them.

'Since you're unable to sit calmly on your arse, you'll be setting out, quick march, with the next *meret*.[20] You are to report to the Honvéd chancellery of the 9th Company... and I'll have those stars of yours torn from that collar...'

I squared up, lifted my chin, coming stiffly to attention, thrust out my chest, brought my heels together sharply, saluted, and then spun around to leave...

'Sooner or later,' the words came flying over my shoulder. 'Goodbye stars! Goodbye family!'

And so I reported to the 9th Company. I didn't set out for the front. No one tore away my stars. I was spared that, and in February they sent me to Žilina with twenty-eight men to guard the barracks there.

For a short while then, I was in command – provisionally, true, but all the same, in command of a handful of men – and, as Napoléon once said, every drummer-boy carries a Marshal's staff in his backpack. My command consisted of assigning and recording the postings of my twenty-eight men cycling on and off guard duty. They watched over the objects, and I watched over them. I spent my time laying on the couch, reading novels. This would have been satisfying enough for me, but there weren't many novels there – actually, only a few – and so I had to look around for something else to do, so that they wouldn't say that all I did was lay on my stomach and cash my cheque from the fatherland. So I looked about for a part-time job and found one: helping out at the post office, working up junk mail and distributing letters. When

....

[20] Magyar: March battalion.

the Carpathians began to yield their victims, I lent a hand in hospital.

At the time, transports of the sick and wounded would arrive daily. Sometimes as many as 800–900. The barracks were set up for 6000 patients. These were a mixture of nationalities: Czechs, Slovaks, Romanians, Magyars, Germans, Ruthenes, Bosnians, Croatians. Winter battles in the Carpathian Mountains took their toll. Crippled arms and legs, frostbitten limbs, rheumatism, pulmonary algidity, frozen stomachs and bowels. Pallid, wasted, unshaven, wrinkled soldiers – young and old. Some of them could still walk, others not. These were borne about on stretchers. Many hadn't even strength enough to lift their heads. Others could, but when they did, they looked around themselves – at us, at the writing on the wall – as if they'd just been awakened from sleep, before closing their eyes again. All were exhausted, sad, apathetic. Those whom a bullet didn't reach, the winter caught up with: the frost, the ice, the freezing water, and the lice that gnawed at them. And there were a lot of lice. More even than the young scriveners and Jews who helped out there. At the disinfection of clothing I saw whole heaps of yellowed, scalded lice on blouse and jacket. When the steam begins to burn them, the lice group together in mortal agony.

We gave each of the sick and wounded a number, stripped him naked, collected his money and whatever else he had on him, registered him and sent him on further to the barbers and the baths. I once walked through the barbers' area. Here, the lice fell like little seeds. The shorn curls seemed to be alive, crawling upon the floor. In the baths it was... girls who soaped up and bathed the naked soldiers. Amongst them I saw some quite nice, homely faces. The soldiers were forbidden to speak with them, walk with them, touch them. Those who broke the rules were locked up. For this work, the girls received fifty crowns a month as well as bed and board. The bathers were covered with scabs, and this too was from lice. In a third room were doctors, operating, bandaging, manipulating.

I made my rounds from bed to bed, checking the little black charts above their poor heads, making sure that the data on the *Kopfzeile*[21] were correct, noting down where each of them had been born, whether they were married or, if single, if they had father or mother, brother or sister, to inform should anything happen to the sick men. I kept my pockets full of cigarettes to pass out to them. Everyone begged for a smoke because three or four days would pass until they'd been completely disinfected. They were unable to buy anything, and generally they were as hungry as wolves.

There were funerals almost every day. Sometimes a wife would be present, or a parent; some were able to come before the man died, while some were held up and only arrived after the funeral. There was a lot of quiet sadness, and loud lamentation, and fulmination, too. There was pain enough to cause it.

War is a dainty morsel for such an implacable, agile, and horrible commanding officer as Death. There is no deserting her ranks, no way to hide from her, no way to bribe her. In vain you offer medicine, coins, sweets, in an attempt to turn her from her strictness, and be lenient. Death is heartless; Death has no soul, and mercilessly she always stretches out her cold hands for the heart, for the soul…

But death isn't the only thing that brings sorrow. Once again it was life that was to cause me pain.

It happened on a rainy afternoon. The falling ropes of rain beat the smoke of the chimneys down upon the pavements sprinkled with cinders and covered with lime. The fumes of the brown coal stank. Russian prisoners of war in clay-spat-

....

[21] German: Information card (placed at the head of the bed, hence the literal rendition 'head-tile.')

tered overcoats were carrying about disinfected clothes. 900 wounded were about to depart. I was standing at the window, gazing outside. We were forbidden to go into town, and I'd just finished reading my novel.

Then I caught sight of Mr Šteindl. As usual, he was scurrying about here and there, so that everyone would see how busy he was. Some people are expert at making small tasks look like major undertakings. Now I saw him near Barracks A/2, then he was by H/11; now he was on the lime-dusted path between the barracks, but no sooner would he scuttle into view than I'd lose sight of him between the quarters. His skinny frame was clad in oversized clothes, while the tall, government-issue cap he wore was a little too small for his broad forehead, his large skull. It made you wonder how such a thin, flimsy person could lift feet shod in such heavy boots, caked in mud from toe to heel, and so shrewdly twist those feet along the path he sped down. Šteindl was a grocer in civilian life, and a supplier of sheep's cheese. Chatty and courteous, as befits his profession. In his mind, perhaps, he was ever behind his counter, and everyone he spoke to was a potential client for sheep's cheese.

I watched him talking, now with this one, now with that. I seemed to hear him chatting to everyone, inquiring of each one and always in two or three tongues.

'Áno. Hej. Igenis.'

'Hogy vagyunk? Ako sa máme?'

And then the answer:

'Dobre. Jól. Tak je dobre. Hej. Hlavná vec je zdravie. Igen.'[22]

His courteousness was such, he was so pleasant, as to be incapable of contradicting anyone. He was Slovak or Magyar, German, Lutheran, or Catholic, according to the given

....

[22]   A melange of small talk in Slovak and Magyar. 'Yes. Hi. Yes indeed. / How are we doing? How are we? / Good / Good / So that's good / Hey / The chief thing is health. / Yes.'

circumstances in which he found himself, the person with whom he was engaged.

He also had an influence on the mess. During Lent, as Easter approached, he wanted *halušky*[23] with sheep's cheese served – so that he might supply the cheese. *Áno. Hey.* He was diligent in noting down the addresses of every solid firm to which he might cater.

He saw me standing by the window and ran over to me.

'I hear you're about to be commanded out... Elvezénylik. Škoda... Sajnálom.'[24]

And he was off again immediately. I gazed around in concern. Besides me in the room there was only Lietavec, a half-deaf, grumpy old batman. He was on his knees between the beds, praying. Another, Juriš, a Lutheran, was sitting on his bed grumbling to himself 'It's really pouring out. By God, how it's pouring!' Through the opening in the roof, raindrops rolled down the stovepipe and sizzled when they fell on the hot plates.

'These two here won't tell me what's going on,' I thought, and I went off to the canteen to have a bottle of red from Munich. 'True enough: A person doesn't have to stink for them to sniff him out... Others reek for three miles round about and yet the air seems to them as fresh as it is in the Tatras... Such a quiet little town is only good for pungent patriots, whom no one'll ever get a whiff of... Somebody's behind this, may the Lord God pay him back in kind...! And once more, devil only knows where I'm off to...'

I ordered myself another bottle for consolation. Šteindl dropped by, too. But he only half-sat on the stool, always tensed, prepared to race off at a moment's notice.

....

[23]   A Slovak dish consisting of macaroni and cabbage, often fried with butter.

[24]   Magyar: 'Conducted away.' 'I'm sorry' (Slovak, Magyar).

'Where'd you hear that, that I'm supposed to be sent away?'

'*Főhadnagy*[25] Fügy said so.'

'You don't know why?'

'You went into Žilina a few times, and there, supposedly, you met up with enemies of the fatherland. That's the reason you didn't even get a *Passierschein*[26] and the prohibition to go into Žilina was decreed.'

'That's it? I understand.'

'But now I'm off. I have a lot of work to do. Do videnia. Viszontlátásra.'[27]

And off he ran. It seemed to me as if he were afraid to be seen sitting next to me. My Pan-Slavism might rub off on him. I called to mind how the Slovaks in Trenčín all kept their distance from me, when I'd returned from the military prison. They didn't even acknowledge my wife when their paths crossed hers. They spoke and corresponded in Magyar, avoiding one another so as not to arouse anyone's suspicion, published manifestos declaring their loyalty, and – only in the darkest of corners, after casting careful glances over their shoulders, did they whisper to one another that the Russians were advancing. Weaklings! Nothing will ever come of you!

Then a *Dienstzettel*[28] arrived with orders for me to report to Trenčín. I went alone.

In Trenčín I was greeted by Lt. Šír:

'Megint eljárt a bagólesője.'[29]

There was no sense trying to plead that I had been as quiet as a deaf-mute; that I had spent all my time in Žilina with my

....

25 Magyar: First Lieutenant.

26 German: Pass, passport.

27 Slovak: 'See you later.' Magyar: 'Cheerio.'

28 German: Service slip.

29 Magyar: 'So the bagpipes are caterwauling again.'

JANKO JESENSKÝ

mouth, as it were, bound and gagged – he wouldn't believe me, or didn't dare believe me – the denunciation had arrived from District.

'Vigyázzon, mert haditörvényszéket kap... A kerületből jött a parancs... Én meg aztán orrot kapok, hogy olyan helyre vezényeltem,'[30] he said angrily.

He ordered me to depart for Veszprém at 9:00.

'Menetlevélben legyen: 9 órakor. Élelmezési jegy... Menetjegy... Gazdasági hivatal,'[31] he dictated, and pointing with his finger at my long, German bayonet, ordered 'Unbuckle that. You're leaving it here!'

Already on 9 April, I found myself in Veszprém. Major Orosz, a short, black-haired, pleasant man, greeted me almost with open arms. He gave me my choice as to what sort of work I preferred – in the office or in the company. Pleasantly surprised, I chose the office. He assigned me to the Territorial Army Command (*népfelkelő parancsnokság*). My commanding officer was Captain Muić, a Croat, fattish and balding, and my direct superior was *őrmester úr*[32] Csomay, a dry, swarthy Magyar with an austere look to him, from whom, later, I rented my flat.

Once, Hodža came by to visit us in the office. While he was there, he slipped a small scrap of paper into my hand, unnoticed. It said that he would be waiting for me at eight in the evening on a certain street, but – either I got the street wrong, or he did – we didn't meet up with each other.

Őrmester úr was also there, writing or doing whatever in the divisional supplementary headquarters office (*hadtest-*

....

[30] Magyar: 'Be careful – there might be a court-martial... The order's come down from District... And then I'll be dragged there by the nose!'

[31] Magyar: 'Scheduled departure: 9:00. Here's your ration voucher... Ticket... Economic office.'

[32] Magyar: 'Sergeant Sir.'

kiegészitő parancsnokság). Later, I paid a visit to his private flat. He was home. Having supper, he handed me some Swedish illustrated magazines to look through while he finished eating. Then, he told me that Major Orosz had warned him that it would be better if we didn't spend any time together.

'All right then, so, be well!'

And we never met after that. I once saw him in the company of other soldiers in some café or other, but I pretended not to.

Once, *őrmester úr* Csomay surprised me with:

'And you – don't put in for advancement to officer.'

'Where did you come up with that? It's never come into my heels, let alone my head, to seek such a thing.'

'Well, it won't work out,' he stressed. 'No, so don't even try.'

'But I never thought of it...'

'It won't work out, it just won't work out, what with that political past of yours,' he repeated, as if I had been squabbling with him. 'It didn't even work out for Hodža, and he had a nice letter of recommendation, praising his correct behaviour.'

'But I'm well aware of the fact, *őrmester*, Sir, that the only stars that belong to folk like me are the ones above us in the sky at night. And those will sooner fall upon our heads than one of those gold morning stars land on our collars. There'll always be clouds enough to obscure it.'

'A magyar haza ellensége, Pan-Slavist, politisch verdächtig...' The thought 'My shadow followed me from Trenčín,' flashed through my mind. 'I'm not going to be coming to work in that office much longer.'

My suspicions were confirmed soon enough. Towards the end of April I was transferred to the 9th Company of the 31st Honvéd Regiment. Captain Muić was very kind to me at my discharge. He wished me 'all the best.' All the others in the office wished me the same. All of them were greatly relieved that it was me, not them, who met with such a fate. The poor bastards had been worried about losing their warm, comfy places. I was already far past that: I no longer cared.

I began to soldier on as a recruit. I got up at four or five. I went out with the company. I lay on my belly 'in paradise,' and gazed at the beetles crawling about. I searched for a lucky four-leaf clover. At the cry 'Előre!'[33] I sprang to my feet and raced toward the invisible enemy with fixed bayonet, to throw myself once more upon my belly to wait for what's next. I dug *fedezéks*, pitched *sátors*, and at *rohans*[34] poked hanging straw dummies, representing Russians, with my bayonet, etc., and returned to barracks. Someone would start singing. Someone would shrug his Mannlicher into a more comfortable position on his shoulder; someone else would make a little hop in order to fall in step with the rest. The left arms of all would swing in rhythm, and our footfalls would thunder together in time to the melody: tramp, tramp, tramp, tramp...

'Apró szeme, apró szeme, van a kukoricának...'
Tramp, tramp...
'Bécsi szappan, de bécsi szappan, kell a honvéd bakának...'
Tramp, tramp...
'Ha megmosdik a bécsi szappan habjával...'
Tramp, tramp...
'Odacsalja, csilicsalogatja, sejhaj! a leányt a szagával.'[35]
Tramp, tramp, tramp, tramp...

The difference between this place and Trenčín lay in this, that there we sang in Slovak, and my wife would be waiting for me after our marches with a ham or a baked duck, fruit,

....

[33] Magyar: 'Forward!'

[34] Magyar: Foxholes; tents; charges.

[35] The incipits of Magyar marching songs: 'Tiny eyes, tiny eyes, has the cob of corn;' 'Viennese soap, ah, Viennese soap, is what the battalion needs;' 'When you have a wash with foamy Viennese soap...' 'How it attracts, how it allures, a maiden's fragrant hair.'

sweets, and all sorts of other things so that, if I was to be sweating so uselessly for the fatherland, I'd have something to build back my strength and something to sweat out again. In Veszprém all such poetry was nothing but a distant memory. Sad and lonely, I would sip my beer in the tavern across the way from the barracks, reminiscing:

> Alone in a tavern with my beer,
> Mine is a sad, sad tale.
> It wouldn't be, if you were here
> Instead of steins of ale.
> Like bitter tears the hoppy foam
> From my moustaches drips.
> O, if I only were at home
> Pressing you to my lips!

Soldiers get very sentimental. Sentimentalism doesn't have to be mute. You can find it in mockery, irony, clamour and din. When we were carrying on the loudest, it was a sure sign that we wanted to stifle the scream that was welling up inside. When we were cynical and coarse, we were merely dressing up our own sorrow in flashy clothes. When we were laughing and gibing, even this was just a mask for our concealed sadness.

One couldn't say anything against the war. But how many silent protests did I witness!

You could see this among nearly everyone who had already been to the front, and had undergone the baptism of fire and blood. I once saw one of these fellows express pity for some beetles that had been knocked from tree-leaves:

'Don't step on them!'

'Why not? They're harmful pests,' came the reply.

'They only want to live,' said their protector.

'And you – you've never done any harm?' spoke up another soldier, in support of the beetle-protector. '…We've killed people, so crush us too while you're at it.'

And the beetles scuttled away safely.

Another time, we were drawn up in two ranks when along came scrambling a little black beetle. He tried to turn right – nothing doing, the road was blocked by boot heels. So he tried to go left, but the toes of boots wouldn't let him pass. So he went on, straight down the line. Then one of the soldiers spurned him with his foot.

'Leave him alone!' said someone who'd seen this. 'Let the poor fellow be.'

And these are men at war; men who had either already killed people, or would shortly be killing them. It's true – when ordered to do so, and in self-defence, so that they wouldn't be killed themselves, whether by those against whom they were sent or against whom they would be marching, or by those who herded them off to war in the first place, to be cut down for king and country. The little beetle found a place in their hearts. King and country? I reckon that these were very distant from them – unseen, unknown. The beetle, on the other hand, with his brief lifespan, was as close to them as their own lives. Sentimentality? All right. But it was also a quiet protest against a senseless war.

Among the troops there were also some Slovaks from the Slovak villages of the Nitra capital region – but they did their best to speak Magyar. 'Don't *beszélj magyarul*, because I see right through you,' I'd say to them with a laugh, even though I had to admit that now wasn't the most appropriate time to be uncovering one's true face, showing how different it was from the desired patriotic mask painted over in red-white-green or black-yellow.

One's mouth had to be painted in the same colours, as well as the words that came out of it. I only spoke in Slovak with Maršan, a young, blond-haired soldier, with peach fuzz instead of whiskers. In civilian life he had been a clerk trainee in the Bánovce People's Bank. He'd been gaoled for half a year or so, for, it seems, he had said something in praise of Princip for having shot Franz Ferdinand. When he arrived at Veszprém, he took to me as a son to his father, and I looked upon him somewhat as a father upon his son. We'd walk about together and we strove to work it so that we'd remain in the same company.

Maršan was a little piece of my former, free life in Bánovce, and a mirror image of my own convictions. Very likely, he found the same things in me. We vowed to stick together at the front; he promised to stay by my side. Unfortunately, he didn't, or couldn't. One 'forward line' separated us forever. I remained behind, he went on, and was killed.

The Russians were retreating from the front, but slowly. Ever new companies romped out of Veszprém for the front to be ground into the mud there.

'Who hasn't been to the front yet?' our company Feldwebel once asked, while we were standing at attention on the barracks parade ground.

I took a step forward. So did Maršan.

'Nobody else?'

No one else made a move.

'So, you'll all go.'

A few days later, we got a new commanding officer, a lanky first lieutenant with green britches and a dark tunic. He had a very slender waist, like a maiden manquée. He introduced himself to us from horseback. In such a way, he wanted to somewhat counterbalance his youth and slenderness, to overawe us. He spoke in a hearty sort of voice and every third word of his brief speech was 'death.'

'I'll personally shoot anyone who refuses to do his duty... Whoever goes off without my permission, I'll shoot him without pity... I don't intend to suffer the slightest blunder. Whoever commits one, well, "kupán vágom. Kiköttetem, hogy a nyelve kilóg... Kupán derítem..."'[36]

....

[36] Magyar: 'I'll bonk him on his nut... I'll throttle him until his tongue

JANKO JESENSKÝ

It seemed to me that this was all for show. That he was just pretending to be so bloody and strict, and that behind all these dreadful words there was a good spirit, laughing, loving, compassionate... maybe a little frightened, which needed to be masked.

He led us out into the fields, where we lay a long time in the grass. Then the captain came, and we marched before him in defile. It had showered a bit in the morning, but then the sun disentangled itself from the clouds, and the day became bright and warm. It was a good-willed company. We defiled in parade fashion even without music. The thunder of our boots was the only sound to be heard. The fattish captain on his horse praised us. His round, red face smiled.

'Jól van, második szakasz... Jól van, negyedik szakasz... Jól van, fiam...'[37]

We were supposed to head out on 25 May. They dressed us in grey on the afternoon of the twenty-second. First, they issued us cloth tarps. We spread these out on the ground before us and placed on them everything they gave us: backpack, bread sack, mess-kit, belts, two pairs of underwear, two pairs of undershirts, winter underwear, top and bottom, cords, puttees, then: clothes, boots. Everyone gathered all this into a bundle, tossed it over his shoulder, and went off to get dressed.

A lot of the men were quite pleased with their new uniforms. Around seven in the evening they left the barracks and went off into town like new men, dressed in grey – real soldiers, ready to be sent off to battle, proud at their consciousness of the fact, looking down their noses at the 'boys in blue.'

. . . .

hangs out... I'll get him.'

[37] Magyar: 'Well done, second platoon... Well done, fourth platoon... Well done, my lad.'

Maršan and I celebrated our 'puffing chests' in a café over iced coffee and chocolate cream puffs, as the very summit of bliss. Then we hastened to empty what was left of the poppy-seed rolls from the package sent by my mother so that – God forbid! – nothing should remain to tempt anyone while we were away. Then we wrote our farewell letters home. Most likely, we lay aside our cynical masks in these last letters of ours; probably, there was a little sadness in them, to which we were driven by the uncertainty of the future that stretched before us. Well? Love exists, after all. It shows up, if ever, in such delicate moments as these.

Replies to our letters came by return post. We luxuriated lovingly over each dear word – most of them resplendent in crowns. My mother was first with the coronation, sending along 30 crowns. Then my brother Fedor sent 30, Vlado 50, and my wife 100 along with a sad telegram: 'If my letter doesn't reach you in time, I can send you a blessing this way, at least, in my name and in Mother's: May God bless you. I'll always be with you in my thoughts. Anna.'

With such precious paper bandages on our bleeding hearts we went from store to store, buying what we needed for the road. Spoon, fork, knife... Sugar? Sugar... Diana candies?... Why?... Because they're good against thirst, supposedly... Chocolates... Biscuits... Cloth gaiters... Salami... Matches... Powdered lemonade... A little cognac... Tallow ointment for the feet... Antiperspirant tincture... Lice powder... Soap... Warming capsules... Still this, still that... What won't those hucksters come up with!

So, vaccinated against cholera, measles, and generally against any sort of unheroic demise, all so that we might wage war as heroes and die a hero's death, we bathed and had a hair-cut and a shave. I had it all taken off – there was no one now for me to please with my five hairs combed over from the right – 'Give me,' I said, 'the convict look.' Then, the oath, church, prayers. Here and there someone went to confession,

88   JANKO JESENSKÝ

that God might forgive him his sins. And now, at last, we could go off to spill some blood. All we were waiting for now was a telegram to tell us where we were to be thrown. When it finally arrived, we were sent to defend a nearby village known as Kedárt – where the enemy was trying to cut off our food supply. Every now and then we would lie about on our stomachs, but generally, we drank cognac, beer, ate and smoked, and marched back home singing.

Finally, at the beginning of June, smartened up, amidst music and cheers, under a storm of flowers, we marched off to the front.

While on the way, it turned out that we hadn't yet been fitted out in quite everything. A little past Čadca they ordered us all out of the wagons and marched us off to a nearby forest. Then, after the singing of 'Isten áld meg,'[38] each of us had to take a clod of earth into our packs.

This was supposed to be a symbol of our love to the motherland. The captain proclaimed that, just like this handful of dirt in our packs, so do we bear in our hearts our love for our dear, beloved motherland. We were, indeed, leaving our dear land now, but not in our souls, our hearts, our mind – in these we would never abandon her, and even if we were to die on her behalf, we would do so gratefully, just so long as she would live on.

Now, if that captain had asked then and there, who among you wanted to go back home, and who wanted to go on to Russia to shoot at people, I'm certain that the entire regiment would have taken the train back.

Those clods of dirt soon crumbled into dust, and that dust slowly sifted away through the canvas. After a little while, there wasn't even a speck of dust left in our packs...

....

[38] 'God bless the Hungarian land,' the Magyar national anthem of Hungary. Words by Ferenc Kölcsey (1790–1838) and music by Ferenc Erkel (1810–1893).

III. CAPTIVITY

It was a bright, dry early evening at the beginning of July. With fixed bayonets, we were bearing down on some Russians who were firing on us, hidden on a wooded hill. We were heading down a gentle slope that led first through some fire-ravaged and abandoned village, and then through sparse fields of rye. It was here that I lost my field shovel. I hesitated a moment, wondering whether or not to go back for it, but I quickly decided not to: 'No one finds good fortune by going back,' I thought. So we arrived at a little dip in the terrain, thickly overgrown with osiers. Just beyond the dip, the harvested field was already full of haystacks…

I halted there, protected by the trunk of a thick tree, thinking to catch my breath when some *szakaszvezető*[39] or other ran up to me, with a scared look on his face, and cried:

'Előre!'

'Right away!' I called back to him, intending all the same to wait a little longer.

Maybe I'd be lucky enough to vanish.

Bullets were whistling all around me. The company to which I belonged had disappeared to my right; I never saw them again.

I remained there alone. When the evening had really fallen, I passed through the little vale, emerging onto an open field. I ran across this and then crawled on my stomach up a

....

[39] Magyar: Sergeant.

small hillock, from which the grain had not yet been harvested. From here, in the dusk, I caught sight of some Russian fatigue caps and linen shirts at the edge of a wood. The Russians were lying prone on their stomachs, firing.

'If I wanted to go over now,' it flashed through my mind, 'they'll light me up. I need to wait until morning, when it'll be light.'

So I retraced my steps to a barn that was on fire. Bullets were rattling against that part of the shingled roof that was not yet afire. It was like a metal rainfall. Hayricks were also blazing. Somewhere off to the side a village was burning. Every now and then, searchlights criss-crossed the fields. I threw myself flat at every flash of light. I don't know if it was from the fire or the moon, but the whole sky was lit up, and the night on this side of the slope glowed as bright as day.

Small-arms fire was popping incessantly. There was no stop to it, and I so yearned for at least a moment's peace. I'd become completely disoriented. I hadn't the foggiest notion where our regiment had got to, or who was shooting, our lads or the Russians, and from which side.

I ran out into the open field, but there, in the light, I was visible to everyone. So back I ran to my burning barn, but here I could be seen even better, and I might get buried in flaming debris should the place collapse. Then I remembered the willow tree with the thick trunk, but I couldn't find it, or the dip in the terrain.

When it began to grow light, I discerned that one of our soldiers was lying near me, clad in a mantle, but face down. He wasn't moving. At first I thought he was asleep but then, I don't know why, it seemed to me that he was dead. I gave him a shake. He didn't make a sound, but I couldn't see blood anywhere.

'So he's asleep,' I thought, and turned away from him.

Bullets were whistling, wheezing and pattering all around me, burying themselves in the soil, striking against tree trunks and branches, tearing away twigs and leaves.

'This is a dangerous place,' I concluded.

I had no mantle myself. In the July heat, I had made a deal with a certain Neumann to carry mine for me, for some thirty kilometres, for the fee of two crowns. The nights in Galicia can be chilly. Especially near dawn it would get quite cold. The sun had not yet come up and my teeth were chattering. It was more from that cold than from danger that I got myself up and, stooping, made my way up the nearest hillock. I crawled on my way, carefully, finally lifting my head to see what was to be found on top.

'Russians!'

I pulled my head down quickly, but one of them had already seen me. He let out a beastly bellow – I reckon that I scared him as much as he me – he thought perhaps that I was trailing an entire company behind me. He shot his rifle. I was close enough to see it flame, but my head was already safely down. The bullet passed overhead.

'Don't shoot! I'm a Slav!' I cried.

'So then, your gun, brother!' he replied.

I tossed my Mannlicher over at his feet.

And the Russian who had shot at me now smiled and indicated a dugout where I should go. The men there surrounded me. They gave me bread and lard. I unpacked the cigars and chocolate that I'd been sent by my brother Vlado, and distributed it them around. I also gave them two tins of meat. One of the soldiers was fascinated by my three-in-one knife, fork, and spoon. He asked me to give it to him as a souvenir. I did. Another one congratulated me:

'The war is over for you now. You'll go to Russia, maybe even to Siberia. It's good in Russia and in Siberia. You can get a pound of white bread for three kopecks; our ladies'll take care of you.'

I was happy to be able to sit a while in safety. The soldiers were nice, well-mannered and courteous. They took nothing from me that I didn't want to give them myself.

A little later one of them said: 'We'll go see his grace the commandant.'

Two soldiers led me to him. The captain was a young man, with tufty whiskers. He also smiled at me and engaged me in conversation, asking me all sorts of things.

Emboldened by his affability, I asked him:

'Why are you Russians retreating?'

He explained to me that they had land enough in Russia. Galicia is a foreign land. They don't need it. And so they're on their way home, bit by bit.

Of course, that wasn't true. But how was a Russian officer supposed to respond to an Austrian prisoner – and one of a lower rank[40] at that?

The officer sent me on farther to Battalion. There I met up with quite a number of other captives, but nobody I knew personally. Czechs, in Russian uniform, exchanged our crowns for roubles, patted us down, and took away our notebooks, letters, and whatever other scraps of writing we had, sent it all to a colonel and translated our statements.

In this way I lost my notebook and my letters from my wife. In vain I pleaded with a Czech lieutenant not to take my notepad, as it contained nothing of military significance. He promised to intervene with the colonel on my behalf. But either he didn't, or the intervention was fruitless. Upon emerging from the office, he spread wide his hands.

'You're going to take command,' he said.

'What?' I asked in surprise.

'You're going to take command of those men. Gather them up,' he said, pointing to the captives. 'You're moving on.'

'Vergattern!' I cried.

....

[40] Jesenský uses the term *chin* here, which in Tsarist Russia indicated social standing, as well as rank in the army. Even in civilian life, Russians were assigned a social level corresponding to military rank.

'Ein, zwei – erstes Paar, ein, zwei – zweites Paar, ein, zwei – drittes Paar... viertes Paar... Doppelreien rechts um!... Direktion geradeaus... Kompanie marsch!'[41]

Such was my last Austrian command.

We were on our way to Russia.

---

[41] German: 'Form up! [...] One, two – first pair, one, two – second pair, one, two – third pair... fourth pair... Double-ranks right face!... Forward... Company, march!'

IV. KHARKOV – TAMBOV

From 3 to 7 July we marched on foot to Chełm. Then, from Chełm we travelled to Kiev[42] by rail.

Everything increased for us according to the saying 'Every little pile begs for more.' The road was endless. There was nowhere to sit, no clean place at all. Everything in the wagon made you itch. One day I found myself sitting at the window looking out at the broad, flat Russian land with its hills, the endless sea of yellow wheat, thatched cottages between trees, Russian churches, flashing as if decked out for parade, with groves of trees reaching up towards their onion domes, wooden railway stations with little garden plots, Russian signage, little shacks with food and hot drinks. Everything the same, monotonous, as far as the eye could see.

If I hadn't been a prisoner of war, and if I had been travelling in an express train with a full wallet, Russia would have been quite pleasing with its Cyrillic alphabet, Russian speech, hay-wagons, long cigarettes and *makhorka*, filled pastries, white bread, low prices for everything, endless tea, but – being as I was, with the last rouble to my name in my bag, travelling in a cattle-car with Magyars for my travelling companions, my mood didn't improve, rather it deflated the more with each station we rolled through.

....

[42] Spelling according to the accepted transliteration current at the time of the composition of the Slovak original.

It seemed to deflate entirely at Kiev, when the Russian soldiers collected the mess-tins from which we'd been drinking our tea, our summer boots, our canteens and all other useful items we had, to sell them back at ten to twelve kopecks a piece to the very same soldiers they'd taken them from in the first place.

My neighbours were all Magyars. There was some Corporal Rózsza, who in civilian life was a secretary for the assurance society Fonciér. He was from Veszprém. *Honvéd*[43] Helbert was the agent of some firm or other in Pest. There was another honvéd named Vrábel from Cluj. All of them were penniless and as hungry as wolves. They watched each morsel as it made its way into my mouth, noting whatever it was I was eating, whether a *pirog* with cabbage or white cheese, or some sort of *pirozhnoye*.[44] I could almost read their minds:

'We see what you're eating. And here we are, licking our lips...'

Angrily, they cursed at each and every moment. Saints were falling from the skies like apples in autumn orchards – the Lord God, Jesus Christ, the Virgin Mary, and other blessed beings. They brought their fathers and mothers into it as well, clawing their way back to their grandparents and even further – until what hair I had stood straight up straight on my head.

Their endless swearing offended me, but I let them carry on, in the assumption that our fate is in God's hands, and if it weren't for fathers and mothers, we'd be seeing neither war nor Russia. But when they started berating the Russians and making fun of them, the blood in my Slavic heart began to boil. And it was thus that I learned that my ardour for Russia hadn't completely cooled.

....

[43] Magyar: Infantryman.
[44] Russian: Small pastry, cake.

We arrived in Kharkov on 14 July.

They billeted us in gigantic barracks at the edge of town. Reddish buildings with red metal roofs and a great courtyard of yellow sand. This was a so-called 'raspredelitelny punkt voyennoplennykh.'[45] It was here that they herded the prisoners of war before dividing them into parties and sending them off to labour in field or wood or factory, as need dictated.

Already when we arrived there were prisoners of war standing in double-ranks with their baggage, and with their mantles tossed over their shoulders. They smoked while they waited, talking and laughing. They were still quite fresh. They were wearing their grey Austrian caps, but without the I.F.J.[46] The name of that majesty had to be torn away. Instead of His Majesty there were only holes. Such is the fate of captives: the farther on they go, the more holes there are.

They began to register us. It so fell out that I became a translator between the Russians and Magyars. They wanted to know our names, our age, our rank, the regiment in which we served, where it was that we were taken into captivity, the state of our health, and what we did in civilian life.

When my turn came and I said that I was a doctor-advocate in civilian life, they expressed some doubt.

'Perhaps you are an advocate. But if so, then you're not a doctor. Or, you might well be a doctor, but if you're a doctor, then you're no advocate. Perhaps you might even be both an advocate and a doctor, but then why are you not an officer? And if that's the way things stand, then maybe you're hardly an advocate, and hardly a doctor. At any rate, it so seems, dear brother, that you are lying to us, right...?'

....

[45] Russian: Prisoner-of-War Distribution Centre.

[46] Latin: Imperator Franciscus Josephus [Emperor Franz Josef I].

It was difficult to explain. I myself don't know why I never took the officer's exam. So I didn't clear up this enigma for them, but I did translate faithfully. I even got an honorarium: a quarter loaf of bread. And a title: *gospodin perevodchik*.[47]

And so I became *gospodin perevodchik*, and I translated every day. Despite the fact that all the Romanian I know is 'Deșteaptă-te, Române'[48] and 'Setreasca,'[49] I even translated from Romanian into Russian. I only needed to ask:

'Unde ješt?' and the Romanian would immediately tell me where he was from. Or:

'Unde to pris?' and he would tell me where he had been taken prisoner.

'Sanatos?'

If he began to scratch behind his ear, that meant that he was ill.

'Plugar?'

If he nodded, then yes, he was a farmer.

Then came the German-speaking Austrians. It was easy to extract from them what the Russians wanted. What's more, I even understood the Teutons. Still more: I began to fill out cards and write reports. I wrote in a nice calligraphic hand, in Cyrillic, such as none of those *unter*[50] gentlemen could. It's true that I slipped up with my 'я' and ypsilons, which in Russian aren't always set where they are in Slovak, but my slip-ups were tender strokes in comparison to the orthography of the Russian scribes. The Russians were satisfied with me and it's quite possible that they came to believe, at last, in my doctoral and legal diplomas, even if I wasn't an officer.

....

[47] Russian: Translator. 'Gospodin' is an honorific.

[48] Romanian: 'Awake, Romanian!'; the Romanian national anthem, lyrics by Andrei Mureșanu (1816–1863), to a traditional melody.

[49] Romanian: 'Long live!'

[50] Russian: Sergeant.

JANKO JESENSKÝ

As a sign of their satisfaction, they rewarded me: I took my soup with them every day, and that soup differed from the captives' soup in that it had meat in it. They also gave me gruel to eat, which differed from prisoners' gruel in that it was larded with *salo*.[51] After dinner we drank tea and talked politics.

The *unter* gentlemen were of the opinion that the fault of everything lay with the Russian generals, and the Russian generals had this fault – they were all Germans.

'O, for example: Rennenkampf. Good old "byl a udral."[52] Or Roschel, the Chief at Warsaw: "Who grabbed the cashbox and took off!"'

'And what a politician was that Peter the Great,' someone said. 'Even a dog would shake his head at it. He's the one that settled the Germans, who grew rich in Russia. They've been here now for two hundred years, and still they can't speak a word of Russian… They'll betray Russia first chance they get…'

I was stunned at these words. That's the way common soldiers talk. That's not good.

In the evenings, the Russians went off to town. I remained in the office alone. I swept the floor, collected the fag-ends of discarded cigarettes, and rolled myself smokes with some rough toilet paper. When it got dark, I lit the office lamp, drew down the shades over the windows, mended holes with needle and thread, crushed lice and wrote poems. Then, usually, I lay down upon the desk at which I sat writing during the day, and with clouded eye gazed about that wide-stretching expanse of Russia wondering whom I should approach so as to be liberated. The names of some Országovci, Hunčík and Krutošik in Moscow came to mind, as did that of Dr Kvačala in Yuryevo – these I remembered.

....

[51] Russian: Fat, lard.

[52] Russian: 'He was, and he ran away.'

'If not one, then the other. If not the second, then the third,' I mused.

I spent one evening writing to them all.

At the time, I still hadn't heard of the Czechoslovak Legions.

I woke up very early in the mornings. The office windows were broken, and the draught blowing through the lowered blinds wouldn't let me sleep. What was more, I was always vexed at the thought of the two worst things I'd have to endure in the morning: the visit to the latrine, and washing up at the well. Both places were always crowded. All the holes in the former were occupied, and around each of the fortunate tenants there hovered five sufferers, with ten more waiting behind them. The stench, which filled the entire courtyard, here stabbed the nostrils and penetrated the brain. There was no disinfectant. Not even a trace of lime or carbolic acid. Sometimes, there were up to 7000 prisoners in the barracks, and only one latrine with some thirty holes and one partition for them all. No privacy. *Palam et publice*,[53] my friends. One might borrow a light from one's neighbour, or whisper into his ear of the joys of the simple pleasure…

There was only one well, too, with a long trough. It had to be besieged like Przemyśl. Everybody wanted water, and whoever finally reached it didn't relinquish his place at the trough until he'd washed all his filth away. The ground at the well was a real bog. Thus, even if one succeeded in getting washed, he still came away again as filthy as a swine. The washing-up wasn't much to speak of anyway – a little water taken in hand, rubbed on one's mouth, one's face, and that was that. It was the same for the Russian officers, with the one difference that a servant brought their water to them in a pail and poured it on their hands. The laundering of clothes was the same as the

....

[53]   Latin: Openly and in public.

washing-up. The water never left the trough, and as a result it was even filthier than the prisoners' clothes. We had no soap. An illusion of laundering, nothing more.

Now and then the scribes would come by and we'd set ourselves to work. They'd bring baked goods, cucumbers, and they treated me. Once, an NCO named Zolotarev bought me a present of an entire packet of tobacco and a pack of rolling papers, for which I was very grateful. Sometimes, I'd get a cigar or a cigarette from my fellow captives, too. I'd cut the cigars into small pieces and I taught myself to roll smokes with any sort of paper.

So it went on, all the while I was *gospodin perevodchik*. But one fine day in July, the scribes vanished. They didn't show up. Most likely, they'd been transferred elsewhere. I was left by myself. Now I belonged to no group; I'd not been entered onto any list – and so they didn't want to give me any bread or gruel. They took away my office lamp, leaving me with nothing but the half-rusted washbasin for gruel, which by then I'd succeeded in desecrating by washing my socks and my feet in it, since I'd soon grown tired of trips to the well and standing there awaiting my turn.

When the battle for daily bread and gruel began for me as well, I'd go off to the kitchen with that washbasin of mine. There, the cook, who was a Czech, would pour me so much that I shared it with a certain Elsasan, who had quite a healthy appetite.

The days were beautiful, hot. We sweated and we stank. Once, in the camp office, I interpreted a request put forth by many of the captives that we be allowed to bathe in the river. The adjutant, a second lieutenant, glanced at me over his shoulder and growled in reply:

'Kuda do chorta? Nelzya!'[54]

....

[54] Russian: 'Where, devil take you? Not possible!'

And so I went away.

Slowly, the barracks grew empty. I was able to occupy whatever free place I liked. No one gave a thought to me; no one checked in on what I was up to. I moved up to the first floor, to a large room, the windows of which gave out onto the street. I wanted to be able to see a portion of the town, at least. At that moment, it happened to be pouring. The poplars beneath the windows were whispering in the wind and rain. The street had turned into a river of cloudy yellow water. Barefoot boys were wading through the flood under umbrellas, carrying baskets, on their way to town. No buying and selling was going on at all in the three *torgovlyas*[55] across the way. Everyone in the barracks was sleeping, squatting, or being as sad as me.

I had three roubles and seventy-five kopecks to my name from my wedding ring, which I'd sold. I might get my ten-day-old beard shaved, buy myself some tobacco of the best quality, or send out for sausage and cucumbers – whatever my heart desired. But I held onto the money with the intent of returning it to Mikhail Mikhailovich Sonin, to whom I'd sold the ring, to buy it back. But I didn't run across him. Zolotarev caught up with me, Matvei Ivanych, an old infantryman, my neighbour in the office where I worked and slept, ran into me on the street and invited me to dinner, but Sonin was nowhere to be found. So I was sad in that big room. I philosophised:

'It's just a thin hoop of gold, whether I have it or no. More important things fall by the wayside. What's all this mushiness about? So I no longer have my ring. I can still preserve my faithfulness, ring or no ring. A little band of gold can't protect me from infidelity... When I get back on my feet I can buy two rings, even... True, it won't be the same one...

....

55 Russian: Market-shacks.

But is it my fault that Sonin's disappeared…? It is sort of a betrayal… But where's the stupid chap got to…?'

The rain lashed against the windows. Water dripped from the sill. The wind whistled at the buckling tiles and made the poplars to sway. That portion of the heavens I could see above the street was one leaden cloud, and not a soul was to be seen in the whole, huge place. There had been times when I was stifled by masses of humanity, and longed for solitude. But solitude can be just as oppressive, and then you long for company. I couldn't hold out any longer. So I went off for a shave and to buy some tobacco, some bread, and some sugar.

It was too bad that I had been so hasty about selling that ring. A few days later, I received a letter from the firm of Hunčík and Krutošik, informing me in cordial terms that my recklessness was about to be entrusted with thirty roubles – which were to be wired my way.

I nearly jumped for joy. If I had, it would have been premature. In Russia, being wired some money doesn't mean the arrival of a postman, who proceeds to count out the sum in cash, on the spot. Rather, it means Russian bureaucracy. And Russian bureaucracy moves at a snail's pace, rather than a telegraphic tempo.

So I took myself to the office indicated. Of course, they told me:

'Posle chetyryokh chasov…'

I came back at quarter to five.

They told me:

'Netu ofitsera…'

So I came back an hour later. And of course the officer still wasn't there. What could they tell me?

'Mozhet byt zavtra.'[56]

....

[56] Russian: 'After four o'clock…'; 'The officer's not here…'; 'Maybe [he'll be] tomorrow.'

But I was under the pressure of time. I still held to the hope of catching up with Mikhail Sonin and getting my ring back. Even with interest, I'd still be out ahead. And here they're telling me *mozhet byt.* What is as much as to say, 'Maybe not tomorrow, either.'

The next day I showed up at the office. No officer. I waited there until he came. When he did, he kindly informed me – in German, so that there would be no misunderstanding:

'Morgen oder übermorgen. Früher nicht.'

'But look – that money was sent by wire,' I made bold enough to note.

'Keine Spur.'[57]

He explained to me that, supposedly, the officer had to go to Squad – that he'd get the money there, and only then could he give it to me.

So, I came back to the office *übermorgen*.

'Dengi zdes?'[58]

'Niets,'[59] came the reply.

A short answer, but to the point.

'Fantastic,' I laughed bitterly. 'It's still at Squad. And Squad still has to vote, I suppose, whether to give me my money or to hang on to it... It'll be two weeks before we learn who'll wind up with those thirty roubles.'

The next day I went back to the office, again. I was a bit embarrassed to be going over there so often, making a pest of myself, but thirty roubles was such a pretty sum that I overcame my reluctance. But no one took any notice of me in the office. It was as if I were a ghost, despite the fact that I sat rooted there like a stump. Finally, a certain courteous

....

[57] Germany: 'Tomorrow or the day after. Not sooner'; 'No trace of it.'

[58] Russian: 'Is the money here?'

[59] German: [*sic*] 'Nothing.'

captain with a benevolent expression on his face had pity on me, and asked, in German, what I was in need of.

I told him everything. He searched for the *povestka*[60] for me. I knew that the money had been wired. The benevolent captain turned to another captain and asked why they were holding onto the money, but that one merely shrugged. Then my captain pointed at me and remarked:

'A vot on zdes.'[61]

From what I could tell, it seemed to me that, perhaps, they were telling the captain that I'd never called for the money, and that they hadn't been able to find me themselves.

'Zavtra poluchite,'[62] the captain assured me.

I clicked my heels in salute, turned, and left.

But the next day was Sunday, so I went back on Monday. The warrant officer in charge of accounts was not there. It wasn't until it was nearly evening that I got hold of him. Even then I wouldn't have got my money if it weren't for my benevolent captain who was there too, fortunately. He gave me twenty-five roubles out of his own pocket.

I was deeply moved. Apologising for coming there so often and pestering them, I explained to him:

'Ya bukvalno bez kopeiki... Net u menya ni odeyala, ni shineli.'

'Pyat rublei poluchite pozzhe.'[63]

'I know I'll never see them,' I wanted to say, but I was happy to have at least twenty-five in my hands.

I made haste to leave lest the captain give the matter some more thought and ask for his money back. The whole affair

....

60 Russian: Chit.

61 Russian: 'But here he is.'

62 Russian: 'Tomorrow you'll get it.'

63 Russian: 'I'm literally without a kopeck to my name. I have neither a blanket, nor an overcoat'; 'You'll get five roubles later.'

filled me with such a dislike of Russian officialdom that I never returned for those five roubles.

I didn't dare go into town. So, upon exiting the Russian notary's, I asked a certain Russian to buy me some sausages, tobacco and bakery items, promising to pay him for his services. I gave him a rouble.

And I never saw rouble, nor soldier, nor food again. He vanished like a stone tossed into a pond.

'So, now that's six roubles vanished into thin air,' I cheered myself.

In order to go into town and get at least a few breaths of free air, I was in need of civilian clothes. Nobody wearing an Austrian uniform would get very far. A little distrustfully, I asked Kuznetsov, a scribe with whom I once worked as *perevodchik*, to buy me some cheap mufti in town – and some second hand but good shoes, because my huge boots would give me away immediately – and some sort of hat, as I'd cause an outrage among the citizens of Kharkov in my hole-riddled Austrian army cap; and otherwise, I'd need a tie, too. I also asked him to buy me some new underclothes, so that I shouldn't die of shame should I go to the baths.

Kuznetsov promised to carry out my request, and took ten roubles from me.

It was quite a while before I saw him again.

'Well,' I began to think, 'another ten has evaporated. That makes sixteen.'

But this time, praise the Lord, I was mistaken. Kuznetsov brought me a new Russian shirt, black (so that it wouldn't get soiled so quickly), colourful shorts with a pattern of tiny pink flowers, a grey cap, a thin, blue suit of clothes of the sort that mechanics wear, and boots, second-hand, but quite presentable to the eye. The whole kit cost twelve roubles and eighty kopecks.

If I didn't go completely grey then, in any case, my hair stood on end. From twenty-five roubles, I was now down to eleven and twenty kopecks.

JANKO JESENSKÝ

But off I went for a *raspiska*,[64] which would allow me to go into town. They gave me the *raspiska*, attaching to it an old soldier with a long, grey beard and immense jackboots.

'He'll be watching over you so you don't get lost,' they said.

First, we went to the baths.

When I stripped off my clothes, I noticed that I was as black as a chimneysweep. I'd sweated along the way, and the black dye of the shirt had bled as a result.

'Will you come in the cabinet along with me?' I asked my escort, seeing him strip naked as well. 'I won't get lost in there.'

But we did in fact bathe together, after which we went to the cafeteria. We ordered pork.

'Well then, Matvei Ignatyevich, seconds?' I asked, wishing to be a good host to my enforced companion.

'It wouldn't hurt.'

'Perhaps another?' I encouraged him after the second portion.

'As for me,' he smiled, 'I can fit it.'

He would have eaten five portions. But I had a yen for some pastries, so off we went to a pastry shop. And then to a tea room. And then to the cinema. Then back to the tea room, and, as it wasn't all that late yet, we went back to the movies.

At parting, while we were shaking hands, Matvei Ignatyevich expressed his satisfaction and assured me that, if I wanted, he'd go with me tomorrow as well.

But on the next day I went into town with Kuznetsov. We had borscht, cutlets, lemonade and black coffee. I paid, as befits a chivalrous fellow. On the third day I took my dinner in town with the Russians again. There was beer and red squash, and afterwards, for digestion, black coffee. In the

....

[64] Russian: Signature on a pass.

evening we went to an orchard to take our tea. In my worker's clothes, I stood quite clearly apart from the company in uniform and the civilians who were decked out like lords.

While on my way home, I discovered with shock that my new-bought boots were falling to pieces. And not only my boots – my roubles too were disappearing. With what was left of them I bought myself a shabby enough coverlet for a rouble twenty-five, but as always, so now, I intended to mend my ways and save my money – now that I had none left. I cursed my civilian togs and grey hat. I was most angered by that marvellous footwear of mine, and longed again for my army boots. Even though they were clumsy and awkward, still they were reliable and comfortable. I would have boxed my own ears had I sold them.

And so I put on my old soldier's shirt again, stuck my cap with the missing Franz Josef I badge back on my head, and was once more transformed from mechanic into prisoner of war.

I wrote a letter of warm thanks to Hunčík for his aid, and moved back to my old office. Once again I began sleeping on my desk beneath the coverlet I'd purchased. I visited with my old Landsturm neighbours: good old bald-headed Timofei Ivanych with his great Russian beard, and shaggy, ill-humoured Stepan Semyonovich Bornikov with that red beard of his own.

Not without good reason the saying goes: 'A red-haired fellow is no good.' Bornikov hated me. He was mean, miserly. He hoarded everything he could get his hands on, to sell later at exorbitant rates. A profiteer. For example, he'd buy pickles in gross and when he sold them, his prices were always higher than anyone else's. He divided the meat in the soup, always, into two portions, so that none would remain for me. Whenever I ate with them, I had to keep close watch that the devil wouldn't tempt my hand to pull a piece of meat from the tureen, or he'd curse me with his eyes. He slurped, he gulped, but what impressed me most was the facility he had of blowing his nose by pressing a thumb against one nostril, then the other, when it was full. I tried to imitate him, to spare my hanky, but I couldn't master it. The other Russians were just as skilled as he.

Timofei Ivanych protected me from Bornikov as well as he might, and complained of him too: that he had to do everything himself, a *yefreitor*, chasing about from early morning on business, and yet from all that he pulled in, he earned nothing at all.

'He won't even offer you any milk,' he said. 'He'd rather it go sour.'

And he extracted a bottle and showed me.

'Such a village-market Jew he is. And he's angry with you, too.'

'Why?'

'Because you don't buy your rolls from him, but from me.'

'Aha! So that's the reason.'

The riddle was solved.

It was because of Bornikov's hatred that I let the old Landsturmers alone. There were only eighteen Magyars in the whole barracks. Allegedly, they refused to perform any hard tasks, and for that reason they were being punished. All of them were *Feldwebels* – sommelier, journalist, business agent, and so forth. Intelligentsia.

One of them named Geréb – a young, swarthy fellow, clean-shaven though somewhat run-down, introduced himself to me as a writer of belles-lettres, poet, publicist, jurist, and socialist.

'I don't write my poems down. I carry them about in my head,' he told me. 'Want to hear some?'

'Sure.'

And off he went, on Magyar literature, Budapest, and from thence he passed on to occultism, telepathy, visions, hallucinations, and back to poetry. He began with some verses of Kiss and finished up with a poem by Ady:

Kipányvázták a lelkemet,
mert ficánkolt csikói tüzben...[65]

'That Ady of yours is tough as a boot,' I said, a little impru-
dently.

But he was already reciting a Magyar translation of Baudelaire. It was as if he hadn't heard me at all.

'And what if I were to recite some Pushkin for you, like
that?' flashed through my mind. For example:

Иль русского царя уже бессильно слово?
Иль нам с Европой спорить ново?
Иль русский от побед отвык?[66]

But at the time it was going poorly on the Russian front.
Warsaw had fallen, and there were rumours that even Kov-
no had been taken. In the *Russkoye slovo*,[67] I'd just read Khvostov's speech in the Duma, during which he thundered
against the German colonists. He argued that, in Russia,
everything was in German hands: the economy, the banks,
industry, diplomacy, the general staff. He proceeded from
thence to mention the court, the Empress.

So I just left well enough alone with my Pushkin citations.

Meanwhile, he'd already moved on to Magyar politics, to
'Nemzeti kaszinó' and 'Országos kaszinó.'[68]

....

[65] 'They mocked my soul / because it capered ablaze like a colt...'

[66] 'Is the word of the Russian Tsar a helpless thing? / Is it new for
us to tussle with Europe? / Has the Russian grown unaccustomed to
victory?' From Pushkin's verse 'Клеветникам России' [To the slan-
derers of Russia, 1831].

[67] Russian: *The Russian Word.*

[68] Magyar: National Casino; Countrywide Casino. Magyar associations promoting the development of Magyar national consciousness.

'Well then, so, after the war is over, will you grant us autonomy?' I interrupted him.

'Soha!'[69] he exclaimed with pathos.

'Well then, you're certainly not a socialist.'

'No? What, then?'

'A chauvinist.'

'That I am,' he stated firmly.

We parted ways, but not for long. The Magyars asked me to teach them Russian.

I agreed, but with some reservations, as my own Russian was none too good. As a matter of fact, my Russian was surely worse than Vajanský's, who thought he knew Russian until he tried it out in Petrograd – at which the Russians stated with enthusiasm that Slovak sounds quite a bit like Russian...

I didn't get too far with the lessons. On one beautiful September morning they gathered us all together, counted us, loaded us onto wagons, and sped us off to Yekaterinoslav. We'd hardly had time to reflect upon this unusual Russian alacrity when we were set to very hard labour in the iron-works. We were supposed to lug around heavy rails, shovel coal, fire the furnaces, dig with spades... We worked day and night in shifts. But we didn't quite ever get the hang of it, and soon they packed us up again and sent us back to Kharkov.

'If you don't want to work, you'll be sent to Siberia,' the Russians said.

The first thing we did upon returning back to Kharkov was to check at the office to see if any mail or parcels had arrived for us. Among other things I found a postcard from Dr Kvačal. The words he wrote sounded in my ears like the song of an archangel, for there it said that I should report to Dr Edzelin, a colleague of his at the University of Kharkov, who would present me with ten roubles.

....

[69] Magyar: 'Never!'

'God bless and keep you, Professor!' I greeted him in spirit. Then I borrowed a nice cape from a certain soldier so as to hide my dirty shirt; Jožko Adamec, who used to be the doorman at Štefánia's in Trenčanske Teplice, lent me his boots, and I was off to the university. The boots were pinching me so that I nearly took them off as I went along. And yet I hobbled and stumbled my way until I got to the uni and found the professor; after the conclusion of his lectures, he came out onto the landing where I was waiting for him. Upon showing him the card from Dr Kvačal he immediately handed over to me those ten roubles.

I was saved. Right away I went out and got myself something to eat. Afterwards, I bought myself some necessities, and took my time getting back to the barracks.

I got back just in time. That very day, that is, 21 September, they packed us into the wagons again. Once more I found myself at a window gazing out upon the Russian landscape. It was a foggy day, rainy and cool. The fields were empty, the trees wet, their leaves yellow. We were all depressed. They had us detrain in Kursk, where they herded us into town and into the courtyard of some great building, where they had us stand all day long, and long into the night – until two in the morning. Somebody found a hay-shed. We crawled inside and buried ourselves in straw. The next day they sent us off again, for Tambov, through Voronezh.

On 26 September, they detrained us in Tambov, which was familiar to me from Lermontov's poem:

> Тамбов на карте генеральной
> Кружком означен не всегда;
> Он прежде город был опальный,
> Теперь же, право, хоть куда.
> Там есть три улицы прямые,
> И фонари и мостовые,
> Там два трактира есть, один

Московский, а другой Берлин.
Там есть еще четыре будки,
При них два будочника есть;
По форме отдают вам честь,
И смена им два раза в сутки;
. . . .
Короче, славный городок.[70]

I saw only a little town with a few wide but disorderly streets; wooden buildings, festooned with poplars – not like ours, tall and slender, but more broad, bushy ones. The streets were thick with mud, and no one was to be seen in them but soldiers.

They didn't put us up in the Moscow or Berlin taverns, but rather in a great, unfinished brick building. Somebody said that it was supposed to be a theatre. There were so many prisoners of war in there already that we hardly were able to find a place for ourselves.

I found myself in the company of a certain Resler, a cadet, an exchange agent in civilian life; Fischer, a young lad in a gala uniform, the mollycoddled son of a merchant in Pest, and Geréb.

I came to know Resler for an idiot on the very next day. Kelemen, an imprisoned shoemaker, failed to come to attention before him when returning his hobnailed boots.

. . . .

[70] From 'Тамбовская казначейша' [The Tambov Treasurer's Wife, 1838] a narrative poem by the Russian romantic poet Mikhail Yuryevich Lermontov (1814–1841). 'On general maps, Tambov / Is not always marked with a dot; / Formerly, it was a town out of favour / Now, it's true, it's quite something. / It has three straight streets, / With lanterns and pavements, / Two taverns, one / Called Moscow, the other Berlin. / It also has four shacks / Two guardhouses among them / They salute from them, pro forma / The guard changing twice a day. / In short, a splendid little town.'

'Hapták!'[71] he growled at him.

Kelemen wasn't in the mood.

'Hapták! Or I'll have you tossed in the jug!' the cadet screeched.

I interposed.

'Cadet, sir, you are an idiot. Do you think that we're in Austria-Hungary? It's a far shout from Vienna to Tambov. We're not going to click our heels here before any cadet...'

We stopped speaking, sleeping next to one another, and playing chess.

Geréb was no better. Back in Kharkov he wouldn't grant us autonomy; here in Tambov he even balked at a Slovak gymnasium. Jožko Adamec had heard from someone that back home, the Slovaks had been promised a Slovak gymnasium, supposedly on account of them being good soldiers. Whatever the case may have been, six Slovaks had presented that demand to the government of Hungary. I passed the news on to Geréb. He assumed a dramatic pose, raised his right hand, and declaimed with determination:

'Soha!'

'Meddig lesz még úr a betyárság?'[72] I asked, quoting that Ady of his.

Fischer scurried about the town scrounging from Jews. He encouraged me to do the same – claim to be a Jew. He wanted me to go to the Russky Torgovo-Promyshlenny Bank[73] – straight to the director.

'He'll support you,' he assured me, 'but only if you're a Jew.'

'I'll give it a try.'

....

[71] Magyar: 'Attention!'

[72] Magyar: 'How long still shall villainy reign?' A line from Ady's 'Magyar jakobinus dala' [Magyar Jacobin song, 1908].

[73] Russian: Russian Merchant and Industrial Bank.

And I really did go. Kuno Mann, the director, a rotund, honest gentleman with glasses, gave me two roubles. I duly entered his name and address in my notebook, promising to repay those two roubles. I still owe him. Fischer scraped together three roubles somewhere, a half-sole and some linen, from which I obtained only some underpants that reached below my knees.

After a good dinner in town, we sat long in the city park, taking pleasure in the emptiness of autumn. Geréb lectured us on Magyar painters:

'Bencúr isn't worth a jot. László Fülöp is an idiot, but Márk, who captures woman on his canvasses in all her sensuality and animality, is a great, original, artist with his own special point of view. Hollóssy and his school are justly renowned... There's this one remarkable painting, *Genij*. You know, there's this sort of embryos, and this here and that there, and that's that *Genij*...'

He kept on with his perorations back at the barracks too, only now he'd moved on to his genius of a boss. What an all-around educated fellow he was: stylist, orator, jurist, and yet he was persecuted by misfortune. From his editorship he went to work for some fellow named Braun at *Nap*,[74] and from there, out of the newspaper racket altogether.

He went on talking far into the night. Was it because we'd had a better sort of dinner, or because it was raining that night, but all the bedbugs were riled up and pricked at us so that we couldn't get to sleep. Only near dawn did those ferocious, bloodthirsty little animals retreat, and then we fell into slumber.

In the morning Geréb asked:

'What was with those bedbugs last night?'

Someone impishly responded:

'You got them angry with your twaddle.'

....

[74] Magyar: *The Sun*. A political daily advocating Hungarian independence, existing from 1905 until 1922. The 'Braun' in question is Sándor Braun (1866–1920), journalist and founder of *The Sun*.

V. TAMBOV – SIBERIA

On 8 October 1915 we were herded once more into cold and filthy freight cars. There was neither stove nor straw inside. It was a cold and bright day. The wind howled in through the cracks. For breakfast I gnawed on some crumbs of black bread and two cloves of garlic. I stank doubly, of garlic and poverty, like an old Tambov Jew. I hadn't a kopeck to my name. I'd run out of *makhorka*. One of my boot soles had come loose and was flapping around like a sore tongue. I wound some cord around it, but that came undone after only a few steps. I had no cloak. Back in the Austrian days I'd given it over to this little Jew, whom I paid to carry it for me on marches, so as not to get overheated. He did a good job of it, at the rate of two crowns for every thirty kilometres. Then we had that tussle with the Russians; the Jew stayed behind and I fell into captivity – without a topcoat. In such a fashion, my luxury came back to bite me.

In the wagon I lay on the racks – that is, the upper slats along the wall – covering myself like a lord with the thin, threadbare blanket that I'd bought in Kharkov for a rouble and twenty-five kopecks on the Russian-and-prisoners' market, which was held there every day.

They were saying that we were on our way to Siberia – Krasnoyarsk. Up until then, I'd known of Siberia only from maps and a little from Russian literature, which I'd read sitting by a warm stove. Now, it appeared to me as a great white spectre, reaching out to pull me close in its freezing embrace. I was shivering, both from the cold and from thinking about that white ghoul…

Every other dinner was stolen from us, and every other twenty-five kopecks, which they gave us as a food allowance, they shoved into their own pockets. Thus, we had a meal only very infrequently. Instead of bread they gave us seven or nine kopecks. On an empty stomach, we froze all the more. Our vital energy dropped day by day, along with the thermometer. I neither undressed nor changed my clothes for weeks on end, nor did I bathe, because of the cold. I stopped struggling against the lice who, it seemed, were warm enough thank you, and who bit me all the more fiercely when I raised my hand against them. I no longer even wanted to get out of the wagon when we'd stop at a station, so as to avoid looking at the market women and their counters with roasted meat, *pirogi*, sausages, loaves of bread, and other pleasant items. I didn't even want to get a whiff of the aromas which floated so irritatingly through the air.

Around me in the wagon there were some who had more than enough clothing and cash. Supposedly, in Przemyśl, right before the capitulation, when they were even burning banknotes just so that they wouldn't fall into the Russians' hands, these fellows sewed thousands into their capes and tunics – and now they were set up, carefree. They stuck together like a coterie of counts. They isolated themselves and buttoned themselves up to the chin. The rest of us, those with whom I most often had to do, were just as wretchedly poor as I.

Like Fischer and Geréb. Back when our bellies were more or less full, we'd sometimes engage in huge arguments. Then, our common poverty quieted us more and more until our conversation was confined to greetings made up of the phrase: 'Kushanya net, deneg net?'[75] At which, he so greeted would respond in the affirmative: 'Kushanya net, deneg net.'

....

[75] Russian: 'No food, no money?'

After such an exchange of pleasantries, we'd usually hang our heads and enter into no further discussion.

Our spirits were lifted a bit when we succeeded in stealing half a rick of straw and shoving it into the wagon, so that we might be a little warmer and the slats beneath us a little softer. Later, when one of our more dexterous mates grubbed up a discarded stove and metal plates from a scrap heap and set it up in the wagon, we had quite a lovely iron stove with stovepipe, which we fired with stolen wood. A sort of quiet exaltation settled down upon us then. Blissfully, we gazed at the little flame glowing in the stove and warming us. It mattered not that it smoked up a storm and that in little time we up on the 'rack' were as cured as smoked hams.

Then one of the POWs, Eliáš Kováč, died on the cot below us. It struck me that he had some nice boots and an overcoat that was almost new.

'It wouldn't be out of order to slip them off him,' I thought. 'What good are they to a dead man? They'll bury them along with him, and a beautiful mantle and pair of good boots will just rot along with him. And they would come in so handy to me! How my mood would improve – how much warmer I'd be!'

But I chased the ghoulish thought from my mind.

Sometime around 16 October snow fell – and never stopped falling thereafter. We crossed the Urals into Asia. Little hills and mountains covered in birch and spruce. We followed the Ural River for quite some time. Snow everywhere. People on sleds.

'If it's not raining back home,' I thought, 'it'll be Indian summer.' And I gazed off into the snow-covered summits.

In Chelyabinsk they added ten kopecks to our dinner allowance. I bought myself a pound of bread for six kopecks, and spent three and a half on *makhorka*. Rolling paper cost a kopeck, so I had to go halves with Daumer, a former waiter. And thus: breakfast and smokes.

In Kurgan they loaded us into wagons that had stoves. If it hadn't been for our stove in the old train, we would've frozen to death by then. But here it was just the opposite problem. It got so bad for us up on the 'rack' that we couldn't take it long before we had to climb down to cool off.

Slowly, slowly we crawled onwards. We passed through Petropavlovsk and arrived in Omsk. It was a bright and cold morning. The eastern sky was ablaze with red.

'Gorit vostok,' I declaimed gloomily in my soul, reading through the telegrams, where 'grokhochut pushki.'[76] I read that Serbia was in hot water: Bulgaria and the Austrian-German armies were pressing it from two sides.

I saw little of Omsk, where Dostoyevsky had suffered. Larger and smaller houses, wooden, not many trees. Nothing but birches. But I wasn't interested in the city as much as I was in the white bread, which was being sold for some five–six kopecks and roast chicken – a rather large one – which could be had for thirty-five. A pound of cooked pork cost thirty, a pound of compressed sugar eighteen–nineteen...

It wasn't so long since I'd greeted Geréb with:

'Kushanya net, deneg net?'

And he in return would reply:

'Kushanya net, deneg net.'

Now, I just waved my hand at that *kushanye*.

I resumed my philosophising in Nikolayevsk, even though the saying goes that hungry men don't talk philosophy. I kept meditating on how it could be possible that when there is neither *kushanye* nor *deneg*, everybody was eating except me and Geréb. But I felt too weak to call the entire gang of my travelling companions onto the carpet.

....

[76] Russian: 'The east is burning'; 'Cannons are rumbling.' Those are lines from poem 'Poltava' (1829) by Alexander Pushkin.

We passed through Irkutsk, a large, beautiful city on the Angara River. What a beautiful region. Tunnel after tunnel. And off in the distance Lake Baikal shimmered like liquid silver. Tall, ragged-toothed white summits, as if sifted with sugar. And to the right, black summits, like pieces of broken chocolate. How much better would it have been if the waves of Lake Baikal weren't flowing like liquid silver, but rather silver was flowing in abundance like the waves of Lake Baikal.

There was no room for us in Krasnoyarsk. So on we went. They let us out in Beryozovka-za-Baikalom.

VI. IN BERYOZOVKA-
ZA-BAIKALOM

It was the morning of 1 November. A little village with a mass of wooden barracks. They said that there were 30,000 prisoners kept there, of various nationalities. The surroundings were hilly – bare, gritty, rocky, and spruce-covered.

It was a beautiful morning, but it was cold. A wind was blowing, and it was biting enough. It smote me rather brazenly, as if it knew that I was without a topcoat and had flimsy, battered boots. It penetrated my shirt and pierced my feet from below. In vain I battled against it like a soldier, swinging my arms as it blew around me and stamping it beneath my feet. In spirit I cursed the Russian way of doing things, which was just the same as it was with us, that is, the lot of the soldier is to walk, walk, or to stand – and when you were to stand, you stood and you stood. And so we stood – firm and surely, just as it's written in the Slovak anthem.[77] First at the station, then at the barracks, then in front of

....

[77] The Slav anthem, rather, or 'Hej, Slovania!' [Hey, Slavs, 1834], words by the Slovak Lutheran pastor Samo Tomášik (1813–1887), set to the music of the 'Mazurek Dąbrowskiego' (composer unknown). Jesenský's reference is to the concluding lines of the third stanza, which read in Slovak: 'My stojíme stále pevne, / ako múry hradné / Čierna zem pohltí toho, / kto odstúpi zradne!' [Firm and surely do we stand / Like a castle's walls / May the black earth swallow him / Who treacherously deserts!]

the barracks where we were to be lodged, then in the lanes between the barracks, then in the barracks themselves, then in front of the barracks again, before our bath, where we were to bathe, and after bathing, we stood in the wind and waited until others got done – some even laundering their linen. We'd had enough, for sure, when we finally got into the shack they'd assigned us.

They jammed sixteen of us into a narrow, oblong room. Cots were ranged in tiers along one of the walls. The corridor down on the floor next to the lowest tier was so narrow that only one person could pass along it at a time. My right side was raw from constantly lying on hard surfaces, and here too the cots were bare, and filthy on top of that – just like all of us. There was one little window that gave out onto the icy and snowy outdoors. But you couldn't see anything because between the outer and inner panes there was a thick, opaque sheet of ice – which would melt under the influence of the interior warmth until it formed a large puddle beneath our cots – a little lake, in fact. Then, the ice would form again, accumulating until it reached the very top of the window. When the moon was out, the ice would glitter and shine in the darkness of our room, which was dark indeed, as they didn't even give us the smallest soldier's lamp for light.

I'd lay there often on my back, fully clothed, gazing at the bright ice and wondering how I might come into the possession of boots and a cloak.

'For God's sake, I won't even be able to go outside like this,' I fretted. 'God, to have a short Russian fur coat, big Russian snow boots, and a *papakha*[78] – that'd be ideal! If I were dressed up as a Russian, I'd get to the porridge sooner. Cash, cash, cash – without money you won't get anywhere. There won't be any coat or boots or furry cap, and the gruel will go

....

[78]   A high cylindrical winter hat made of fur.

to a mangy mutt, or they'll scrape all the fat out of it; we'll drink our tea bitter, unsweetened, because they'll swipe my sugar cubes; I'll get no bigger portion of meat than your little finger, because they'll steal three quarters of the portion; I'll get less and less bread because they'll be thieving that, too… I have to make some money. But how? I trained as a lawyer. What good is a lawyer's education here? If only I were a cobbler or a tailor, or at least a Gypsy musician. There's a pass to the good life, with boots… A fee for sewing trousers – and music for the sobbing soul is always in demand. All these pay better than law-complaints or a graveside eulogy. It's true that I've written letters for some prisoners, and when I read the Russian papers, I tell them what's in the news – but I'm not going to ask them to pay me for that…'

But when Geréb saw that I knew how to read Russian, that I understood what I read, and that I'm able to relate it to others, he came up to me and said:

'Listen – you've got to be a little practical here. Let them pay you for every article you read, every letter you write. The prisoners are really interested in what's going on at the fronts and in the rear. They'll hand over a kopeck, or two, or even three, gladly.'

I laughed at the suggestion.

'No, really,' he went on. 'We'll go from barrack to barrack and read them the news for a fee.'

'No, no, that's not for me,' I said, my pride taking voice. Then: 'I don't even have start-up capital,' I said, turning the idea over in my mind. 'Where'll we get the papers we need to buy?' I asked at last, admitting the possibility.

'If you don't want to walk about the barracks,' Geréb coaxed me, 'I'll do it for you. You translate the news for me, and I'll go read at the different barracks. I'll provide us with the *Russkoye slovo*, paper and pencil, and we'll divide the profits.'

'It's kind of desperate,' I said.

'Let's give it a go,' Geréb insisted.

And so, in this way, the first oral news service in Beryo-zovka was founded, and I made my first money. Geréb brought in thirty or forty, even fifty kopecks every day. I improved my standard of living with half of my honorarium, which is to say I had sugar in my tea, sifted powdered sugar on my gruel, smeared my bread with butter – some days I even allowed myself an extra supper: noodles with poppyseed or nuts, now and then some goulash made from a cat or some other domestic animal they'd caught... The prisoners were pretty good at cooking up and seasoning such things, which they sold at steep prices. Such an extra supper cost some fifteen to twenty kopecks. I also had some sizeable expenses in that I'd send my linen off to be laundered. The cook I sent it to wouldn't wash drawers for less than five kopecks, while a kerchief cost one, and a small hand towel – three.

And lo and behold, even in such poverty, I took on lordly airs. I sent out my linen to be laundered instead of washing it myself, I dissolved sugar cubes in my tea (instead of holding a cube between my teeth and sipping the tea over it, as the Russians did); I treated myself to some fine suppers instead of satisfying myself with the watery soup (or soupy water) that they gave us for our evening 'meal.' On account of all that high life, I wasn't able to save up the two roubles that I needed to telegram home and ask them to send me some money. I hesitated before borrowing from the Przemyśl magnates, for I reckoned that the sight of my unkempt beard wouldn't win me much from them, and that my lack of a greatcoat and those decomposing boots of mine – which I hadn't yet had time to exchange for new ones – would knock the very idea of a loan right out of their heads.

It's true that the Russians came around the barracks to note down what anyone needed, at which time I requested a greatcoat and boots – but those requests merely remained on paper. I went from pillar to post about the offices until I succeeded in acquiring a Chinese mantle, that is, a long quilted frock with sleeves, of grey colour, which reached my heels. I looked a fright in it, but at least I was a little warmer and had something to cover myself with as I lay upon my cheap and threadbare blanket. It's true that, meanwhile, I had sold one of my undershirts for forty kopecks, but that Chinese frock enlarged my inventory by a nice piece of cloth.

'Now, just boots, two roubles for a telegram, and I'll be more or less set up,' I cheered myself in spirit. 'I'll earn enough for daily expenses by translating the news and writing letters – thirty or forty kopecks a day, if the Good Lord preserve my health.'

But a nice fur coat is a surer defence against the Siberian weather than the Good Lord. The Chinese frock arrived late. I started to feel the cold and my head began to pound. Nor was my stomach in the best shape after all those cats and dogs. I started to be plagued by feverish dreams and I grew weak. I went off to visit the doctor. He gave me quinine. I cooled down my head with snow and slowly the headaches passed away, as did the shivers, after about a week. I started to think that I was well again. The bright, starry Siberian nights once more began to gladden my eyes with their huge moons, as did the pleasant winter mornings – green at dawn, then grey, becoming still and sunny days with the temperature hovering between 12 and 15 degrees below; and the surrounding hills, grey with frost like Russian *papakha*. Even my dreams were first-rate. Once more I seemed to be home, eating *koláče*[79] and chocolate pastries – which were signs of hunger. And then the lice. I'd find ten or fifteen a day. Such a tiny speck of a nit would grow, over the space of one night, into quite a beast, and just changing clothes didn't suffice. But I kept up with writing telegrams and translating articles from the *Russkoye slovo* and

....

[79] *Koláče* are sweet pastries popular amongst the Czechs and Slovaks.

the *Irkutskaya zhizn*,[80] cashing in my fifteen or twenty kopecks from Geréb. In a word, I was back to health.

Once, even Strážmajster Béla Sárközy, who had also been at Przemyśl, and had the reputation of being a moneyed chap, engaged me in conversation. I'd always thought him to be a rather pitiless cynic, and lo and behold, how wrong I was. He loaned me five roubles, a portion of which I used to telegraph home.

I sent a telegram to my wife, informing her that I was in good health, that all was well with me, but that it would all be a good bit better if I had at least a hundred roubles in my pocket; and if not a hundred, at least thirty – just like a student might write to his father. I wrote about fifteen other letters to people I knew and some I didn't. Among others, I wrote a letter to Bohdan Pavlů, of whom I'd heard that he was in Petrograd, editing the periodical *Čechoslovák*. I asked if it would be possible for him to help me to come among them, or at least get somewhere near. I also asked after Ivan and Igor Daxner, who were also in captivity.

Geréb was bringing in fewer and fewer kopecks with each passing day, although I was translating strenuously, and that, not just telegrams from the battlefield, but whole articles. For example, B. Mikhailovsky's thoughts on Serbia, Radko Dimitriev's long essay on the Bulgarian nation, the reflections of Nemirovich-Danchenko, also concerning Bulgaria, and others. At the same time I observed that my distributor was somehow spending more money than I was. He was having double portions of extra supper, shelling out funds here and there. I on the other hand was in debt for one extra goulash, short two kopecks for cigarettes, and yet, when you get right down to it, I'm the one doing the heavy lifting and not you, you wretched automaton, who only blabber out what I set in your larynx, devil take you!

....

[80] Russian: *The Irkutsk Life.*

One time, he chided me for overlooking a supposedly very interesting article.

'Well, you know, you're asking a lot for those nine kopecks of yours,' I snapped in reply. 'Translate it yourself, why don't you?'

'That'll be it for the news, then,' he warned.

'So what. Any business that can't stay afloat goes under.'

'But that'll be it for us, as well.'

'So, down we go, then.'

'And today, they're preparing *gombóce*. There'll be fresh black coffee, too,' he coaxed, wanting us to continue on with our joint venture. 'And you've gotten so thin lately. You need to put some meat on those bones.'

But I wasn't in the mood for *gombóce*, or *knédliky*, as we call dumplings in Slovak. For three or four days now, I'd been feeling shaky again, and when you've got the ague, you're neither hungry nor tempted by food. All the same, it was as if all the cooks were conspiring against me with the suppers they were preparing. There was goulash, *halušky* with cabbage – my favourites – and here my stomach was up in arms. I always passed on three fourths of my portions to Geréb.

'It'll be the same with those *gombóce*,' I thought to myself. 'You won't tempt me with that.'

All the same, I translated the latest news and Geréb took around enough of them that I had my dumplings and coffee too.

Later that night I had a high fever. I was constantly thirsty and I had the sweats. Rummaging around for the cold tea that the captives often kept in their flasks, I nearly drank down some kerosene by mistake. Near morning, I placed some compresses on my bosom and over my heart to cool it down and stop its racing. My head was spinning and I felt so groggy and weak that I could barely remain on my feet.

In the morning, it left me. In the evening I was already eating some sour potato soup, and for extras I had *halušky* with poppyseed, followed by *paprikáš*[81] and finishing up with goulash. The illness disappeared. At least so it seemed to me.

I had peace and quiet from the end of November until 9 December. Meanwhile, I received not one, but two telegrams from my wife, in which she informed me that she was sending me some money. Of course, whether that money would actually get to me without losing its way and winding up in someone else's pocket, or if indeed it got to me, when exactly that would be – this was all a distant melody. But the telegrams themselves were good signs. When I asked Strážmajster Ďurovič for a loan of two roubles, so that I might send a telegram to my wife, he gave me ten, with the explanation that he hadn't anything smaller on him. He entrusted me with such a large sum and I, bonehead that I am, did not betray his trust. Instead of ten roubles I returned him only six. But although my honesty was relative, it was honesty all the same. Thanks to my wife's telegrams, even Volunteer Fischer appeared on the horizon, though at a distance, for I still didn't have the money in hand. Szirmay, my cot-neighbour, who rolled and sold cigarettes, urged them upon me, saying that I could pay for them later. My other neighbour, Kelemen, funded me supper. In short, my credit rose to unbelievable heights and I felt again as I did before my law exam, and for a long time thereafter, when I lived on future bills of exchange, honoured by all Slovak banks and their branches.

Telegrams weren't enough for a cloak and boots, true enough, but they were worth at least so much that I was able to set aside our oral news service, satisfying myself alone with the news I got from the papers, without spreading it through the barracks and alarming the other captives with what I read. For it was desperate news indeed and fostered no hope

....

[81] A dish popular in Slovakia and Hungary, consisting of a sauce of red peppers (hence the name), often with meat.

JANKO JESENSKÝ

for a quick end to the war. On the contrary: the entanglement of events just got worse and worse, and the inferno spread ever more wildly. Anyone and everyone was tossing fuel on the flames, which no one was putting out.

At the start of December the winter turned sharper. The temperature dropped to 27–30 degrees below zero. The dawns could be magnificent, for they glowed with a rose-coloured light, and the mountain summits were as white as if coated with lime. The prisoners who weren't careful got frostbitten ears and noses. We hustled more than one of our comrades outside and into the snow, to rub his nose with snow when we noticed him returning with an appendage a bit too white-coloured. The Russian soldiers still drilled, but civilian passers-by covered their faces with fur mufflers.

I was still shaking with my fever. I lay on my cot and curled into a ball beneath my blanket. One evening I wanted to go outside, but I hadn't taken more than a few steps before my head began to spin and I fell senseless onto a cot. I was out for a while. The others rubbed my hands and my brow with water. Kelemen gave me some Hoffman Drops. Someone ran off for the doctor.

And that's how I landed in hospital. It was a hospital manned entirely by physicians who were also prisoners of war. It was really just a sickroom, a so-called *maródizba*, large and high-ceilinged, with three Russian pot-bellied stoves. The only things of brick here were the chimneys leading off from those stoves; otherwise, the whole barrack was made of wood. The rafters were supported on posts and along the walls of the room, there were four rows of wooden beds with mattresses, and on them the sick men lay. Those who had been operated on were moaning, here and there; many were coughing, and some were fast asleep. Almost everyone who found himself here was, it seemed, suffering from a solid case of ague and fever as I was, and worn away with it.

My fever subsided as the night passed. The next morning brought a beautiful Siberian day. I lay there on my sky-blue mattress, with which I was greatly pleased. I leaned my head against the wall and wrote. In the morning they gave us tea with sugar. Before dinner, we each got a piece of white bread – some patients were even given milk. We were brought our supper from company: soup, meat, and porridge. For supper they gave us a piece of white bread again and caraway soup. I drank two bowls. Each of us also got one egg apiece. It was warm in that room. Even the WC was heated, and there was toilet paper. It was simply marvellous. In the evening they measured my temperature: normal.

The doctor came by and examined me, tapping me here and there. He asked me to turn over onto my back and, it seemed, to take some deep breaths. I did, and he listened. He told me to turn on my side and breathe again. He held my side, and I breathed. I stuck out my tongue. He took my pulse and noted everything down on a card.

'You haven't been ill with any long-term ailment?' he asked.

'No,' I said. 'I had typhus more than twenty years ago.'

But I didn't know what was wrong with me.

'Is it the flu, doctor?'

'It's the flu,' he confirmed.

But it had to be something more serious, because for a long time I walked around in a funk, joyless and rather apathetic. I grew so thin that I was just skin and bones. My muscles went flabby and my mood soured. Later, my legs began to pain me, my fingers got swollen, and they also hurt.

I returned to my company on the third day. They all greeted me warmly. They told me that a telegram had arrived for me.

It was from my wife, urging me to reply to her earlier wires.

My telegram to her was still laying at the censor's. I had handed it in before I fell ill with that fever, and somehow didn't get it back – but perhaps because I didn't try hard enough. I'd spent those four roubles from Ďurovič, and once more had no more money with which to pay for a telegram. So I took the first telegram from my wife out of my pocket – the one in which she gave notice about the money, and went off to Strážmajster Sárközy to ask for another three roubles. He gave them gladly and at last I was able to properly hand my telegram over to the post to be sent out.

But the groschen from my wife never seemed to arrive. Christmas came round, and – nothing. We treated ourselves to goulash on Christmas Eve. Russia honoured us with salt water and one potato in a metal washbasin, for lunch. The night was a bad one: the wind howled so, it seemed poised to lift the barracks off their foundations and carry us away with them. We were shivering with cold. We slept fully dressed, which was to the advantage of no one but the lice, who sipped on our thin blood in warmth and comfort, multiplying rapidly, despite our constant persecutions of them, mercilessly crushing them and burning out their nests concealed in our seams with matches.

At last, after New Year's, my dreams finally came true. The Austrian Red Cross came among the prisoners and dressed them as well as they knew how. I received a military parade mantle of a reddish colour and high-laced boots, with beautiful thick soles.

'O, this'll be parade-ground elegant!' I thought to myself, but there was no mirror anywhere on which I might feast my eyes on my new look. 'And now, if just a few of those roubles came in, everything'd be almost all in order...'

And then, just like in a bedtime story, the thought had barely crossed my mind before I was brought word from the post office of the arrival of some thirty roubles, and again of eight roubles and forty kopecks. The first came from Bohdan Pavlů, the second from my mother back in Martin. It's true that it took them some two weeks to finally pay it out to me – in

Russia, nothing moves quickly – but this was something more than mere hope that I'd actually receive enough for myself, and to pay back those on whose credit I'd been living.

'And now, if only the money sent me by my wife would come, I'd be a wealthy man.'

And then fifty roubles arrived from her.

'And now, just a tiny bit of freedom!' I bartered in my mind.

And lo! I was summoned to Battalion. Handshakes and smiles. They had me sit down.

'You're being given your freedom,' an officer told me. 'We've received word from Petrograd that you've translated nearly all of Pushkin into Slovak. Is that true?'

'Well,' I replied. 'A good bit…' I confirmed.

In reality, I'd only translated his story 'The Tale of the Fisherman and the Fish.'[82] As a fifth-former. When I was just learning Russian. It was never published. 'Who thought up this con?' I wondered.

'You're a poet,' the officer prodded me. 'You'll get a private room and a *propusk*[83] here in camp until we can transport you to central Russia, so that you'll have freedom of movement even now.'

I saluted, clicking my heels together smartly, military-fashion, and the officer shook my hand once more.

I was honoured. A grubby Austrian POW shaking the hand of a proud Russian officer.

They really did want to give me my own private room with a bed, but that would mean evicting some older Austrian strážmajster, and I wouldn't have that. So I remained among my old friends.

....

[82] A verse fairy-story based on the 'The Fisherman and his Wife' by the Brothers Grimm. Published in 1835, the title in Russian reads 'Сказка о рыбаке и рыбке.'

[83] Russian: Pass.

I also really obtained the *propusk,* which allowed me to wander around Beryozovka from seven in the morning until seven at night. I wanted to try it out immediately. I made my way to the village, but there I was nearly run through with a bayonet. I showed them the *propusk* with all its stamps.

'We can't trust *propusks,*' growled the soldier with the bayonet in reply.

So I went back. A stout bayonet will always carry the day against paper and human flesh.

'Just like back home,' I thought. 'Law is on the side of the paper, but it' s the bayonet that's really in charge.'

Slowly, March arrived. Once a debtor, I now became a creditor myself. I paid back Ďurovič, Sárközy, Kelemen and Szermay, honestly. Then Volunteer Fischer happened by. Once more, he was just waiting for some money to arrive from Pest, but since it wasn't coming, could I help him out a bit? I gave him a couple of roubles. Then it was my assistant editor and distributor of the oral news service, Geréb. I knew what he was after before he even opened his mouth. I gave him some, too. This one came, and that one.

'That's enough,' I said. 'I'm supposed to be leaving for Russia, and I need some cash myself.'

But even if I'd sewn the money into the most intimate corner of my greasy undershirt, I'd have to rip it out and share it all the same.

'The gluttons!' I muttered.

It was going well for me – a capitalist with a full belly, new greatcoat, gorgeous boots and *propusk.*

VII. BERYOZOVKA – VORONEZH

I was lying on my cot listening to the Germans singing 'Edler Adler.' 'Fein, fein schmeckt uns der Wein... Servus du...'[84] etc., when a certain Magyar showed up inside our barracks and told me to get my things together and report to the major at his office. It was about eight in the evening. I got up a little grumpily, threw on my greatcoat and went. I knew that I was to be sent off to Russia, but I also knew that I had fifty roubles waiting for me at the post office, which my wife had sent me, and that if I wouldn't be able to collect them, they would either be stolen, or, in the best possible case, sent after me – and then it would take at least a year until I got my hands on them.

And so I requested that my trip be put off for one day. But the Russians, who had forgotten already that I had translated 'all' of Pushkin into Slovak, refused to comply with my request. The order said that I was to be ready at 9:00 that evening, when an escort would arrive for me.

And that's what happened. My escort came at 9:00, outfitted with gun, banderoles across his chest, and bayonet. And off we went. It was a beautiful, still night. The moon shone and little clouds slid across the sky like coils of smoke. The road was frozen, covered with snow, our footsteps crunched and squeaked and our breath steamed before our faces as if we were smoking pipes. We waited at the station until maybe

....

[84]   German: 'Fine, fine, the wine tastes to us... Here's to you.'

JANKO JESENSKÝ

1:30 in the morning. Then a little window in the booking office lit up, opened, and my escort presented the man there with our marching orders.

Fortunately for me, the marching orders had been improperly filled out. For sure, instead of listing the aim of my journey as Voronezh, where I was supposed to be heading, it read something like Vladivostok or Harbin. It was impossible to rectify the error that night, so we trudged back to camp.

Thus the Lord God Himself intervened in my journey so that I could collect my fifty roubles. Of course, it cost me a lot of effort, a lot of rushing from pillar to post, a lot of sweat until I was permitted to withdraw them from the post office out of the regular order, but I got them at last, and all the same we left on the next night.

There's lots of everything in Russia: lots of porridge, lots of bread, lots of flies, lice, bedbugs, and lots of travellers. The passenger wagon was filled to bursting. I got a place right up near the ceiling. My hands were swollen and pained me. It was difficult for me to climb up to the heights, and difficult for me to lower myself into the depths. As if this pain wasn't enough, I was still having stomach problems. I had to make the trip to the *ubornaya*[85] again and again. And the *ubornaya* was always occupied. The need for haste was excruciating, and it was pure torture to wait my turn. Although there was a sign there reading 'mozhno polzovatsya'[86] for fifteen minutes, it seemed to me that everyone in front of me was determined on sitting there until we reached Voronezh.

Once, in a real emergency, I made my way to another wagon. Pure elegance here: clean, electric lighting, plush seats – all occupied by high-ranking Russian officers. My hair stood on end. I wanted to evaporate, but before I could

....

[85]   Russian: WC.

[86]   Russian: 'Can be used.'

a Russian guard rushed up to me, poking his bayonet at my bosom.

'Well then,' I said to myself. 'I made it through combat unscathed, and now I'm supposed to kick the bucket here? For such a little peccadillo? What – is the Tsar among them, or what?!'

I began trying to explain to the guard how it came to be that I had suddenly appeared there, and what I was after. As soon as he heard my Slavic speech he calmed down, lowered his gun and said, mercifully:

'Idi!'[87]

We passed through Chelyabinsk. The masses of travellers grew no less. Only at Irkutsk did the wagon thin out a bit and I was able to change places from the uppermost tier to floor-level. The exchange wasn't entirely favourable. From the upper 'étages,' muddy, hobnailed boots with heel irons were always hanging right above my head; I had to protect my nut constantly. Hardly a moment passed without someone climbing up or lowering himself down. There was a constant blizzard of seeds, apple cores, straw, greasy papers, crusts. People were always sitting down on my bench and making me straighten up when I wanted to stretch out prone. The pain in my arms now spread throughout all of my bones, my neck, my head.

But *joie de vivre* would not allow me to grow languid. I bought and read the news from the *Russkoye slovo, Solntse Rossii, Novoye vremya, Zhenshchina, Novy Satiricon, Ves mir*[88] and other such periodicals.

I read the more interesting articles and humoresques aloud to the Russians, whenever the tireless balalaika player

....

[87] Russian: 'Go then.'

[88] Russian: *The Russian Word; The Sun of Russia; New Time; Woman; The New Satiricon; The Whole World.*

JANKO JESENSKÝ

paused plinking his one and only note for a minute, or loaned his admirable instrument to someone in a farther corner of the wagon. My audience consisted of a cobbler travelling with three pairs of boots, a soldier with fat, greasy cheeks, who was always chewing on something, a young gendarme with a lisp, whose response to everything was always the same: 'da' or 'ha,' and another gendarme with bad teeth who drank his tea unsweetened and gnawed on hard crusts given him by some civilian or other.

Archishchevo, Samara, Syzran, Penza, Kozlov. Everywhere, changes of trains and exhausting periods of waiting. My travelling companions changed, and I was cast now on the first tier, now on the floor, and once again right beneath the ceiling amidst the crates and sacks, where I had to lash myself in securely so that I wouldn't tumble down should sleep come upon me in that position.

Approaching Voronezh, there were so many people that I had to stand squeezed so tightly amongst three fat women that I could hardly breathe.

We finally arrived in Voronezh at 8:00 or so on the morning of 21 March. Aching, fatigued from lack of sleep, wrought-up, half-dead, I got off the train, dragging my baggage with one hand. The fresh air returned to me the half of my life that I'd lost, and after I'd washed up at the station and drank down a couple of mugs of hot tea, I came back to life entirely. I hired an *izvozchik*[89] and for forty kopecks sledded off with my convoy to the 'upravleniye voinskogo nachalnika'[90] It was my first sleigh ride in Russia. The *voinsky nachalnik* questioned me, and then handed me an *udostovereniye*[91] declaring me 'provisionally liberated within the administra-

....

[89] Russian: Cabman.

[90] Russian: Military commander's office.

[91] Russian: Certificate, identity card.

tive regions of the Voronezh guberniya, as attested to by this signature and the seals affixed thereunto…'

And so I and my convoy parted company. I thanked him for watching over me, gave him a little something, and thus became free, 'provisionally,' and only 'within the administrative regions of the Voronezh guberniya.'

VIII. VORONEZH

Freedom is like a girlfriend. You've got to support her, or she'll be unfaithful to you. And the more valuable she is, the more she costs you.

Up until now, the Russian state had more or less taken care of me. I had a roof over my head, and 'no need to forage – we've got our porridge.'[92] From now on, I had to take care of my bread and board myself.

They chased me away from the barracks and the kitchen door was closed in my face with the words:

'You've been released. You may go on your way. Just make sure we have your address.'

It's true that I still had a few roubles in my pocket, but – well then? A little room with some modest furnishings and a stove as tiny as a dwarf cost thirty roubles a month. Go find yourself a place!

'At least let me remain in the barracks until I find a flat and some patron or other,' I asked.

'Oof! You'll need to make a request in writing for that.'

'That's great,' I exulted. 'Until they attend to that in the chancelleries, half a year will pass, and perhaps the war will be over before then.'

So I submitted my written request, and repaired to the office of a sawbones named Pyotr Kazakov, a pudgy, broad-shouldered and gay young fellow with a shock of black

....

[92] In Slovak: 'tú kašu – mať našu' [this gruel here – is our mother].

hair, the sort that artists have, and moustaches as thin as two skinny caterpillars beneath his broad nose.

The doctor's office was a large, light-filled space with two rows of beds, an iron stove in the centre of the room, the long stove-pipe of which stretched through the ceiling, and innumerable cages all along the walls and at the windows.

For Kazakov was a great lover of birds. Some twenty different songbirds chattered, leapt about, and sang in ten of those cages. There was a clatter of chirping there just like in the woods, especially in the morning. I would gaze at these little creatures: each one of them sent forth one sound or another. Only the famous lark kept quiet. The first few days of his captivity, he kept hopping about, batting himself against the bars, wanting out. Then he just kept impatiently pacing back and forth in the cage, never uttering a sound. The poor thing!

The doctor talked to the birds, whistled, and sang along with them, and I along with him.

Besides Kazakov and me, there were two other soldiers there: greyish, bearded Landsturmers of the same sort as Timofei Ivanych and Bornikov. They were very pious. Every morning I watched from my bed as they bowed in the direction of the icons in the corner and made the Sign of the Cross, first standing, then on their knees, and finally touching their foreheads to the floor. I felt something squeeze at my heart.

They also knew how to blow their noses as expertly as my comrades in Kharkov, but their table manners were impeccable. They'd have two or three slurps of their soup before banging their wooden spoons down on the table, as if they wanted no more. Whoa! How hot! But this was just a breather, a pause so that no one would think them wolfishly hungry. After the pause they'd take up their spoons again, slurp another two or three times, and then bang their spoons down again. This slurp-and-bang, slurp-and-bang, was like a drill. They'd picked it up from Kazakov. I didn't want to be any worse, so I began to adapt myself to them, slurping and banging.

In the evenings, we'd usually cook our own suppers on the iron stove. We'd cook sausages, eggs, and boil water for tea. I did my part for the common table, bringing sausages, rolls, eggs, butter and sugar from town, along with carrots for the birds. Every now and then Kazakov and I went off to a cafeteria for borscht and cutlets.

Going to the market like this almost every day, I would look around to see where signs were hanging with 'Rooms to Let.' But I couldn't get up the courage to go into the buildings. In my Jewish cap, with that reddish greatcoat with double lapels and metal buttons on the shoulders and back, puttees and huge boots, presented me by the Austrian Red Cross, you could tell that I was a foreigner from two kilometres away. I figured that every Russian would chase me away from the threshold, to say nothing of inviting me in.

Voronezh is a big city. Businesses everywhere, a large post office, a permanent theatre, confectionery shops, hotels, cinemas, and three or four parks. A bust of Koltsov in Koltsov Park, a statue of Ivan Savich Nikitin – Russian poet and native of Voronezh – as a dried-up, tense old man of about fifty with long hair, a narrow beard, and arm hanging, as if fainting, before him. Farther on was the statue of Peter the Great in the park named for him, wearing a snowy *papakha* on his head; thick whiskers, grim brows, and an anchor in his right hand. He was pointing somewhere with his left. History can tell us where, but it seemed to me that he was pointing at a park bench, of which only the backrest was protruding from the snow. It was as if he were saying:

'In Germany they clear away the snow and cart it out of the city to give the sun a little hand. So that spring might come along a little more quickly, along with dry pavements. But you lot do nothing? Your main street, Dvoryanskaya, is still covered in ice and the cobbles are already dry beneath! In Germany, they'd break up that ice and cart it off! They'd have a nice dry road. But you? You even let this *papakha* of snow here on my head. That's how you honour me?'

'That's it,' I said, confirming Peter's suspicions.

'Why not?' the Russians wondered. 'The sun'll do it without any help from us. And we're at war with Germany. We're not going to do anything they do!'

So the road stayed just as it was, under the ice. Toward afternoon, the ice melted and the water mixed in with dirt to form a mud covering for the drying cobbles. It was muddy and wet everywhere. They only cleared it away from the rails of the horse-tram. The exhausted little horse slipped along between the rails, the coachman with his frozen, icicle-stiff whiskers was shouting, ringing his bell and zipping his little whip over the horse's back, and people would dance around morning and evening through half-frozen water and mud.

I took my breakfast in Tifental's pastry shop. Good coffee, and especially chocolate, didn't pair well with my exterior appearance. But the Russians didn't make a fuss about it. Undisturbed myself, I busied myself with my correspondence, and then read the *Russkoye slovo*. I was hoping to find there the end of the war, so that I wouldn't have to rent a room. I was elated in spirit to read of Haase's speech against the war... 'There will be neither victor nor vanquished, and further bloodshed is nothing but insanity...' And I grew irate at those who shouted Haase down and wouldn't allow him to speak.

'Those jokers in warm rooms!' I fulminated against them, and continued to read:

'Turtsiya ishchet mira...'[93] But England won't even hear of a separate peace... The *sovet soyuznikov*[94] in France maintain

....

[93] Russian: 'Turkey seeks peace.'

[94] Russian: Allied council.

that an advance must be attempted on all fronts... There will be war until Germany admits it's beaten...

'They can wait!' I laughed to myself, thinking bitterly that they're all crawling around peace like cats circling hot porridge, afraid of taking a bite so as not to singe their whiskers. 'And those Russians, those Russians, those Russians! *Artilleriiskaya perestrelka*,[95] and the result: zero, or two zeros, or what's contained in two zeros,' I thought angrily. 'They stand rooted to the spot like trees on the hills. The devil take them! The whole war stands still as long as the Russians don't move, and here we're waiting for it to be over and done with! And the end won't come, and I'll have to go and rent myself a room...'

I received word from Petrograd that the Daxners were in Bobrov, but that one of them, Vaňo, was often in Voronezh: Ostrozhny bugor 44. I went there and, by a happy coincidence, found him at home. He'd just arrived from Bobrov.

He was freshly shaven, his hair nicely combed, in a white collar with lacquered shoes of grey deer leather on his feet. He had a visiting card pinned to the door reading 'Ivan Ivanovich fon Daxner,' with a little crown.

'How elegant you are, Vaňo!' I said, after rubbing my eyes and assuring myself that indeed it was he.

'I have a position in a bank. And on top of that, an *ofitserskoye zhalovaniye*.[96] I'm getting by, more or less. I have no intention of going home, so I have to look for a permanent source of bread. And you – you want to go home?'

'What would I do here with my legal degree?'

'I'll find you a place. But as you are now – that'd be impossible.'

He turned me round, checking out my clothing front and back with expert eye.

....

[95]   Russian: Artillery barrage.

[96]   Russian: Officer's salary or pension.

'I'll give you some clothes. I've just bought some new ones.'

'Since you bought them, you need them!'

'I'll buy others.'

He showed them to me. Beautiful things – a dark blue double-breasted suit. It was a great temptation. But it passed through my mind that, if you want to preserve a friendship, neither a borrower nor a lender be. There was a mirror in the room. I glanced at myself, and just couldn't resist.

'Seriously?' I asked Vaňo once more, in case he might change his mind.

'Seriously. It's nothing.'

'Well, if it's nothing, I'll take it.'

'Please do!'

I measured the length of the pant-legs, grasping them at the ends and spreading them along my side.

'Good?' he asked.

'Good! Thanks, Vaňo. You're a prince.'

Spending the night there was a more difficult undertaking. There was neither bed nor couch for me in that little room.

'We'll find a room for both of us tomorrow,' Vaňo said. 'And here are seven vouchers for dinner at the "Moscow" cafeteria.'

'I've got three roubles twenty. Please – they're yours.'

That got him fairly riled.

'We'll put it towards the clothes,' I said.

'We're not putting anything towards anything.'

'Vaňo, you're more than a prince!' I gushed, overjoyed at having such noble relatives.

Toward evening we went out looking for a room. It was a wet season. The streets were choked with yellow fog; you could hardly make out people or buildings. My right leg was paining me. I could barely drag it behind me: leftovers from my Siberian illness – rheumatism.

When Vaňo noticed how hard it was for me to walk, he took the task of finding us lodgings on his own shoulders.

A week passed, and – nothing.

And this time I was mistaken concerning the sluggishness of Russian officialdom. My petition to be permitted to remain in the barracks was decided rapidly. Kazakov brought me the news of my request being denied. I had to leave.

'Once you're freed, you have nothing to look for among soldiers.'

The question of lodgings took on a new urgency. So we hit the streets again and checked out the To Let signs by turns.

In one such place they showed us a beautiful room. Warm, with its own bath, an *ubornaya* with porcelain fixtures, potted palms, chairs, étagères, albums, pictures, and a nice, fat, feather bed with red coverings – thirty roubles.

'Shall we take it?' Vaňo asked.

'We shall!'

We handed over a deposit.

I was to move right in. When I did, they ushered me into a room that was nearly empty, with naked walls, no furniture, no mattress on the bed, which stood there like a skeleton.

'This...' I stammered, 'this isn't the room...'

'It is,' replied a fat old woman with a black cap on her head and eczema on her yellow face. 'We just took the furniture away.'

'But why?'

'You rented an unfurnished apartment.'

'You want thirty roubles for this? I'd like our deposit back, please.'

I thought that this would get the furniture back in; instead, I was handed the ten roubles.

In another place, right before I was to move in, they told me that the room had been let to someone else. In a third, they let me know that they had not been aware of the fact that we were *voyennoplennyye avstriyaki*[97] and that they could not risk renting a place to us and coming under suspicion themselves. In the fourth place, they couldn't decide whether to rent us the front room or the one in the back. When Vaňo was there, the old woman in make-up was willing to cede the front room, but when I came by, there was no question of that. It was obvious that Vaňo had made a better impression on her than I.

'Where is that young friend of yours?... You don't have any galoshes? You need to buy some... I'll rent you the back room...'

Walking about in search of rooms began to seriously pall on me. Once, there was this old woman who took me for an old man. I kissed her hand so that she would see that I knew how to behave, wishing to bribe her a bit with a token of good upbringing. All in vain: she wasn't impressed, and gave me the back room.

Her husband, a tall, thin, grey-haired gentleman, must have been a teacher in his earlier life. He immediately explained to me:

'This is a screen. Behind it is a bed. You lay your head down here.'

He brought up a pillow as big as a walnut.

'This pillow is what you rest your head on. Not your feet. This is how you draw the shades. You turn the knob this way when you want to open the door... Here is a lamp. Turn the rowel to the left if it's too bright, and to the right if it's burning too low... If you want to douse it completely, turn the rowel to the left and puff at the flame from above.'

I nodded my head to show that I understood, although I hadn't the foggiest idea as to why he was explaining all this to me. After all, I hadn't been living in a gypsy wagon all my life up until now.

....

[97] Russian: Austrian prisoners of war.

JANKO JESENSKÝ

'This here is a washbasin,' he went on. 'You pour water into it like this... This jug here is for water, and water is what we wash ourselves with...'

'What do you know!' I interrupted him. 'Back home, we wash ourselves in grain alcohol.'

He had no idea that I was joking.

'Here they use grain alcohol to make vodka,' he explained in serious tones. And all of a sudden, he asked: 'Have you ever tasted vodka?'

'Nope.'

He brought some over and poured me a shot. If not for the vodka, I'd've figured he took me for an idiot.

Still, my anger didn't pass. The next morning, while I was still sleeping behind the screen, I was awakened by a screech. I began to listen with one ear, as it were. It was the door screeching, just like Kazakov's birds. And now they began to bustle about through the room, jangling keys, rattling bins, dragging something heavy across the floor, pouring water, swishing and sweeping.

The old man poked his curious head in behind the screen a few times.

'What bloody-minded people!' I fumed. Here they treat their *kvartirant*[98] right indeed! Won't even let him sleep!

Someone thumped against the screen and sent it rocking back and forth.

'They'll throw it down on me before long to wake me up! On purpose, the pests!' I cursed in my soul and, throwing off the bedclothes, I leapt to my feet.

When I was dressed and about to head out for breakfast, the man of the house grabbed ahold of my coattails.

'You've got to buy some galoshes,' he said. 'Those shoes of yours, take them off nicely when you get back and set them

....

[98] Russian: Lodger.

at the wall beneath the coat-tree… Hang your coat up here and that way you'll keep it dry and clean.'

'With pleasure. But at your expense…'

'And your *odeyalo*[99] is also bad. You need to buy a new one.'

'Anything else?'

'You have to leave here early in the morning and not come back till evening. You see, the holidays are on their way. We've got a lot of *bolshaya rabota* and you'd *meshat*[100] us all up if you were to stay in the room all day long.

I tore myself out of his grip and went off into town to have a look at the 'To Let' signs.

It was brutal outside. Snow and rain were falling. A sharp wind was blowing, tossing the cold raindrops into my face. My feet were soaked. I wasn't too enthusiastic about such a stroll. I looked at the other passers-by and noticed that everyone was wearing galoshes, even those with boots on. I went to Tifental's. I had my breakfast, read the *Russkoye slovo* from cover to cover, and went out again.

I'd killed a lot of things in Russia: bedbugs, lice, flies, fleas, and now I was killing time. I couldn't get back into my flat. I rang the bell and knocked against the door in vain. They couldn't hear a thing for all that *bolshaya rabota*. I went for another breakfast and read through the *Russkoye slovo* from cover to cover backwards. So that they wouldn't turn me out into the street, I picked at two or three crumbs of pastry every fifteen minutes, gazing out the window. But in Russia it's not like it is back home, where you can spend the whole night in a café for the price of a black coffee. Here, people come in, slurp and gobble what they need, and go away again. I already had maybe ten *pirozhnyye*[101] in me, so like it or not, it was time to go.

....

[99] Russian: Blanket.

[100] Russian: Big work; to disturb, to get in our way.

[101] Russian: Cakes, pastries.

The snow turned into rain and it was still just eleven o'clock. I returned to the flat but, once again, I had no luck in getting anyone's attention.

'The beasts!' I swore and went off for an appetiser.

And then for dinner. After dinner, for a black coffee at the Zhan Café on Dvoryanskaya, then off on another walk, then for a café au lait and one more stroll. I was on my way to ruin: I'd just run through four roubles. However, as evening fell, I met up with Vaňo Daxner. He had news for me: he'd found a flat at Dubnitskaya 15.

'Pack up, get your money back from those fools, and let them have a piece of your mind!' he instructed me.

So I hired a carriage to get me back to my place as quickly as possible. We went so fast on my account that the horse lost a shoe and the *izvozchik* wouldn't go on any farther with a shoeless horse. What was I to do? I got out of the carriage, paid my fare, and went off to look for a horse with all of his hooves shod.

The new flat was beautiful. To reach the room you had to pass through a sort of half-salon, half-dining room, but it was worth it – the chamber was quite large, clean and bright. There was a huge French window. Flowers on the sill: geraniums, and a bit farther from the window, arbor vitae, rose-laurels, cacti. An icon with a lamp burning before it. A painting of Cleopatra pressing the asp to her breast, a *Pesnya lyubvi*[102] depicting two people very much in love, then two more Madonnas, two vases with flowers. In a word, 'the flashing of a flower in spring,'[103] on all hands, but that which

....

[102] Russian: Song of love.

[103] A reference to the song 'Kde domův moj' [Where my Homeland is'] from the comic opera *Fidlovačka* (1834), with words by Josef Katetán Tyl (1808–1856). Line four of stanza one reads *v sadě skví se jara květ* [in the garden flashes the spring flower]. The song was later adopted as the national anthem of the Czechoslovak Republic.

pleased me the most was that the floor beneath the beds was swept clean and there were no suspicious stains on the walls.

There was a little table with a lamp. During the day the view gave onto metal roofs; at night, the sky sparkled with stars and bright windows when the lights began to glow behind them in the rooms.

What does a person need to be at peace with the world? One person might say: good health. But good health and empty pockets are like a bare foot on ice. Another person might say: freedom. But freedom in poverty is like licking honey through a glass pane. Yet another might say: a roof over your head, a full stomach, a cigarette, and, yes, just such a table and lamp in a warm, quiet room with a cup of hot tea and a good book… But is any of that possible without money? No. For that sort of peace you need the same thing you need to make war: money, money, money.

Back home, my wife had no income to speak of. With those hundred roubles that she sent me in Siberia, her well had run dry. It is true that Professor Kvačal wrote to me in Voronezh that he was sending me an additional ten roubles; Messrs Hunčík and Kutošík sent me twenty more, but that was all too little. Petrograd wasn't responding to my plea for a job there. Kiev was silent, Moscow deaf.

Ivan Ivanovich Országh made good on his word, however. He provided me with a line of credit for five hundred roubles, for five months. I doffed my Jewish cap and bowed to him from afar in gratitude when he sent me the first fifty. They arrived like rain falling on the parched earth. I breathed with life renewed and my hope glowed a luscious green, like clover.

'In five months' time, the war will be over for sure,' I reckoned. 'I won't even have time to go through the whole loan.'

In Russia, salaries are paid and accounts settled on the twentieth of the month. Whether so or whether no, by the twentieth of that month, all I had left of those fifty roubles was fifty-eight kopecks. One morning I was awakened by a loud cry. Somebody was yelling in the neighbouring half-salon, half-dining room:

'Ya dvoryanin!'

At which another hoarse voice shouted back:

'A ya kamerger!'[104]

'Ya dvoryanin.'

'Ya kamerger.'

And so it went on for a full five minutes. At last, the 'dvoryanin' told the 'kamerger:'

'Vy bolvan!'[105]

In such a way did the man of the house and Vaňo Daxner argue about which of them had the greater title. The man of the house was the 'dvoryanin,' and fon Daxner the 'kamerger.' The nobleman refused to recognise Vaňo's chamberlaincy, and for that reason he bestowed upon him the completely undeserved title of 'blockhead.'

The quarrel had brewed up because we had not paid our rent fully beforehand, that is, for twenty days; we'd only paid for fifteen. You understand: we already had nothing of what we had before, and we still didn't have what we were waiting on.

After this unpleasantness, the flowers, the palms, the cacti and the geraniums began to disappear from our rooms. The vases took a powder, and in their wake one table and two chairs cleared out as well; the paintings slid off the walls and tottered out the door. When almost everything had aban-

....

[104] Russian: 'I'm a nobleman! And I'm a chamberlain!' Russian society at the time was divided into civil ranks, corresponding to ranks in the military. The so-called Table of Ranks had been instituted by Peter the Great in his efforts to replace the bloodline aristocracy of the boyars, with whom he constantly had to struggle, with a new meritocracy loyal to the throne.

[105] Russian: 'You're a blockhead!'

doned the premises, so did we; out the front door, into the street, from whence we moved into a new flat on Pyatnitskaya St.

I didn't remain there long. Vaňo's brother Igor showed up one day, gave me a grim stare over the rim of the monocle he wore, and proceeded to adduce many important reasons – his 'baggage' was of greater volume than mine, which was much lighter, and in consequence, it would be much easier for me to move on than for him – so that this was exactly what came about; I resigned my bed to him, and moved off to Sinitsinsky Lane, where I took a room from Madame Neonila Mikhailovna Nagurskaya, a divorcée.

It was a small room and cost fifteen roubles. Just about the size of my cell nr. 13 in the military prison in Bratislava, with this one difference: that here I had a window and the door was unlocked. One little chair, a little table, a bed, a coatrack, and that's that. My window gave out onto a courtyard overgrown with grass, the white enclosure of the grounds of a church with a steeple, a slip of the river beyond the city, and, in the distance, scattered little woods.

A shaggy dog named Ryabchik wagged his tail at me when first I leaned out of the window. My first friend. Then some young lady in a red dressing-gown came out through a door – hair undone, bare feet – and tossed some water out of a washbasin. I saluted her military fashion. She shot a gloomy look in my direction and didn't return the greeting. My first enemy.

I sat down on the bed. There were maybe five flies buzzing about the room. It sounded as if someone were playing *fortissimo* on an organ. The first defect. Some rather unintelligent crows... Why aren't they flying off to the front? They'd be better off there. The second defect. But the third, fourth, fifth and tenth defects were the bells. They rang those bells from morning till night – something that was especially unbearable on the Sabbath and on the eves of holy days. Bells from various steeples echoed one another like village dogs. A real racket. My hands flew to my head and I cried out in my soul:

'The gap between here and Heaven is huge. You need a lot of bells to fill that vacuum and arrive at last at the Kingdom of Heaven... He must be an old, deaf staff general who has lived through so many wars and is now sleeping somewhere on a couch of cloud. He's been pensioned off, and no longer has thunder and lightning at his disposal; no more downpours with which to drown all those earthly kings, generals, strategists who have destroyed and continue to destroy the Kingdom of God on earth!'

The bells rang and rang. The people blessed themselves. I tried to stuff my ears.

But despite all these flaws, the flat had its good points, too.

Madame Nagurskaya was the good spirit of the premises. Not too tall, about forty or so, with smooth skin, black hair smartly combed, dark eyes and black eyebrows. A familiar sort among us: a mare that labours from dawn until dusk. She dusted, she swept, she cooked, she served. She had her hands full with her elderly father, an oldster of about seventy, who went out 'to the bazaar' every day, or otherwise drowsed all day long at the stove. Besides him there was her daughter Marusha Ivanovna, a gay, pink, thin little girl with supposedly bad lungs. She coughed a lot and worked, poor thing, as a scribe for some notary.

There was also a *kvartirant* named Mikhail Mikhailovich Pustovalov. He was a teacher, a nice young man, with a large library in his spacious room.

Madame Nagurskaya spun around like a bobbin, running about here and there, with a sharp, fresh, tiny tread, but she also managed to pause a bit for a chat, to laugh whole-heartedly or to complain about how much there always was to pay and how little money there always was to pay it with.

She never went out.

'Ne khochu ispugat lyudei,'[106] she would say.

She would always bring me something: *pierogi* filled with cherries, in a thick cherry sauce with cream, strawberries, compote, cutlets with macaroni, 'Soldier's Goulash,' milk, candies. She was ever chewing *semechki*,[107] spitting the husks into her palm and thrusting them into her pocket. Sometimes she'd be sitting with her daughter Marusha in the room next door, and I, lying on my bed, book in hand, would listen to them crunching seeds and talking in low voices, deep into the night.

Every now and then, she'd spill a handful of those seeds into my palm with the warning not to spit the shells onto the floor, because she'd have to sweep them up.

Once, I'd made a little mess and went off to find a broom and dustpan. I found the first, but the latter was nowhere to be seen. But I'd noticed that the lady of the house scooped up the dust from the floor with old letters or a cover torn from one of Pustovalov's books.

Pustovalov set his library at my disposal. During the day I would read various newspapers on park benches, while at home in the evenings, I would read, now Balmont, now Bryusov, now Izmailov's *Literaturny Olimp*, now Kogan's *Literaturnyye ocherki*, or the *Etymology of the Russian Language,* or Sergeyenko's study *How Count L.N. Tolstoy Lives and Works*, or Merezhkovsky's *Death of the Gods* and Andreyev's *Anathema*.

There was music, too. Mamselle Marie would play some songs from Little Russia on the piano. Some of them were similar to ours. Listening to these, I would be transported, past the mountains and valleys, home.

From time to time our entire little society would gather in my room and we would part from one another only at

....

[106] Russian: 'I don't want to startle anyone.'

[107] Russian: Sunflower seeds.

JANKO JESENSKÝ

midnight, or at one, at two – there was no end to our discussions.

The women chuckled at my Russian. I would say that they were not speaking in a literary style, and were wolfish with their words, for they gobbled down at least half of every one they pronounced. Pustovalov, usually, talked politics.

'Our government is a bad one. Our farmers can obtain no land. Everything is in the hands of the *pomeshchiks*...[108] If nothing gets better after the war, there'll be a *bunt*...[109] Devil take it,' he would chafe, 'we've got might; we're a great mass, we have the power, and yet we're nothing but toys in the hands of a few individuals... Nobody wants war, and yet they whip us to it, like a herd of cattle... Everyone wants reform, and reform never comes...'

He spoke of the Decembrists, and of the 1905 Revolution. He gave me the speech of Herzenstein, the murdered deputy of the Duma, 'Are the Peasants in Need of Land?' so that I might become familiar with that issue. He brought me Gorky's *Man* – a poetic fantasy concerning the destiny of humanity. It made him angry that in higher schools, and even in technical schools, religion was still being taught.

'Everywhere God, God, God, and priest, priest, priest... The Russian wastes half of each day blessing himself.'

'If it were only that,' I thought to myself – but it was all of those religious *gelenksübung*:[110] and the image of those Landsturmers in Kozakov's office passed through my mind.

And thus our evenings flowed on, quietly, like a little stream crossing through a vale, until, suddenly, a boulder tumbled into the gentle waters from somewhere and the stream began to swell and burble for being dammed. Some-

....

[108] Russian: Squires, landowners.

[109] Russian: Revolt.

[110] German: Joint-bends, i.e. calisthenics.

thing happened that wasn't supposed to happen. Madame Nagurskaya began to ignore me. She would go off to town early in the morning without first making me tea or bringing me rolls. *Pierogi* with cherries and cream, eggs, strawberries, *bliny* had all disappeared. The spiders wove their webs in the corners of the room unmolested. No more letters dusty from taking the sweepings of my floor, nor did anyone tear a cover away from Mr Pustovalov's books to use as a dustpan. Old Mikhail Mikhailovich had evaporated somewhere. I no longer saw him drowsing at the stove or leaving for town with a basket to do his shopping. Some sort of tragedy was being played out. The household order was turned upside-down.

Mamselle Marie stated that the old gentleman had gotten angry and went on strike. It seems that that's his way – his nose gets out of joint once a month.

I asked my neighbour the teacher what was going on with our housemistress.

He shrugged his shoulders and replied to all of my complaints with:

'Let it be. We can make our own tea.'

'All right, but who'll be doing the cleaning?'

'We ourselves.'

'Nice,' I said. 'But why, why, why? Whatever's happened? Before – everything, and now – nothing.'

Once more, he merely shrugged.

I went over to the girl and asked her. She laughed and nodded toward my neighbour's door.

'He bought her a hat. Since then she hasn't been able to sit still. She wants to show it to everybody.'

'So that's the way it is?'

And in this way I came to understand three things:

1) Madame Nagurskaya and Mr Pustovalov were sweet on each other.

2) Miss Marusya just couldn't see that. She'd rather that it was her that Mr Pustovalov was sweet on.

3) Two women were battling over our teacher. So I must put up my sword, whether that be for the favours of Madame Neonila or those of Miss Marusya.

The upshot of it all was the bitterest of conclusions:

'Farewell *pierogi!*'

I waved my hand in resignation. One more valuable item lost forever.

While this idyll was playing out on Sinitsinsky Lane, some strange news arrived from Hungary. The Magyars, it seems, would like to conclude a separate peace. Our commentators argued that this was because the Magyars wished to preserve the whole country intact, without losing Slovakia and Transylvania. Slovakia, therefore, was in danger. Sazanov, it seems, caught on to the Magyar tricks, but Stürmer, the Germanophile, was all for the separate peace.

The word in Russia was that Károlyi was trying to establish a new party, the aim of which was Hungary's absolute independence from Austria. Supposedly, a lot of meetings were taking place in Szeged, Temesvár, and Arad, all in favour of the separate peace. Germany, supposedly, was doing everything in its power to counteract this 'stremleniye narodov k miru, prinimayushcheye trevozhny kharakter…'[111] But even so, Károlyi's party was growing and Franz Josef himself left for Pest, where there was quite a bit of unrest.

Some hellish bombs were dropped on that 'stremleniye narodov k miru.' Romania and Italy seceded, the Romanians occupied Kronshtadt, Petrožén, Čik-Seredu, Kézdi-Vásárhely, and so on.

The war was getting tangled up, like a ball of cotton yarn. What sort of stocking might result from this, and when, flitted through the minds of us all.

....

[111] Russian: 'Aspiration of the nations to peace, which are assuming an alarming character.'

We began to swarm, like ants when someone thrusts a stick into their anthill.

There was a whole crowd of unemployed brothers in Voronezh at the time. We'd meet up, now in the Petrovsky Park, now in the Koltzovsky or Semeiny Park, and then we'd go off to the Moskovskaya eatery together, or the Warsaw, or the Polish cafeteria.

A person would tumble out onto the street from his lodgings in the morning, just like a drop of rain, without the foggiest idea of which way he'd be rolling, what current would be sweeping him up, or where he'd end up at last.

Our society was made up of engineers and artists: Engineer Vašek, Engineer Novotný, Engineer Štěpánek, and then there was Engineer Koželský, who had an established household and a job and therefore had no need of cafeterias or parks; Čížek the sculptor, Hrdlička the painter, now and then the Daxners, and me – always. Our group also included a lady: Sofia Vladimirovna, a young, petite, black-haired Russian girl with bobbed hair.

Everyone stood out somehow. Engineer Vašek by his courtliness and by virtue of the fact that he was living with Sofia Vladimirovna, Engineer Štěpánek on account of his paleness, slenderness, his always being opposed to something and his discontent; Čížek the sculptor by his ever-present smoking jacket, rubber collars and cuffs, which on account of his vibrant gesticulations while speaking were constantly popping out from under his coat-sleeves. He kept pressing these down, now on the edge of the table, now on the back of a chair, and when he was doing neither one nor the other, he would be pulling them up under his coat sleeves. His cuffs would snap and flutter when the 'sculptor' was speaking of his thousands:

'I have all the old silver and copper coins. I could trick out nine ladies from tip to toe in Russian duds… There in that bank I have three thousand roubles, in another two, and in a third, one thousand.'

From time to time he would be seized by a fit of gallantry. Once he invited us out for wine. The wine was old, sweet, red, and dear. It was a real shame that no one reciprocated, and thus we remained, so to speak, at just one bottle.

Hrdlička the painter went about with us only when we went for a swim, and then only so as to study the forms of the naked women bathing there, from the riverbank. I never saw any of his pictures, but Engineer Novotný averred that his missus was an excellent cook, indeed, a real artist in the kitchen, at least insofar as the volume of dishes was concerned: supposedly, one could consume up to thirty dumplings there for just fifty kopecks.

Engineer Novotný, a plump, swarthy fellow with a sun-tanned face, a thick mop of dark hair and round, full cheeks, was conspicuous among us mainly because of his practicality and humour. A pleasant chap, he would grab you by the coat and begin: 'It was like the time I once played a joke on a certain barber... You see, there was this general who was to come on a visit – a real fishing enthusiast he was. This barber of ours was also an avid fisherman, so I say to him, "The general who's coming is a big fisherman like you, but he's always eager to learn more about the craft. You could be his teacher, but I warn you: he's a real stickler for uniforms, so you better provide yourself." So the barber goes flying about after a uniform, telling everyone that he's going to teach the general how to fish. The general comes by, really, and the barber in uniform is veritably tripping over his heels and constantly explaining, "You do that this way, general sir; that's done like this, general sir..." and on and on until the fuming general falls into a frenzy and doesn't he chase him off with his fishing pole...!'

Or, during a conversation, he'd suddenly place his hand upon your knee: '...So this pensioner drops his line into the water and sits there waiting, waiting, waiting. And there's no fish, no fish, no fish biting. So I run off to buy a herring. I go back and the old fellow's still sitting there waiting. 'Maybe you need a fresh worm?' I say. 'Look – I'll watch your pole here; you go off for some worms." He does. Meanwhile, I hang the herring on his hook by the tail, and cry out "I got a bite!" The pensioner runs up... Pulls... and lands a fish caught by the tail...'

'Ha, ha, ha!' we all laugh.

'So I went on with a straight face: "This has never happened before, that a fish was caught by the tail. We need to go see the authorities, and then take the fish and the hook off to a museum"...'

'Ha, ha, ha!'

He was an inexhaustible font of anecdotes. He'd start on a new one before he'd quite finished telling the last. This was a gourmet dessert, pleasant, and easily digestible, to our modest meals. It seemed that everyone liked Novotný.

Once I complained to him:

'The waitress won't give me any sugar. Says they have none.'

'She always gives some to me.'

'How is that?'

'I always say to her "Kystihand!"'[112]

What set Sofia Vladimirovna apart was that she would invite us to tea, with cheesecake, sweet rolls, farmer's cheese, butter, scrambled eggs, ham and eggs, black coffee and the like, and then she'd start grumbling with a laugh:

'Czechs are all sly little wretches. They're always plotting. "You give, he gives, and I pay – with your money so it doesn't cost me a cent..." A Czech invites you to tea, but make sure you bring over some sugar and pastries, otherwise he'll guard that spoonful of sugar like crown evidence and then he'll tell one and all that he hosted you... You borrow cigarettes and

....

[112] Probably a corruption of the German *Küsse deine Hand* [Kiss your hand].

JANKO JESENSKÝ

count up the matches… That's what supper's like at a Czech's place – pure mathematics: so much water for the soup, so much chives, five scrapes of seasoning, so much meat for five and so much flour for five dumplings… I'm not fond of your ways…'

'I once ate thirty dumplings at a Czech woman's table,' Novotný protested.

'It's all because of the situation we happen to be in at the moment,' Štěpánek answered back. 'We're temporarily impoverished.'

'Oh, sure!' said Sofia Vladimirovna, not retreating an inch. 'But even if he were a millionaire, a Czech is going to sum up your portion of cherries, slice an egg in three and still reckon on what his friends toss in the pot.'

'You know nothing of us. The Czechs are selfless, but wise: not wastrels like you Russians. They were able to collect millions for their schools, their theatre…'

'That's just my point – everyone gets a slice, no one gets the whole of anything.'

'Everything for all. Everybody gets something… You don't know us at all… You've never been in our country. How can you say such things?' they cried, offended.

'I base my opinions on my observations of you.'

'That's a mistake. We're shipwrecks.'

'Every man bears within him the character of his race.'

Sofia Vladimirovna said all these things with a laugh, but she was serious. She seemed to forget, poor girl, that it was a Czech, Engineer Vašek, who was keeping her, and that the snacks she was treating us to had been paid for by a Czech.

But we kept our mouths shut, for if we'd mentioned that, we would've ruined everything.

'Why does she say such things exactly then, when she's hosting us?' I asked myself. 'It sounds as if she wanted us to contribute next time – this one bringing some sugar, that one some pastries, and someone else the salami.'

But I didn't play that trump either, for that would've caused grave offence too.

Once I came across her in Peter's Park. She was waiting for Vašek. As we spoke of this and that, I asked her straight out:

'Do you really find the Czechs so unsympathetic?'

'Not at all,' she responded. 'They're real *molodtsy*,[113] but they can also be really petty amongst themselves. Engineer Novotný looks askance at Engineer Štěpánek because he puts so much sugar in his tea. Štěpánek gets down on Novotný because he devours everything that's set before him, and even cleans up Hrdlíčika's plate (thirty dumplings!). That high and mighty friend of yours complained to me once about you wearing his shirts, and that he has to support you (O, the chivalrous fellow!) even though he's got his own younger brother to take care of. Mrs Koželská bad-mouths me on account of Vašek, Koželský her husband won't even recognise me in the street, Vašek, of course, is angry at Koželský... Pettiness to the very core. I'm not fond of people like that.'

'Then you'll never be fond of anyone, Sofia Vladimirovna.'

'No?'

'No. You measure people against the ideal, whereas you ought to use a ruler with centimetres. According to your system every person is petty. You need earthly measuring sticks to take the measure of human beings – by centimetre or by inch.'

She laughed.

I laughed too, but I was angry in spirit. I, on my part, took the measure of my cousin, who wanted to impress a Russian lady with the clothes he donated and the seven coupons to the Moscow Cafeteria he bestowed as largesse. My measuring stick was simple enough: a tailor's measure, and I'd have been

....

[113] Russian: Fine boys.

quite happy to take it to my noble benefactor, Chamberlain fon Daxner, and how!

And the Czechs – sly little wretches!

Our whole society, me included, was wretched. Immense events were going on all around us and we were just squandering our strength and wasting our time.

Tisza was fulminating back in Hungary: uproot all the Slavic nations before their descendants destroy our children!

The Czechs were already joining the Družina[114] in great numbers. Czech officers – 'volunteers' – came to Voronezh as well, travelling from Bobrov to Kiev. We talked with them a bit.

'Not too many Slovaks have joined up,' they said. 'Four, to every ten Czechs.'

'We're a small nation,' we replied.

'Money-grubbing intelligentsia,' somebody said.

'What Slovaks?' another person said. 'Slovaks are Czechs.'

'And Czechs Slovaks,' I responded.

We were actually expressing the thought behind the Czechoslovak theory. From our conversations it became clear that this would be something that binds as well as divides, a seed of unity and a core of dispute. How things would unfold would depend upon the stronger party, which is to say, upon the Czechs.

Not long after this, Dr Daxner arrived from Bobrov in the wake of the Czechs.

'What we need,' he told us, 'is for America to send us at least a battalion of Slovak volunteers. We'll set ourselves at their head and create a separate Slovak regiment.'

I tried to imagine what that regiment would look like, which 'we' were to head.

'Czechoslovak unity and a separate Slovak regiment: there's the first hole punched in the union,' I opined.

....

[114]   Czech: Company, the forerunner of the Czechoslovak Legions.

Then an American brochure concerning the Czechoslovak question fell into my hands. The author concluded with:

'We (Slovaks) can't simply be poured into the Czech nation. However, firmly holding on to our home rule, we can create one Czecho-Slovak kingdom.'

'We haven't a thing yet, and here we're one step away from demanding autonomy.'

The debates commenced. Ideas were exchanged; they criss-crossed, they crystallised.

At that time I was already corresponding with Jožek Gregor, who was in Kiev, working for the Soyuz zemskikh gorodov.[115] He wrote to me that the Union of Czechoslovak Citizens had been enquiring about me in all the military bureaux. Wouldn't I like to come to Kiev?

'It seems to me,' he wrote, 'that you're not too keen on coming to Kiev to zanimatsya nashimi delami.'[116]

And here I was only waiting patiently for a transfer.

Then I received word from the Union of Czechoslovak Associations that they wanted me in Kiev to work in the Union administration.

So, once more I had to venture into Russian officialdom. They couldn't sort out anything. I couldn't move an inch without official Russian permission, or an order. So I went off to the office where I was registered, but they knew nothing about any of this there.

In one of his letters to me, Jožko wrote: 'I'm sending You the original staff communiqué (don't lose it!) wherewith they are ordering you to report here. Get yourself to the Regional Military Commandant's Office there in Voronezh, show

....

[115] Russian: Union of *zemstvo* cities. The *zemstvo* was an administrative unit introduced in nineteenth century Russia, following upon agricultural reform.

[116] Russian: 'Busy yourself with our work.'

them the communiqué, and demand that they send you here immediately.

'When you arrive, you'll be an editor of the official Union gazette. It's understood that you'll receive an officer's wage from the Union, as is the case of everyone who works for them, whether or not they had an officer's rank in the army. Hell, you editors will be getting even more, at least for any belles-lettres you compose besides your regular column. You'll be put in charge of a Slovak column, with three Czechs working on Czech topics and columns in common. Don't worry – we'll be able to handle it; we'll write what we need to write.

'The regional military commander should already have been in touch with You, because he'd received that communiqué himself.

'As for the rest of the things that concern us, both public and private, we'll talk it all over when you get here. Don't dilly-dally thinking it all through; get yourself here full of trust in the success of our ideals. Don't be afraid of fighting again. So what if we go warring once more? We (You and I) have already had a full life; you have to die someday, and there's more glory to death on the battlefield than death in bed. And in any case, it suits us writers to return to our liberated fatherland as soldiers and leaders of men. Of course, it's possible that they won't have any need of us oldsters, and that we'll be returning in "civvies," not Russian uniforms.

'All things shall be revealed unto you. Come as quickly as you can. You are impatiently awaited by Your devoted Jožo.'

'I have had some experience with journalism in Siberia,' I laughed to myself. And so that my old friend should have no doubts about my willingness to further 'the success of our ideals' by my service, even if that meant the army again, I went off as usual to query those who had already said so many times to me here that 'they didn't know anything.' And it was true enough – again they were in the dark.

Meanwhile, the post office had found out where I lived. Letters began to arrive. I even received two packages that my wife had sent to Beryozovka. They included winter clothes (it was summer) and heavy winter socks (it was July). These cheered me a great deal, although some thievish hands had thinned them out quite perfectly. But the thief in question was still honest enough as to leave something for me. And Mama – poor thing – managed to scrape together eighteen roubles, twice. Mr Ján Hraško was successful in presenting me with a pair of summer suits. And our patron, Mr Ján Országh, kept his word and faithfully sent along fifty roubles each month. It was only the military offices that were frozen. I would have handed over to them my entire wardrobe if only it would warm them up and make their icy rigidity thaw.

And these were no empty words. My wardrobe at the time was something that no bourgeois gentleman would sniff at in disdain. In sum:

10 shirts (as much as that, as they are the most visible to the eye); 5 pairs of trousers (as few as that, for they're less visible); 6 collars (each laundered every two weeks); 1 pair of cuffs (used only when invited to tea at Sofia Vladimirovna's); 2 towels (each with two ends and a middle, so, six actually; or rather twelve, as they are all two sided); 5 handkerchiefs (for use only after blowing one's nose to the side); 7 pairs of socks (all with holes, plugged with toes); 2 little dish towels (for a change); 1 heavy wrap (Ivan's. Wasn't he right, after all?); 1 summer suit (Hraško's); 1 blue winter suit (Ivan's. He wasn't lying, after all!); 1 suit of reddish velour (from home); 2 sweaters (from home); 1 winter greatcoat (from the Red Cross); 1 military tunic (*tempi passati*); 1 pair of military breeches (*tempi passati*); 1 military cap (always on my head); 1 pair of boots (from Siberia, always on my feet, without puttees); 2 bowties (long and large ones, if you please) and 2 rubber collars (good, when the others were in the wash).

Well, then!

Madame Nagurskaya gazed at me in wonder, especially when I dressed up in the reddish velour togs sent to me from home. Mikhail Mikhailovich took the fabric between thumb and forefinger, smacked his lips and enthused:

'So soft. We don't have that sort of stuff here.'

And Miss Marusya was also a little more benign towards me – once, she even invited me to accompany her to the theatre in Semeiny Gardens, so she might be squired by a real cavalier.

When we returned home around midnight, Madame Neonila, I saw, had brought in a teapot, some warmed-over cutlets and some compote. She sat down with mademoiselle and spoke of her own youth.

'Now I'm thirty-five. All my love is directed toward my father and my daughter… Between me and Mikhail Nikolayevich there's nothing now but letters.'

Miss Marusya grimaced.

'What is it?' I asked.

'You know, I'm ashamed to go see him. I'm in debt to him for about four hundred roubles.'

I felt sorry for her.

Our company broke up around two in the morning.

I had a hard time sleeping that night. I would drowse and then, without a reason, start awake, drenched in sweat. The room was completely dark. In the silence I heard something like someone sitting at the table and turning the pages of a large book with heavy pages. Then it seemed as if these were being rolled into cornets. The sounds would cease and begin again. I raised my head and tensed my hearing. I wasn't mistaken. The turning of the pages went on and on. A mouse maybe, or a cockroach, I thought. But the sounds were coming from the table, and there was no book or any thick paper there…

I lit my lamp. The sounds ceased immediately. There was nothing lying on the table, nor, thank God, was there anyone sitting there. The clocks struck three, then four, and still I couldn't sleep. It's my stomach, I reasoned. Warmed-over cutlets.

The next night, after midnight, something shrieked above my head. I sat up quickly in bed again. I listened for the turning of heavy paper. Nothing. All was quiet. Nothing, nowhere.

'Something bad's in the offing,' I thought.

And I was right. That afternoon, my left hand began to puff up in the region of my wrist. I had been having fevered dreams – it was that, which woke me up in the middle of the night and deceived me with those illusory sounds.

Then the *Voronezhsky telegraf*[117] arrived with the news that the Czechoslovak 'deyatel i pisatel'[118] Svetozár Hurban Vajanský had died in Turčiansky Sv. Martin, in Vengrii.[119] A little trifle of news, but for us a bouquet of gratitude in honour of his love of the Russians. So, our dear father – dead! I'll never see him again striding up the road in his tall Russian cap of karakul, with his grey beard, forked and so Russian-looking; in his jacket, striding with his birch cane. He'd drop in at the Brittany pub for a beaker of Martinské beer. Sometimes he'd hold court for a while... We felt in our souls that he was our crowned Slovak king, a poet-king, journalist, novelist, critic... He'd lift his great, chronometric watch on its thick chain to his eyes to read the time. That watch was a gift of gratitude presented to him by the Slovak people. Of all the wealth he owned and dispersed to others, only that watch he would never part with. They also glanced impatiently at their watches – those ungrateful ones who wished to tear him from his modest Slovak throne – from our humble souls, made bold by him. They didn't succeed. They only fouled themselves in the process. Nor

....

[117] Russian: *The Voronezh Telegraph.*
[118] Russian: Activist and writer.
[119] Russian: Hungary.

JANKO JESENSKÝ

will they separate him from us even in death. Wherever there will be culture in the world, culture and love of one's brethren, there he will be – he will be that culture.

September came along…

It was then that I was summoned to the office of the regional military commandant, where I was informed that, at last, the *bumaga*[120] had arrived, according to which I was to be transferred to Kiev.

Madame Nagurskaya boiled some eggs for me to take on my journey; she also gave me compote, rolls and salt. Then, along with Miss Marusya and the teacher Pustovalov, she escorted me on my way.

Not only death separates us from others forever – life can, too.

'We'll hardly see each other again, however long we live, O my dear Russian souls!' I thought, and even said something like that when I thanked them for taking such care of me.

'Come see us, when the war is over!' I called out to them at parting.

'And you come back here!' they replied.

It was in a sad mood that I hired an *izvozchik* at the stand near the Municipal Theatre and had him drive me to the barracks, where, according to instructions, I was to rap at the window past which the convoy that was to accompany me to Kiev was sleeping.

I knocked once and listened for an answer. Nothing. As silent as the grave. I knocked again, and a third time. Then a soldier on guard, who was making his rounds around the perimeter of the barracks, came running up and grabbed me by the arm:

'Nelzya!'[121]

....

120 Russian: Document.

121 Russian: 'You mustn't!'

When I told him what I was there for, he made a fist and banged on the window himself. The convoy responded.

'Vo!'[122] the guard laughed.

And so about a half hour later the window opened and in it, my guide appeared: a small, fat chap, as round as a ball, wearing a mantle, girt with a long bayonet.

His face was like a ball, and he bounced through the window like a ball, bouncing before the carriage and then onto the coach box. When the guard saw what was going on – that the convoy's exit from the barracks was not according to regulations, he ran after us, crying from afar:

'Nelzya! Nelzya!'

I tried to convince him, first with words, and then with kopecks, that since *gospodin unter* was already at the reins, he shouldn't be such a stickler for the rules. After all, he'd only wanted to shorten his route, hopping through the window like that, rather than coming through the front door. The guard took the money, but he pulled the convoy down off of the coach box anyway, and made him go back into the barracks just as he'd left it – through the window. Then he closed the window behind him so that he should now be pleased to make use of the proper way out. A window is to be looked through, not jumped out of, and a door is not to be looked through, but passed through.

'That's all we need!' the guard fumed through his bristling whiskers.

The shamed convoy came back out through the door, huffing as if to cool his oatmeal. As soon as we'd passed out of earshot, he burst out with 'Durak kakoi-to!'[123]

It was one in the morning of 5 September when I left Voronezh.

....

122 Russian: 'Inside there!'

123 Russian: 'What an idiot that one is!'

IX. KIEV

I was once escorted from Trenčín to Bratislava by four soldiers with bayonets. From Beryozovka-za-Baikalom to Voronezh I was accompanied by only one, but he also had a *shtyk*[124] on his gun. From Voronezh to Kiev my companion was also a young Russian soldier, but his bayonet was merely dangling from his belt.

In the first case, I was being led to the firing squad as a traitor. In the second, I was being sent to 'residence at liberty' in Voronezh, but as a liberated person of the lowest class. In the third case, I was already raw Czechoslovak material, designated for the Union of Czechoslovak Associations in Russia, headquartered in Kiev.

Such was my path from 'slavery to freedom.'

We arrived in Kiev on 6 September (new style). It was eight in the morning. The sky was a cheery blue, the air nice and warm. Up in the hills lay the city amidst the trees, and still higher up was a hill covered in churches with their onion domes. At the foot of the hills rushed the great river Dnieper. But such was the horrid crush of people at the station that I hadn't much time for gawping up at the hills and all around me. With difficulty, we pushed our way to the tram. The tram was also packed with people clinging to its sides like flies to a honey cake.

'Vasily Ivanych,' I said, 'let's find us an *izvozchik*.'

....

[124]   Russian: Bayonet.

'Khorosho.'[125]

We hadn't much of a choice. We climbed onto the first available cab. The *izvozchik* was as meagre and old as his little horse, who stumbled forward on spindly, crooked legs. At the foot of the first hill he halted and wouldn't budge for all the world. The *izvozchik* snapped the reins and threatened with the whip, but, when the little horse refused to respond, he had us get out, explaining that he couldn't cart us up the hill. He has to spare the horse. He asked for a rouble. Both of us thought the route quite a short one for such a fare, but we're going to argue with an Orthodox believer? I gave him his rouble and we went off on foot to the *raspredelitelny punkt*.[126]

Here also we were to be subjected to a trial of patience.

We got there at 10:00 and reported our presence immediately. They told us that the commandant would be coming in to work in an hour or two, at which time he'd dispatch us. Aha! Welcome home... We knew all about those two-hour waits. We went off for breakfast. When we returned in an hour's time, again the fellow told us – yes, in an hour or two, the commandant will be here. So we went off into town to *pogulyat*.[127] An hour later we reported again, but, once more, the commandant *yeshche net*.[128] Come back in an hour or two. We went off for dinner. The afternoon was no different than the morning. It wasn't until four o'clock that we got our *bumaga*, and with it, a soldier who led us off to the Union, where I was handed over, as is sometimes the case, upon receipt.

The spacious locale occupied by the Union was filled almost entirely with soldiers. Czechs in Russian uniform. Ensigns, lieutenants, volunteers. One of them took me in

....

[125]   Russian: Good, OK.

[126]   Russian: Distribution point.

[127]   Russian: Have a bit of a stroll.

[128]   Russian: Still wasn't there.

hand and announced that a great task was awaiting me, the details of which brother Jožo Gregor would fill in for me. And immediately they sent someone to fetch him from the Hotel Praga.

About fifteen minutes later, he was there.

He hadn't changed. He was dressed in civilian clothes; that same oval face and balding head, his hair was grown out at the sides and behind; he sported a small untrimmed beard, thick whiskers and bushy eyebrows. He had those same smiling grey eyes. It was that same modest chap with his friendly way of speaking, his words without braggadocio or boldness. But there were more strands of grey in his whiskers, and it seemed as if his eyebrows bent a little critically when he turned his gaze upon me. Perhaps because he remembered me as a youngster – filled out, round of face – and here there was an older man standing before him, thinned out, with a swarthy, sun-burnt, bony face and drooping ears.

I still hadn't completely recovered from my Siberian typhus (*typhus recurrens*) and I walked around as if in a fever. I couldn't process events and impressions immediately and directly, but as if strained through a sieve. Nothing cheered me. I was a gloomy pessimist and somehow couldn't shake myself awake.

'Were going to publish a paper!' he said with enthusiasm. '*Slovak Voices*, as an addendum to the *Čechoslovan*. You, Janč, and me. Three pages... Jančeks in Moscow, agitating there... We've got to bestir our people. Give them direction... You'll live with me...'

And taking me by the arm, he led me to his flat. We walked a long distance – somewhere past Krutoi Spusk, even. He showed me a room on the second floor of a building in a quiet street, with windows giving out onto a park with a great lawn. Everything was clean and cosy.

'Thirty roubles a month, with service.'

I lifted my right hand over my head to scratch my left ear – Lutheran style, as the saying goes.

'Well, what do you think? We'll both be pulling an officer's salary. Sixty-two roubles, each of us. It's not much in Kiev, true, but if we live modestly, we'll do fine.

'I guess we will.'

Then, as an example of his idea of modest living, he took me to some grand restaurant on Khreshchatik and ordered goose. He insisted on paying himself.

We smoked and feasted deep into the night.

In this way we prepared ourselves for our journalistic careers.

On the next day, Švihovský, the editor of the *Čechoslovan*, greeted me warmly and introduced me to my 'editorial colleagues' Žd'arský and Dýma.

As far as our outward appearance is concerned, only Švihovský looked proper. Dressed in a good quality dark suit, with a black hat, broad and soft, of the type worn by Socialists, from first sight he looked quite the chief. Smiling, clean-shaven, stout, with a radiant face. Editor Dýma had a great, rotund, black beard, which was to compensate for the sparse hair on his (too) high forehead and bald brows. He would have been impressive in both height and girth, but the picture was ruined somewhat by a battered greenish coat reaching to his thighs and, particularly, the belt round his stomach with the huge stud right at the navel. I suppose that the belt was there to keep his pants up – it could serve no other purpose, it certainly was no ornament. He usually kept his head covered by a soft Jewish-style hat of uncertain colour, also there to cover that high forehead. Žd'arský, a short, thin blond sporting a Russian goatee, the Don Juan of the *Čechoslovan,* wore an ash-grey Austrian officer's greatcoat that reached past his knees, and a military blouse dyed black. He kept his pant-legs tucked inside short boots with worn rubber heels. At the time, Gregor had quite an elegant autumn promenade coat of houndstooth. It was not dingy at all, but its buttons were poorly sewn on – more than one of them was an invalid, broken in half and holding on for dear life. Where he had obtained this coat, I have no idea, but at a quick glance it seemed the very best of all our gear (besides that of the chief, of course). I continued to go about in my 'crucifer' mantle, which I'd received from the Red Cross in Siberia (hence the nickname). So that it wouldn't look like an Austrian military cloak, I tore off the buttons and epaulettes, the belt on the back, and in this way I achieved the appearance of a spacious, broad raglan, but only at a first, quick glance. Otherwise, the white linen fur-lined pocket, which shone whenever I put it on or took it off, as well as the numbered insignia on the pockets, mercilessly revealed its – and my own – pedigree. For this reason, I only wore it when I absolutely had to. And so the vain and self-conscious person is always thinking himself to be the centre of everyone's attention; meanwhile, no one takes any notice of him at all.

The editorial offices were quite like us: provisional, waiting on better times. A corridor with a telephone. The corridor was always full and the telephone was always ringing. And the editors were talkers rather than writers. Jožo Gregor had the best idea, going off to the park to write his articles. But he could permit himself a luxury like that – he was an old-timer here.

I on the other hand was a newcomer. And however tempted I was to follow Jožo's example, I felt it incumbent upon me to remain seated behind the editorial desk.

And thus began my career in the news.

It was Editor Dýma who introduced me into the arcane world of journalism. He would clip the news from the *Národní politika*,[129] which I would translate into Slovak.

This was nothing new. I did the same thing back in Siberia, only there I was translating from Russian into Magyar.

....

[129] A Czech daily published in the years 1883–1945.

A few days later Jožo said to me:

'We need you to write some political columns, editorials.'

'But, brother,' I objected, 'I've never written an editorial in my life. I'm a dolt as far as that's concerned.'

'You have to.'

'Please! You're setting in front of a stove a person who can't tell the difference between carrots and celery, and telling him to cook. I need to learn myself, first; get my bearings a bit. I don't know anything about the various factions, currents.'

'There's only one current – the Czechoslovak.'

'But there are a lot of whirlpools in that stream: hidden currents, cross-currents, undertows, shallows...'

'See how much you know? Write about that.'

What was I to do?

So I dunked my pen in the inkwell and set the nib against the clean sheet of paper. And I dunked it again, tapped off the excess, and placed the nib to the paper again. I waited a moment. Then I shook my head and put the pen aside.

I was pinched by an inner discord. There was this kind of general grumbling inside me – like Jews at prayer in a synagogue. This one bellows, that one bellows back, and again the grumbling. The noise grows. The voices increase, and the gesticulations are ever more numerous, ever faster, until you think they're going to start tearing at each other's hair...

Nobody was good enough, and everyone wanted to be the best.

Take Deputy Dürich for example.

We had a code: the so-called Kiev Memorial. M.R. Štefánik and Josef Dürich signed it on behalf of the Czechoslovak National Council. As did Václav Vandrák, on behalf of the Union of Czechoslovak Associations in Russia as its president, along with the secretary Ján Volf, while the emissary Gustáv Košík signed it for the Slovak League in America.

This memorial read that, 'taking into account the geographic dispersion of the Czechoslovak element and the necessity of a unified political direction, and, furthermore, the increase in intensity of armed resistance and the entire political action of the Czechs and Slovaks living abroad, and that the leaders of the nation beyond the Carpathians lack the competence to organise Czechoslovak matters, both militarily and in regard to the prisoners of war, leadership in these matters is hereby consigned to the Czechoslovak National Council as an inseparable part of their diplomatic and political activity. The deputy chairman of the Czechoslovak National Council, Mr Josef Dürich, has arrived in Russia to become the representative of the National Council in Russia. As such, he is hereby invested with the power to speak in the name of that Council and should be considered the representative of the Czechoslovak nation in Russia.' Etc.

The memorial was quite clear; the people less so.

Grumbling everywhere, always.

The Union was grumbling that the most important matters, that is, those pertaining to the military and the prisoners of war, had been taken out of their hands. The opposition in Petrograd was grumbling at the fact that the Union still existed, and was poking its fingers into its pot. Somebody was shouting about Dürich running a regiment of idiocy in Petrograd and aiming at setting up his own, independent National Council under the aegis and with the financial support of the Russian government. That he was appointing as his collaborators figures the like of Priklonskij, clerk for Czechoslovak Affairs at the Foreign Ministry, a former consul in Pest, and an enemy of Professor Masaryk and the union of the Czechs and Slovaks... The ministerial council had already voted to adopt a subvention... Incredible! ... Now, while it is true that we are dependent in everything upon Tsarist Russia, still we want to be independent. The money would come in handy, sure, but not from Russia – that would mean Russian control and we want no Russian control... And it's also true that most of us are in Russia. So the leadership should be located in

Russia. But of course we already have a centre of leadership in Paris with Professor Masaryk at its head, so what Dürich is doing is driving a wedge into our singlemindedness; it means a leadership divided in two... There can be nothing in Russia save a branch of the National Council. Just as the Kiev Memorial reads... But not with Dürich in charge. He's a traitor...

And so, in the end, the representative of the Czechoslovak nation became an 'Austrian spy.'

Štefánik is working in Petrograd for the establishment of a branch of the National Council in Russia, and Koníček and Štěpánek are going the rounds of the Czechs and Slovaks in Russia. No good will come of that. Those two are representatives of the Tsarophile current. Black-hundredists! Down with them!

There was a Russian-Slovak society in Moscow 'dedicated to the memory of Štúr.' Devil take it! What? Devil take Štúr? Why? What's he ever done? Bristly Janko Sršeň is bristling with ire, Dr Markovič's stirring the pot: Štúr must be sent flying. All of these guvnors are after turning Slovakia into a Russian governate.[130]

Delegate Košík doesn't know who he belongs to. Like a seesaw: now Štúr's on top, now he's below. Now here, now there. How, where, with whom is he now?

The Union got its collaborators from among the prisoners of war. From their number arose the Congregation of Associates. The aim of the Congregation was to saw through the branch upon which the Union chiefs were sitting – the majority of them Czechs in Russia – so that they might break their necks. What have they in common with Dürich? And they, poor wretches, didn't know themselves whether they

....

[130] Jesenský here indulges in some puns, most of which are untranslatable into English. The name Sršeň (hornet) is a close homonym to the verb *sršať* [to bristle, to sparkle] such as here *srší hnevom* [to bristle, or splutter, with rage]; Dr Markovič *štúra* – he 'pokes about' or 'puts his two cents in,' a verb which glances off the poet's last name.

were better off grabbing onto Dürich's coattails or those of Štefánik. They were indigestible fare for the weak stomach, and just such indigestible, warm, fresh bread straight out of the oven was Petrograd with its young and warm opposition for the stomachs of the gentlemen heading the Union. Devil take them all!

The recruiting of the Czechoslovak army was to be entrusted to General Červinka. 'General Červinka... General Červinka...' the grumbling resumed... 'He's supposed to organise the army? But he's ill-inclined toward the Czechs. Speaking of them, he said that half of them were Austrophiles, and the other half absolutely unable to take such an important matter in hand. Only a real Russian general is capable of that.' There you have him. The whole truth. And that's the reason he's intriguing against the Union. He tore a fragment of an article out of the *Čechoslovan* in order to prove how vilely the Czechs slander the Russian army. The news censor was nonplussed. He had to submit the entire article to justify his claim, and what he succeeded in proving was that the article was actually a hymn of praise to Russia... Drown him in a teaspoon of water!

Here again Koutňák gave the Unionists a tongue-lashing in the *Czechoslovak*, edited by Pavlů, who inspired the article. Koutňák gets a literal slap in the face, Pavlů a moral one. A letter of boycott aimed at him is making the rounds for signature. La, la! Shades of Ban, when the lawyers there signed that letter declaring their break with me, because of my being an enemy of the Magyar fatherland.

So Pavlů comes to Kiev with a note of conciliation and an olive branch in his beak. He cools his heels at the Hotel Savoy, waiting in vain for some agents of the Union to arrive, snorting into his feed-bag; no one came.

Papoušek, a historiographer, a black-haired, thin, nice young fellow, surprises me with the news that Pavlů is asking for me.

I ran right over.

He was having supper. He'd put on a few pounds and lost some hair since I last saw him, when he was an editor in Pest. A fat, red neck above his collar, with a soft, full sausage spilling over the back. An open, broad face. Eyeglasses. A kind of well-fed, well-clad professor. He extended his hand without rising.

'Jožo hasn't come over?' I asked.

He laughed.

'Where hast thou left Philemon, o Baucis?... You don't know?... Today, you won't even find him with a cop. He hasn't come, and he won't. He's broken the links that bound us. He signed the boycott "manifesto" against me... Poisoned by the Union... Those gentlemen don't know how to do anything except poison people. Worthless, pusillanimous ignoramuses, without any authority whatsoever. If it hadn't been for us in Petersburg supporting them, they wouldn't mean a thing at all.'

He shifted in his seat and, leaning on the other side of the little chair, pulled a clipping out of his wallet.

'The article against the Union was published without my knowledge, but now I stand behind it, since I can't escape it.'

He laid out all sorts of political programmes before me. He said that it was not out of the question that the Czechs and Moravians might acknowledge the autonomy of Hungary, leaving the Slovaks in the same position as now... Koníček, Štěpánek, etc. want a Russian guberniya. The idiots. Everyone would be against that: the French, the British, and the Italians. Nobody would be happy with a Russia that stretched so far west. Russia herself didn't give a rap for us. Their main concern is Tsargrad – Constantinople. Neither Dr Kvačala nor those stumblebums in the Štúr society understand that.

'Our banner is the only viable one,' he said, bringing his political lecture to a close. 'Only thus will England, France, and Italy get behind us.'

He spoke as if he were reading from a book. Now in Russian, now in Czech, now in Slovak. He shifted from one language to another, smoothly, without halting or stumbling. He didn't mix in words either. In Czech he used the ř, hard, and in Russian and Slovak, r, softly.[131] I was happy with him. 'He'll turn out to be a great man,' I thought to myself.

I also learned from him that it was he who helped liberate me, getting me the *propusk* that sprang me from Siberia by identifying me as a translator of Pushkin.

'I thank you, from the bottom of my heart. And for those thirty roubles that you sent me.'

'Don't thank me – thank the stamps and seals. I used every one I could get my hands on. They're what sprung you...'

Right after him, Štefánik was to pass through Kiev.

We went to have a look at him.

Short, with a large face, a pale complexion, a fat nose set in deep creases and light blue eyes. He was dressed in the uniform of a French major. He spoke with consideration, softly, gently, and persuasively. Courtly, noble manners. He gave the impression of a globetrotter – as if he'd already left his Slovak homeland behind him, exchanging it for the world entire. What was found at the foot of the Tatras was pretty, but petty, to him, like a child's toy, which must be set aside now that we've grown out of the short pants of boyhood, now that big events are brewing. But no narrow-mindedness, please. Let us be broad-minded.

....

[131] Ř, a hard consonant in Czech and Polish (where it is spelt *rz*), does not exist in Slovak, where it is replaced by the soft consonant *r*. For example, the word 'river' in Czech and Polish: *řeka, rzeka,* is pronounced *rieka* in Slovak (and in Russian). Given the near-identicality of Czech and Slovak, it would be easy to trip up in pronunciation and word use when quickly shifting from one language to the other; Pavlů's eloquence is highlighted by his ability to seamlessly avoid such traps.

This impression was confirmed by the fact that he'd never learned to speak proper Slovak. He spoke 'Nitra' Slovak, with a hard vocalisation.

I agreed with him, except for those words of mitigation. I said:

'Look, all of our struggle against the Magyars, up until now, has been for "means." They wanted to tear the tools from our hands, like depriving a sculptor of his chisel, a painter of his brush, an orator of his tongue, a poet of the word, a nation of its culture… Means, all means, and for what? For well-being? For peace and quiet…? This isn't going to work with us, who have lived by the slogan "All for our Slovak speech, our Slovak culture…" If it's all going to be nothing more than a tool, well, let's just speak German or Magyar and all of our insurrection is pointless…'

A debate might have ensued, but then they introduced some sort of descendant of Napoléon the Great or some Bourbon or other; we paid our respects and were led out.

We went off to the editorial offices. There was a meeting in progress. It was like the roof was on fire: such smoke and cries.

Žďársky said:

'The *Čechoslovan* is to be shut down! It's going to be called the *Národní noviny*…[132] Švihovský won't be the editor. I ask why? Is it because the *Čechoslovan* is already well-known and has been appearing for seven months? Catastrophe. They haven't even consulted us editors. Are we a newspaper, or what? We're beginning to organise. We journalists will take it on. I move that we send a memorandum to the Union with these very contents…'

The motion was passed. But now here's something else dreadful: supposedly, Pavlů is going to be in charge of all Czechoslovak printing in Russia. That swelling idiot!

....

[132] Czech: *National News*.

And one more thing: Štefánik is to arbitrate in the suit between Pavlů and the Union! We don't want Štefánik for a judge! What sort of arbiter is he? That would be a pretty thing! He's already stated that he's a personal friend of Pavlů's. And above all, he thinks he's a head taller than the rest of us. We don't want any Štefánik as a judge!

Then Košík and Vladimír Hurban came up with a beautiful idea: to found our own, separate, Slovak periodical. Their argument was quite reasonable: '…Two Czechs keep us in the shade, and when they add *Slovak Voices* as a supplement to the *Čechoslovan*, it's them that prepare it, and so it becomes *Czech Voices* instead. Slovaks don't yet have sufficient trust toward the Czechs, and so it'll be better if independent Slovak Voices say that we're looking to unite with the Czechs…'

'No, in no case whatsoever!' Vondrák and Tuček protested, 'that'd be separatism!'

'Separatism, again!' I seethed in my spirit. 'All the fleas we carry around in our shirt will be called separatists yet! How dare we carry around our own fleas with us like that? It's against the principle of unity.'

And now, Dr Hojo's screeching from faraway Moscow that even Slovaks here in Russia can only be led by such Slovaks as were recognised as leaders back in Hungary.

'Right,' I said. 'We'll send for Dula straight away. He's got to tell everyone back home how gallantly the Slovaks are fighting on behalf of their beloved king and dear Hungarian fatherland, so that little Cinderella Slovakia be recognised. And yet we here must scream and trumpet and beat our drums and fire our cannons to convince everyone that gallant fighting on behalf of the Hungarian king is anything but gallantry, and loyalty to him is disloyalty to our own cause, honouring an oath to him is dishonour and the very betrayal of virtue. Everyone at home is shouted down. They've hidden themselves in their burrows, where they tremble and keep quiet. For that very reason, whatever we say here can't start from loyalty. Our words can't be round and empty like a zero, ready to roll up to the feet of the Magyars so they might kick them aside and scream into our face: "Gyáva népnek nincs hazája!"[133] Štefánik's not enough for you…?'

But my job was to write. And so once more I took pen in hand – and wrote.

With me, it was like that old English joke. There was this merchant named Abel, and he painted his name above his shop door. But the people pronounced it 'Habel.' So he painted it over to read 'Habel.' And they started to pronounce it "abel.' And so…

I wrote in praise of Kiev. And they read it as if I were tearing down Petrograd. I praised Petrograd, and they read it as if I'd written 'Down with Kiev!' I praised Pavlů, and that was read as an attack on the Union. I praised Vondrák, and they said I was tossing grenades at the Petrograd opposition. Once I saw old Dürich, haggard and grey, standing all by himself in the Hotel Praga, abandoned and ignored by one and all. I felt bad for him, and so I set off in his direction – and those who saw me interpreted that as treason against the Czechoslovak cause. I strove to be considerate toward the Štúr association, and they said I was in favour of a governate. I said that a separate Slovak journal was needed, and soon there were those who cried 'Aha! Separatism!' I wrote that the Slovaks wanted this, the Slovaks wanted that, and they parsed it thus: 'Who gave him the right to speak on behalf of the nation?'

And if I wrote that, in the face of all this discord, the one thing that was clear to me was that everybody wants to help the nation to succeed, and that only their directions and methods differed – that both Dürich and the governists, the Štúrists and the Unionists, and the Petrograd opposition all want to deliver the nation from political servitude

....

[133] Magyar: 'Cowardly people have no homeland.'

JANKO JESENSKÝ

to Germans and Magyars, and if the governists wanted to subject us to the Russians, at least Russians were better than Germans and Magyars, and that even Russia will change; the Tsar-dictator will not rule it forever; that there will be a constitution – hey, there's already a Duma, and elections, and so on... They would have said: 'Who's he peddling that lemonade to, that sentimental, spineless scribbler? The task of a journalist is to take his pen and run through anyone who doesn't agree with his point of view! There needs to be one plan, one direction! That Tsarist fledgling! That Black Hundreder!'

I shivered at the thought and never wrote such a thing. But the following epigram did come from my pen:

Would you say that their plan was working
Where one is leaping, one is lurking?
Giddup, Giddup, my black pony!
Whips are cracking... brakes are groaning,
And all the while the wagon's stuck –
Up to its axles in the muck.
No matter how the pony strains,
We're stuck – while ten hands jerk the reins.

That farm will sink in debt and losses
Where carters act like... horse's arses.

But even here I got it wrong. Not as far as agriculture is concerned, maybe, but as for politics...

Only grass grows quietly. At least, we humans can't hear it. But it's only there to be mown down. When a house is being built, the goal is one and the same: to set it firmly so that it will stand. And how much shouting and hammering and quarrelling do you hear while it's under construction! But it's in all that hollering and hammering and quarrelling that you find the concord of the construction process.

The philosopher says: 'Democracy is discussion.' True. But it's just as true when I say that we understand this in a British fashion: 'Let's be democrats, and go at each other's throat.'

*

Let's let democracy be, then; let them dispute, and as those 'gentlemen' argue, it all reminds me of a humorous thing that happened to me. It's an old story, but at the time it was new. Too bad it'll be about boots and mantles again, but there's nothing I can do about that. Alongside all national issues, everyday, vital questions such as 'What'll we wear on our backs and on our feet?' are also to be found.

In Russia, we celebrated the holidays twice: ours, and those of the Russians. As I've already said, in 1915, in Siberia, we celebrated our Christmas with 'extra goulash' at fifteen kopecks along with the state-provided warm water and one potato, which we got for free. For Orthodox Christmas, they gave us some fast-day fish soup, which only stank of fish.

Christmas 1916 found me in Kiev. Here too it was a sad Christmas for me. No one marked the day. It was pouring rain outside. I came back from the editorial offices around four in the afternoon. The room was unheated. I sat at the table and stared out the window, the way one often does when lost in thought – out into the distance. It grew dark. Past the window, the twisted branches of trees in the nearby garden grew black. Past the garden, a lamp was glowing in one of the windows of a tall building across the way. Beneath the lamp you could see something white: a table set, and around it some hazy pale blotches – peoples' faces. It was silent in my room. The only thing to be heard in the room next door was the owner of the house tapping at an adding machine from time to time and the drops of rain falling against the window. I didn't light the lamp. I lay down on my bed, hoping to sleep through all of Christmas Eve.

JANKO JESENSKÝ

Thirteen days later, Russian Christmas came around, cloudy as well, but in the end, it cheered me up.

In Kiev we had quite a few Russian Czechs who were Orthodox. And even if they weren't, they celebrated along with the Russians. Some of them remembered on that beautiful night their lonely, abandoned countrymen who held to the old faith.

That evening, I was invited to the Červenýs', and on Christmas Day to the Živockýs'.

I was lying on my bed when the invitation came. Not from laziness or because I was tired out after a wakeful night. It all had to do with boots.

Jaroslav Hašek, the humorist, also frequented the editorial offices of *Čechoslovan*, but usually at night, so as to stretch his legs out on some editorial desk and pillow his head on a pile of newsprint, of which there was more than enough there to be found. We rarely met. People said of him that he often got drunk and caused scandals in bars, but that he was an excellent writer of humorous stories. I don't know how it happened, but one day we found ourselves in the offices during the daylight hours. He went about dressed in uniform, with a pale, puffy face, with tiny eyes above his round cheeks: his was almost a woman's face, on which hair would not grow, or at least so it seemed to me. He inspected the feet of every person in the place, and everyone who walked in. His boots were in bad shape. One of his big toes seemed to be peeping out and nodding at me.

'Brother, you have another pair of boots,' he said, grabbing me by the sleeve.

'How do you know?'

'Yesterday you were in army boots, and today you've got civilian ones on.'

'That's true.'

'I'd buy those army boots off you.'

'All right.'

And in this way my high-laced boots, which I was given by the Austrian Red Cross way back in Beryozovka-za-Baikalom, for which in Voronezh I didn't wish to buy galoshes, even though that was a condition for renting a room, came into Hašek's possession.

It was a silly thing to do. Not because I should have known that I wouldn't get a kopeck out of Hašek in exchange for them – at bottom, I did know that – but as a former soldier, I should have thought about reserves. Life is a war and in this war, sometimes boots become casualties. For now I had only one pair, and the time came round when they were in need of repair.

They were taken off to the cobblers' by our old serving-woman Shura, who always had a kerchief on her head, twisted, as if her teeth were hurting, and a woollen scarf on her shoulders. She was a half-German, half-Ukrainian, half-Polish woman unable to speak any of these languages properly, but honest, and eager to serve, as one said at the time.

I could have bought myself a new pair, but that would've cost thirty roubles. I could have bought some cheaper ones, but for that I'd have to stand in line for at least a whole day waiting for a ration *kartochka*[134] for the boots, and another day, in another line, *kartochka* in hand, in order to get the boots themselves. So as to avoid all such tiresome difficulties I could have borrowed the thirty roubles I needed. Maybe Živocký would lend me them, maybe not. Maybe Švihovský would give me the 'needful,' but then again, maybe not. Jožo Gregor would give me them for sure, but he didn't have any. That's the way it always is. The most willing to give are those who have nothing to offer. Such being the case, it seemed the simplest thing was to lay about in bed and wait until the *sapozhnik*[135] fixed the boots I had.

....

[134] Russian: Card.

[135] Russian: Cobbler.

I lay about like that one whole day. No boots. As familiar as I was with the pace of Russian life, I shrugged and waited: tomorrow, and if not tomorrow, then the day after, and if not then, the third day will see the arrival of the boots. The dinner was to be on the fourth day, and supper on the fifth. Time enough.

I began to worry on the third day.

'Well then, Shura. Trot off to Foma's and have him send back my boots to me.'

And Shura went, but when she came back in the evening, it was only to tell me that she didn't have the boots.

'Here's your eight roubles,' she said, somehow embarrassed.

'Keep them. You'll go back for them in the morning.'

'Foma said that the boots were leaky,' she whispered hoarsely, before plugging one nostril until her nose was flattened against her face, and blowing it clean. 'Then Foma said that he fixed them and gave them to the boy to deliver them. And boots *net*, boy *net*.'

'For God's sake! Where'd the boy take them?'

'I jus' said: the boy's gone too.'

'With the boots?'

'With the boots.'

'That's theft!' I hollered, leaping from the bed. 'I'll get dressed and go myself. You'll take me there!'

But then, immediately, I sat back down. I can't go anywhere in socks! I thought about it for a while and then jumped up again. I went over to the chest and opened it up, hoping for some miracle. I found the pinstriped suit that Hrašek gave me hanging there, along with the dark blue winter suit that Ivan Daxner sacrificed on my behalf. I saw myself reflected in the fabric, it shone so. There hung my Austrian military tunic as well, but, for God's sake, for the dear Lord God's sake, for the sake of Our Lord and Saviour Jesus Christ, there wasn't even a bedroom slipper to be found there.

'You know what, Shura?' I said to her energetically, closing the chest. 'You go right back there and tell him that according to all the laws that pertain all throughout the civilised world, and so, in Russia too, the *sapozhnik* is responsible for my boots. And he needs to provide me with those boots, or twenty roubles in damages.'

And off she went. I was so agitated that I didn't fall asleep until midnight. And when I did fall asleep, I dreamt that I was running along Khreshchatik barefoot.

Shura was back the next morning.

'Foma didn't even want to listen to me. He's the one he says who's suffered a loss, not *gospodin doktor*. Material and labour he's lost. That's eight roubles… You, *gospodin doktor*, have your loss, and he has his. That's as he puts it, only Christian.'

'Christian is thou shalt not steal!' I bellowed at Shura. 'I'm not required to believe his story that the boy lost my boots… Devil take it! That *sapozhnik* of yours took them and pawned them and drank up the proceeds. The old thief! I'm off to the *mirovoi*.[136] They'll show him what's what!'

Sure! Go right off to the *mirovoi* – barefoot!

'Shura! Go back and tell him one more time that I'll have him locked up if he doesn't send back my boots!'

I waited impatiently until Shura got back around one in the afternoon.

'He'll pay when the *mirovoi* orders him to, and only then. But he demands that you reimburse him for his loss.'

I spread wide my arms and let them fall to my sides in resignation.

'You can't win with an idiot!'

'Imenno,'[137] Shura hastened to agree.

....

[136] Russian: Low-level court.
[137] Russian: Exactly.

'The bandit! I'm getting dressed up right now and going over there myself.'

So go already if you like – barefoot through the water and the mud... And Jožo's out there chasing round somewhere at breakneck speed, everywhere except for coming home. Where's he now? He's grabbed someone by the arm to chat or he's stomping around the Hotel Praga... He'd loan me his boots. Or he might go off to that picker and stealer himself... What can a simple old hag like Shura accomplish? That old shyster of a cobbler could run circles round her.

I never thought a person could be so helpless, so abject, without shoes. I'd never have been close to believing that one wretched pair of boots could make a person so happy. If only that execrable, stupid Shura were standing there now with my boots in her hands, I'd kiss her smack on the lips. 'Cos that there kiss would mean Russian Christmas Eve at the Červenýs': fast-day soup, grits, fish, apple tarts, cheroots, beer, and good company with Dýma, Žďárský, Jožo Gregor, and a real feast the next day at the Živockýs': first hors d'oeuvres, suckling pig, ham, wine, and then solid food with soup, some sort of hare and sweets, black coffee... The lady of the house, a Serb, would play some Russian songs at the piano, and while we were singing, they'd be passing round the tea, the pastries, *torts*, nuts...

But no kisses. Shura stood there before me, but with no boots in her hands. My heart shrivelled in pain and I gazed at the old thing in front of me with her head bound up in that woollen scarf, her wide hips and fat legs, fabric mukluks on her feet with rope soles, high flaps and tongues...

Hey!... What if Shura would loan me her Sunday boots? Maybe they'd fit... Those are village feet she's got, farmer's feet, real 'gimpers'[138] as we call them.

....

[138]   The word in Slovak is 'čapty.'

'Shura…' I began in dulcet tones. 'Are you going to church today?'

'Yup.'

'And tomorrow?'

'Yup.'

'What would it take for you to stay home?'

'You mean in money?'

'In money.'

'Well, for five roubles, I wouldn't move an inch.'

'And what do you wear on your feet on holy days?'

'Boots.'

'Show me.'

She brought them in.

Beautiful boots. Almost completely new. Stiff, shiny, long boots, nicely pleated at the ankle, good soles, not too thick, and rubber heels, no metalling – in short, elegant, city-wear, and they didn't stink.

'Will you lend them to me? … You owe it to me, you know. You're the one that took my boots to Foma.'

She began to giggle so, that her back shook and her belly wobbled. The few teeth that remained in her mouth shone white when she opened her mouth to laugh.

'I'll give you a rouble.'

'So, together that'll be six, what with me staying home tomorrow.'

'All right.'

But the boots wouldn't go on my foot, which got stuck in the pleats at the ankle.

'You're putting your foot in crookedly,' Shura admonished me. So I straightened out my foot, grabbed the boot by both flaps, and squeezed it in at last. Shoop! Only the heel wouldn't budge, and remained jammed against the back, with space between it and the inner sole. Shura walked around me, laughing.

'You put the left boot on your right foot!'

'Stop laughing, Shura. I know what high-tops are all about. Already as a boy I'd wear Polish britches and high boots.'

I pulled off the boot and hurled it at the floor.

'Shura! Give me your mukluks! You're to blame for all this. I'll try them on.'

The mukluks fit me well. When I pulled my trouser legs over them, the wrappings were hidden nicely. We cleaned up the toes and polished them. You could tell that they had once been lacquered.

'I just won't be able to hitch my pant-legs up,' I thought. 'I'll just keep my feet under the table, bent, toes to the floor, and the devil himself won't be the wiser,' I thought, taking pleasure in the mukluks.

'Shurochka, my dear, will you lend them to me?'

And dear Shurochka loaned them to me. And so we went off, first to Foma the shoemaker.

It was four o'clock. The streetlights had already been lit. A wispy yellow sphere of mist surrounded the lights. The cobbles shone like polished boots. The shops along the way were shutting down, going dark. We found ourselves in a shabby, muddy courtyard, walking along the wall toward a low wooden door. Shura knocked, rattled the knob, pushed against the door with her shoulder, but no luck. Locked up.

'We could stay here knocking until Three Kings,' she said.

She wanted to non-plus me with that, but I felt quite good standing there in her mukluks. They were soft, warm, and comfortable.

I pulled out two roubles.

'Here, Shurochka. I'll return your mukluks to you after Three Kings, then.' And leaving her standing there, I went up Krutoi Spusk to the top, and from there to Khreshchatik, from Khreshchatik to Vladimirskaya via Fundukleyevskaya, slowly toward the Červenýs'...

*

Misfortune comes in pairs, and Russia is no exception to the rule. Misery after misery stands here like old women in *ochered*.[139] You take care of one, here comes another, and another.

After the boots, which the *sapozhnik* stole instead of repairing (and after nearly having to pay reparations for the soles and the labour), the time came for my valuable coat.

It was a short, nice little winter coat that I wore at home when driving a wagon in the village. Back when it arrived I was angry with my wife for not sending me my long, city coat. But I cheered myself with the thought that, anyway, I could now get rid of my reddish 'crusader' mantle, which I'd tried to make over into a raglan, but in which I looked like an Austrian when I was doing all I could to look Russian.

The Russians are the most winter-loving people you'll ever come across. Here, everybody has to make himself over into a bear so as to be warm outdoors. Even in Kiev a *shuba*[140] was de rigueur, fur-lined inside and out. So I arranged, at least, for a collar of karakul to be sewn on, and bought myself a black hat of the same material. I had new boots and galoshes, gigantic gloves, a short little pipe at my lips, and even mufflers on my ears, otherwise unnecessary given the hat. Whoever caught sight of me would never guess that it was me, co-editor of the Slovak portion of the world-famous *Čechoslovan*. He'd rather have thought me the director of some bank, even if rather a wretched bank, who, even if he hadn't enough funds for fur linings and a long leather coat, is at least able to afford a fur collar and short winter wrap reaching to the knees.

Even the locale we frequented was chic: the Hotel Praga. We came here, it is true, only for coffee. For dinner or sup-

....

139   Russian: Queue.

140   Russian: Fur coat.

per – only when someone invited us, guaranteeing to pick up the tab, something that happened only very infrequently. We ourselves dared come here on our own account only now and then, after the twentieth of the month, when we'd received our salaries, and that, only once or twice, for borsht with sour cream, cutlets with roasted potatoes and carrots, a mug of something or some sort of ministerial schnitzel.

The great, bright hall with its gigantic windows on Vladimirskaya St, with drapes, plush couches along the walls, tables covered in white tablecloths, and electric lamps… The grand mirror… A place clean, pleasant, warm. As I entered I always involuntarily gave my purse a squeeze, to make sure I had it with me, so that I could pay for what I consumed. I adjusted my collar, my neckcloth; I'd glance at my hands to make sure that they were clean, at my nails, sadly, regretting that I hadn't yet bathed. Such a genteel public, distinguished, quiet. One hardly spoke there above a whisper, as if in a conspiracy, or as if one were awaiting the monarch himself. Only the local Czechs strolled about lazily, drinking their beer, politicking, playing chess, and the only sounds that pierced the solemn silence were their 'check! check!'s and still louder 'mate!'s, the rattle of the toppled pieces, and their loud rearranging for another contest, the tapping of the knight about the board, and now and then a brief dispute or some laughter at a bad move.

We were served by Latvian girls, all of them handsome, young, and, as it was said, virgins untouched – but all gay and always smiling. Except for the most beautiful of them, with her straw-coloured hair and white skin. That 'white swan' always went about with a serious mien, as if very concerned with something.

So we would come here and hash out various editorial matters over coffee. There were many such questions, so one often sat about in the Hotel Praga, drinking buckets of coffee. Usually, we had all the problems of the world solved while the bigshot leaders were still wringing their hands over them. They never came by to consult us, and accordingly most often brought the matters to a different conclusion than we had imagined. Then, to placate our wounded pride, we would go back again for some more coffee. And so it turned out that we sat more often in the café than in the editorial offices.

At first I sat there in my short winter coat, that is to say, first in it, and then on it or alongside it when it got too warm – so that it wouldn't go astray. I would throw it over the backrest of the chair and lean against it, as one leans upon a faithful friend, or at least I would rest my hand upon its thick wadded back; sometimes I would take its sleeve in my hand, so that no stranger's arm might dare venture inside. Nothing terrible, eh? Just a concealed distrust of the whole world.

Now, in some respects Russians are very delicate. When a Russian stretches out his hand to you, it goes without saying that first he takes off his glove. A citizen of our land will extend his hand to you without doing so, even if he's wearing a boxing mitt. When he walks along the pavement, a Russian is so delicate that he neither whistles nor sings as does a person back home – and that right into your ear so that you fairly leap out of your skin. When a Russian smokes a cigarette, he exhales the smoke upward, above your head, and fans away the smoke with his hands so as not to suffocate you; amongst us the smokers blow the raunchiest exhaust right into your face so that your eyes water. Once at the Solovtsov Theatre they refused to believe that we had tickets for the front row, because we weren't all done up in black formal wear, and Jožo Gregor was leaning his elbow ostentatiously on the balustrade and cupping his ear with his hand so as to hear better. To enter an elegant café or restaurant in a winter coat also spoke against one. I saw that the patrons would leave their coats in the hallway on the hangers provided there, and take off their galoshes before entering, but my distrust, as quiet as it was, was just as great.

Once, someone even remarked to me:

'You know, they might be offended at that. It's as if you thought the place were prowled by people in search of coats. As if they didn't have their own.'

'There are such as have, and such as haven't,' I remarked.

'Everyone has, in Russia. Have you ever seen a Russian without a winter coat?'

I glanced out onto the street through the window. He had a point. There was so much fur walking around out there, it looked as if someone had unlocked all the cages of a wild menagerie. There a fox, there a bear, there a wild ram, a rabbit, a cat and who knows what else. Fur *papakchas* the size of small apartments were on their heads. Even the ladies' galoshes were furry.

So from then on I began leaving my winter coat on a hook. I'd throw my hat and gloves into one of the pockets along with my ear muffs, taking along with me only my pipe, and peeling off my beautiful galoshes as well. But, providentially, I took care always to hang it next to some *shuba* of lordly fur. I thought to myself that if any winter coat was suddenly to grow a pair of legs and hoof it, it would sooner be a *shuba* with a furry lining than my little coat furred with cotton padding. And just as providentially, I would frequently stroll out of the café proper to have a look in the foyer and make sure that my coat was still hanging there next to the *shuba*. If the latter were no longer there, I would rehang it somewhere else, for the sake of better company and security. My little winter coat would hang there, humbly and quietly, not making the slightest movement. Satisfied, I'd go back in. After a certain while, I didn't even give it a second thought when I came across it among other coats. It seemed a very natural thing to me that, since I'd hung it somewhere, hang there it must.

Until once when I glanced in its direction... squinted... and – the coat was not on the hook where I'd hung it. Nor was it on the second, the third, or the thirtieth. A cold shiver ran down my spine. I began to rummage through all the coats to check and see if it wasn't underneath this or that one. It was nowhere. I pawed through all the hangers ten times. I searched the floor – maybe it had fallen? No. I don't know why – perhaps I was in such despair – I lifted my eyes toward the ceiling. Maybe it had fluttered upwards, and was now hanging from the lamp? For a brief second a comforting thought passed through my mind, that perhaps I was merely dreaming, and that I would be waking right up to find myself clad in my little winter coat. But there was Jožo Gregor standing a bit further on, as large as life, clearing his throat so loudly that it could be no dream. He was waiting for me. I searched him with my eyes to ascertain whether all this might not be some joke of his, and he was concealing my coat on his person. But no – he was dressed up in his brindled promenade coat with those invalids of buttons. I went back into the room where I'd been sitting to see if the coat wasn't there, although I knew quite well that I'd taken it off and hung it up. Of course, there wasn't a single hair of the coat to be found there. Nor were any of the patrons wearing it. It was gone. Lost. Vanished. They stole it from me, along with my hat, my gloves, and my ear muffs. And once more I was as bare as I had been in Siberia. Another Akaky Akakiyevich.[141]

Then it flashed through my mind that when I was on my way to the Praga the cold had already been tearing at my cheeks; my ears were freezing and my nose was practically stopped up by the bitter air.

And now the evening was drawing on. The cold was only getting worse…

....

[141] A character in Nikolai Gogol's novella *The Overcoat* (1842). He is a low-ranking official who one day finds himself in exactly the same situation.

JANKO JESENSKÝ

I stood there in the foyer, stiff, as if I were already frozen. Even my words were frozen in my throat. God forbid a word should escape my mouth.

'What're you standing there for like that?' Jožo urged impatiently. 'Come on, already!'

'My coat's been pinched,' I finally babbled out after a long pause.

'What!'

'It's gone. Swiped.'

'Did you have a good look?' he said, beginning to rummage through the coats himself.

'I did. Don't bother looking. A fact's a fact. The only thing that surprises me is – look what beautiful *shubas* are hanging there... Here fox, here beaver, there polecat... And it's mine they take.

Jožo, the good soul, began to comfort me. It was just a mistake, for sure. Whoever took it is sure to bring it right back, as soon as he realises his error... And Mencer the hotelier is also responsible. He has to reimburse me for the coat.

'But you can't go out into the cold like that. I'll run home to get your greatcoat. Wait here. You have to, anyway. And when the guests all leave and a coat remains, it's yours.'

I shot out my hand and halted him:

'Don't be long.'

Then Živocký passed through the foyer. Two metres tall and one metre wide. Behind him came Mencer, the tenant of the Hotel Praga. Short, fat, big-bellied, he didn't even reach Živocký's shoulders. They saw that we were standing in the foyer, as if we were talking something over and didn't know what to do. My nose seemed somewhat longer than usual, and my chin fell onto my tie. Above my eyebrows and across my forehead there were seven deep wrinkles. Jožo looked upon me in anguish. He took Mencer by the arm and began explaining to him in good faith that there was disorder in the cloakroom, that this and that that, a coat was stolen, and the doctor here can't go away like this. He's going to have to get a new coat somehow.

Mencer snorted. That signified a laugh, and we know what a laugh like that means. It means: 'Whose coat was stolen? Yours or mine? Not mine, but yours. And so it's up to you to find the thief. Did I lose my coat, or did you lose yours? You did. And as the saying goes: losers weepers, peel your peepers. Whoever's lost something, let him go and look for it. It's me missing a coat, or you? It's you. So it's your problem.'

'You're responsible for it,' I ventured. 'The theft occurred in your establishment. In your cloakroom.'

'I'm sorry,' Mencer contradicted me. 'But if someone stole your watch in my dining room, am I responsible for that, too?'

'That's quite another matter. The watch was in my pocket...'

'Let's say that you placed it on the table...'

This would have developed into a legal dispute that might have lasted into the wee hours had Mr Živocký not got involved.

'I have a fox jacket. I'll lend it to you until you settle your matter.'

I glanced at the giant. I lacked some twenty-six cm to make it to two metres. As far as difference in our girth is concerned, let's say ten.

'I'll lend you a bowler, too,' Mr Živocký went on gaily.

I turned away from the cynical Mencer, bringing the dispute to an end and placed my hand into the bear paw of Živocký as a sign of my accepting his offer and a token of my gratitude. Indeed, my heart was somewhat lighter. In the end, one can always come across a good person.

We waited quite a while until the jacket and trilby arrived. The latter was already going a bit green; the band was somewhat greasy, here and there it bore scars of ancient battles and the wrinkles that result from a wild youth, but it fit me well if I cocked it backwards or rested it on the bridge of my nose.

JANKO JESENSKÝ

The jacket was huge. It reached my ankles. It's even possible that I swept the pavement with it, but that didn't matter. I didn't care. Sure, I couldn't see my feet, but I didn't look down at them much. The shoulders draped down over my elbows, the sleeves nearly reached my knees and I could've wound the thing around me twice. The slit in the back dangled between my calves. *Nichego!*[142] At least I was warm.

Jožo admired my new look. He said I was a real gentleman, from top to toe. Živocký nearly died laughing, at first. But then he said, quite seriously:

'I had no idea it was still in such good shape.'

That evening we went to the café in Fundukleyevskaya with the intention of going on to the theatre at eight.

Then, at an electric lamp-post, a *gorodovoi*[143] halted me.

'Where're you off to?' he accosted me in Russian.

'What business is this of yours?'

'Where are you going?' he repeated his question, ignoring my own.

So this was serious.

'The café. What's it to you?' I repeated my own question. Cop or no cop, that's not the way to approach people.

'Where'd you get that *shuba*?'

'What's it to you then?'

'Come with me.'

Jožo began explaining the matter to him, but Živocký halted him, squeezing him with one hand, pushing the cop aside with the other, and growling out at him, haughtily, coldly, and briefly.

'It's my *shuba*. Let's go.'

Upon my soul, if not for Živocký, they'd've locked me up for seemingly having stolen a jacket.

....

[142] Russian: 'That's nothing!'

[143] Russian: Policeman.

When you're down, you don't give a fig for ridicule. One more surprise was waiting on me in the café. When I slipped off the jacket, I looked like a young fox – the lining of the jacket had shed all of the old fox fur onto my coat. I almost had the urge to drop down on all fours. It took me three whole days to brush it all off...

*

The winter was slowly coming to an end, the weather fickle. Now it was ten degrees below zero (Celsius), with a biting north wind on a sunny day, now came a thaw and it was ten degrees above. New snow would fall on the old sallow layers of slush. Sleds were in operation again. The snow-clearers were out in swarms with their shovels, and the air was filled with their clinking. But not for long. The south wind would blow, the sun would come out warm, and there would be another thaw. Sleds were replaced by coaches. The roads were covered in water. The heaps of snow alongside the pavements turned black again, and day by day they grew smaller. Passers-by could be seen past them, going this way and that. St Joseph came, but he didn't smile upon us like he did at home. He lay down in bed, coughing. He had a cold and a sore throat. Cold compresses were applied against his fever and he caterwauled all over Kiev.

In a word, it was a sharp wrestling bout, with Spring gaining in strength, but Winter stubborn and raging in the throes of its final agony.

There was fighting going on in the natural world; fighting among people. A revolution erupted in Petrograd. The news reported that the Russians had taken Petrograd from the Germans, who supposedly had been conniving there to foment a revolution so as to force the Russians into accepting a separate peace. But the Russians were victorious. Petrograd was in the hands of the Russian revolutionaries.

JANKO JESENSKÝ

In Kiev, all along the rivulets of spring there were red currents of people. Red colour against the lessening snow-banks, as if flowerbeds blossoming. Demonstrations. Ukrainians, Poles, Jews, with shouting, music, singing, slogans on placards. Meetings. Speeches. 'Da zdravstvuyet svobodnaya Rossiya!'[144] Walls and fences were covered with nothing but *vozzvaniya*[145] – resolutions, greetings, memoranda. The Vremennoye pravitelstvo[146] of Professor Milyukov.

Among us too meeting followed hard upon meeting, one summit hot on the heels of another. Like children playing tag. You're it – now you're it. Now the functionaries of the Union, now the congregation of the collaborators; now the secret Black Hand, now the journalists' union; here the Slovaks, there the Poles, and there a confidential dinner party.

Štefánik, cooking up some plans for the organisation of the Czechoslovak National Council branch in Russia, went off to Romania, appointing B. Čermak as his plenipotentiary.

Instead of one National Council we had the Union of Czechoslovak Associations, the Congregation of Union Collaborators, Dürich's National Council, Čermak's provisional office of the National Council Branch, and various other groupings of the POWs, larger and smaller ones, with their own autonomous wills.

Milyukov might well scratch his head.

Štefánik demanded that he recognise the Czechoslovak National Council headed by Masaryk and its Branch in Russia; Dürich demanded recognition for his National Council; Vondrák, the presiding officer of the Union of Czechoslovak Associations in Russia, sent greetings to Milyukov on behalf of the Union and demanded the re-establishment

---

[144]   Russian: 'Long live free Russia!'

[145]   Russian: Appeals, proclamations.

[146]   Russian: Provisional government.

of the Union in its old powers to liberate faithful Czechs and Slovaks from captivity, to find them employment in the defence industry, and to accept volunteers for the front; the recognition of the Union as the representative and organising body of the nation in Russia – and so he demanded all of those rights of which the Kiev Accord had deprived him. The Congregation of Union Collaborators was opposed to the gentlemen in charge of the Union, and, at a stormy meeting, resolved to send a telegram to Milyukov demanding that he recognise the Czechoslovak National Council headed by Masaryk as the unique and supreme political representative of the Czechoslovak nation, confirming the Branch as established in Russia according to the proposal of Štefánik, so that Dürich's National Council should be definitively eliminated. Various POW groupings also put their heads together and sent off their own resolutions to the Minister of Foreign Affairs.

Milyukov brushed aside the telegrams and said:

'Let's wait until Masaryk gets here... Let's wait and see what the Congress says.'

But Professor Masaryk himself was buried in a blizzard of paper. He couldn't take it any longer; he telegraphed back to say that he was on his way, and that until he arrived, he demanded the obedience of Vondrák and Pavlů and Čermak. He sent a telegram to Milyukov too, saying that Dürich had been excluded from the National Council, sending his greetings as well to the 'great Russian revolution, which signifies order and victory... The liberation of the Czech lands along with Slovakia shall be realised with the rebirth of Russia... Free Russia is a mortal blow to Prussianism... Free Russia means the death of Austria-Hungary, that hypocritical and treacherous enemy of the Slavs. Free Russia signifies the strengthening of the Entente...'

Milyukov replied with thanks.

Preparations were being made for the Congress and the meetings were frenzied. Conventions, consultations, councils. As I sang to myself at the editorial offices: 'All the meetings, meetings, meetings are on track,/ And of meetings, meetings, meetings there's no lack.'

The grand opening was scheduled for 6 May.

A resolution was passed proclaiming that 'The Czechoslovak National Council, under the leadership of Professor T.G. Masaryk, is the supreme organ of the Czechoslovak national and political action, and, therefore, it is the obligation of every Czech and Slovak to submit himself to its authority. Let the Provisional Russian Government and all appropriate official organs be notified of this decision.'

The Congress sent its greetings to Milyukov.

Milyukov sent his greetings to the Congress.

The Congress even sent greetings to Slovakia and the Slovaks at home, and this too was to be noted in the news... And then scattered all over Slovakia from the air, by aeroplane. We were supposed to see to the publication. *Slovak Voices* was to be transferred to Petrograd as a separate periodical.

At the conclusion of it all, a group photograph and then farewell.

Now, every idea is beautiful, but when people start to bring it to life, they always soil it with their dirty human hands. The idea doesn't quite know how to tread the earth among people in its ideal beauty. It topples over, it comes to ruin.

Russian freedom!

That's the way it always goes: when you're setting things in order, the result is disorder. We'd swept clean our own little hut, set up our kit, and declared who was head of the household. Dürich's National Council was tossed out on the rubbish heap. The former prompter, Priklonskij, all but had him arrested. Provisional order. But as for Russia? Russia is a little larger *kvartira* than ours, and the disorder there was a little greater too. And then even the servant girls began to demonstrate. They demanded a six-hour workday, two free days per week, and the right to treat guests as their equals. Soldiers began smoking openly as they strolled about; they stopped saluting the upper ranks, and when they did, it was just pro forma, with *légèrité*, no more clicking of heels, with cigarette in hand – if not still dangling from their lips. Some of the officers would call them to order and, quite upset, dress them down for their carelessness and lack of respect towards their superior officers, while others just waved a hand and said 'Naplevat!'[147]

'Smirno!'[148] roared a certain officer at a soldier who passed him by without saluting, cigarette still at his lips. The soldier halted. 'You can smoke if you like, but me, as your superior officer, you have to salute!'

A militia officer then butted in, saying that you can't address a soldier in such familiar terms, but the officer bawled back:

'Keep your nose out of our business!'

The revolutionary militiaman was there, it's true, to preserve order, and, philosophising about the law of equality among all people, was just about to take the officer in hand and toss him in the jug. But then the soldier boy standing there *smirno* tosses his smoke away and says:

'Sir! Permission to thump the lout on his mug for sticking his nose into our business, sir!'

So tradition and the old order still carried the day,

But the thorns continued to grow, and the newspapers began writing about the *rasstroi*[149] in the army and anarchy at home. Instead of one government, there were two: the 'Vremennoye pravitelstvo' and the 'Sovet rabochikh i soldatskikh deputatov.'[150] And these could never find a middle ground.

....

[147] Russian: 'The hell with it!' (Literally: 'spit on it!').

[148] Russian: 'Attention!'

[149] Russian: Unravelling.

[150] Russian: Provisional government; Soviet of workers' and soldiers'

Each one set up obstacles before the other. The slogan 'Voina do pobednogo kontsa' was shouted down by 'Mir!'[151] Wherever Lenin, like some invisible bacillus of cholera, passed, he left in his wake the corpses of all resolutions made up until then, the overturning of elemental principles and convictions. No Russia, no state, no family, no private wealth, no nationalism, no victory, no honour, only peace, peace, peace, 'vo chto by to ni stalo.'[152] 'Grab nagrablennoye!'[153] He played on the most vicious human instincts. Be a beast!

Milyukov left his post as foreign minister.

The Italians, the French, and the British were advancing on all fronts. Only the Russian front stagnated; all quiet there. But if it had only just kept quiet and stagnated, that would still be more or less all right. But the Russians shot their own who wanted to advance! They fraternised with the Germans, exchanging goods with them in the trenches, and deserted the front *en masse* to return home for their share in the looting of the estates of the nobles and the wealthy. Every day, some 12,000 deserters passed through Kiev.

Guchkov declared that Russia was 'na krayu gibeli.'[154] In the *Evening Gazette*, Leonid Andreyev wrote of cataclysm. Kerensky spoke, and spoke, and spoke.

Revolution and liberty gave way to anarchy.

Black posters went up everywhere:

'Smert burzhuazii!'

'Da zdravstvuyet svobodnaya kommuna!'[155]

....

deputies.

[151] Russian: 'War until final victory!'; 'Peace!'

[152] Russian: 'At all costs.'

[153] Russian: 'Take from those who have unlawfully taken!'

[154] Russian: On the brink of death.

[155] Russian: 'Death to the bourgeoisie!'; 'Long live the free Commune!'

People were already walking about the streets with *khanjali* and revolvers, sabres, bombs, and crying:

'K rasprave s kapitalistami!'[156]

Instead of dispersing the screaming, 150-headed hydra of a mob, the militia cautioned the citizenry not to irritate the demonstrators.

Kronstadt declared itself an independent republic, defying the provisional government, arresting its officials and holding them in dungeons, sending off a cheekily defiant ultimatum to the council of ministers.

The army was an 'undemocratic establishment.' Nothing but superior officers, chiefs, commandants, differentiations, and ranks, ranks, ranks. One star, two, three, and the rest were just to heed what they say. Where do you have equality amongst people here? Equality is a laughing stock in the army, just like fraternity, just like democracy.

And now one began seeing the gentleman officers themselves walking about with mess tins in search of rations. Standing, waiting in line along with all the other soldiers until their turn came. And the common soldiers would laugh at them, making them the butt of their jokes.

At the front, there were even murders. The soldiers there had started killing their own superior officers.

Travel was impossible. The trains were all chock-full of soldiers. To the very chassis. The station waiting rooms were barracks. Soldiers everywhere. The officers were standing about, weary, sleep-deprived. All the soldiers were sleeping, sprawled out all over the waiting rooms and second class dining halls.

At a frontline meeting in Odessa, General Shcherbachev argued in vain that the army was beginning to fall apart, and that would be synonymous with the unravelling of Russia herself. The commander in chief argued in vain that Russia is 'na

---

[156] Russian: 'Time to settle scores with the capitalists!'

krayu gibeli.' In vain, Brusilov published an order that ended with the words:

'I demand that the most energetic measures be taken for the immediate suppression of all unjustifiable anarchy.'

But the plague was advancing.

All the while that immense fires were raging on the front and human blood was being pumped at them as from fire hoses to put them out, the winds fanned the sparks and ashes and we to the rear sensed nothing but the smoke from the burnt fields. We saw neither the blood nor the flames; nothing came to our attention save the ash that was borne on the winds like paper tatters, which harmed no one when they fell upon their shoulders. But today fire and blood were surging to the rear. All of Russia was aflame. Wherever one looked, all one saw was inferno, looting, revolt, murder, and blood. The revolution was falling apart. Estates were drowned in red, burnt to ash. The flames shot their long tongues toward the skies. Fire warmed, chivvied, burned, and destroyed…

*

The Congress of Czechs and Slovaks in Kiev had elected me a member of the information and propaganda division of the National Council Branch in Russia. As such, I was to shift my residence to Petrograd, where *Slovak Voices* had already begun appearing as a periodical in its own right.

I received a telegram from Hurban. In Russian, he wrote:

'Come immediately. Identity card upon arrival. Ask funds of Union. First number of paper already out. Have Gregor send manuscripts. Very desirable columns, themes not present political but national life in comparison to future free development. Gurban.'[157]

....

[157] Hurban is writing in Russian; there is no 'h' in Russian, and so his

For those days, it was a rather clear message.

So off I went to the Mezhdunarodnoye obshchestvo spal-nykh vagonov[158] and made myself a reservation for 16 June.

I still had to rush that Congress resolution and greeting to Slovakia through the Čechoslovan printery. They'd been 'printing' it since the beginning of May. Up until the time of which I'm speaking now, among my daily tasks was a trip to the printery to urge on that greeting, and to hear the eager promises that yes, yes, it's coming, it's coming, and this had been going on for two months now. It seemed to me that the Czechs considered the keeping of one's word to be something of a 'bourgeois prejudice.' For variety's sake I would visit a different official at the printery every day.

One day I went to see Chalupa.

'That's in Grunt's hands.'

So I went off to Grunt.

'That's Švihovský's business.'

I went to see Švihovský.

'It's Chalupa you want to see for that.'

And so I went to Chalupa. Etc.

I might've worn my legs down to the knees and – still no article. So I greeted Slovakia myself in the quiet of my soul thinking that, when I get back home, I'll greet her in person.

So I made my preparations to leave, and that day I met up with Duchaj who told me that he was getting a Slovak Congress together.

'But there just was one, only two months ago.'

'That was a Czechoslovak Congress. We want a purely Slovak one.'

Vajanský's poem flashed through my mind:

....
name would be transliterated thus: *Gurban.*

[158] Russian: International Association of Sleeping Carriages.

Down the road the panting Slovak clatters
Upon the wretch's back: but rags and tatters;
He heard quite well the archangelic songs,
But was held up, untangling his boot-thongs.

'What for?' I asked.

'Everybody's holding congresses except us Slovaks.'

'So what now?'

'I wrote an article about the Congress and Braun told me it's already being set for print. I'm going there to urge them on.'

'What did you say? Who? Braun?'

'Braun. The editor.'

'Braun... Braun...'

I didn't even know about him. One more post to hie to from the last pillar. Now it'll be Braun, Chalupa, Grunt, Švihovský, Braun... Da capo al fine.

But Braun informed Duchaj that some Slovaks told him that there wasn't going to be any such congress, because that would mean Slovak separatism.

We gave some thought to what Slovaks that might have been. There were only three of us in Kiev. Vlado Daxner? He was sitting at home cutting apart an old shirt, sewing himself a cap from the pieces. Haša? Impossible. He spent the whole day bathing in the Dnieper. He hardly fit the bill. And I was working feverishly on greeting Slovakia... None of us had spoken with Braun. So, who? We went over the other Slovaks: Braun, Chalupa, Grunt, Švihovský... Braun... *Da capo al fine.*

The article about the Slovak Congress was never published. The Congress never took place. And quite wisely... When we return, we'll have a sitting for ourselves in Slovakia.

The girl who took the reservation for my ticket to Petrograd for 16 June surprised me with the news that someone had already picked it up in my name. Somebody tall, she seemed to remember, and red-haired.

'Who did I tell about my journey?' I asked myself. 'Red-haired, tall… Chalupa! Should I go to him, dress him down, hold him responsible? He'd be certain to blame it on Grunt, and Grunt on Švihovský…'

I made another reservation for 4 July.

X. IN PETROGRAD

I've traversed the length and breadth of Russia by wagon and ship, by turns. I have enough unpleasant memories, for sure.

So, I set off for Petrograd in an international wagon, second class. I travelled in high style. Instead of arriving at eleven in the morning as planned, I got to my destination at seven in the evening. But, in Russia, a delay of eight hours by train is *nichego*. It's not even worth mentioning.

Glory be to God! I found my friends Janko Sršeň and Vlado Hurban, the editor-in-chief of *Slovak Voices*, waiting for me at the station. Otherwise I would have been completely fleeced as soon as I stepped off the train by Comrades *nosilshchik* and *izvozchik*.[159]

Hurban went from *izvozchik* to *izvozchik* to strike the best deal. One of them wanted eight roubles, and another six, for a drive of only twenty minutes. Finally, he found one who would take four. Voodoo! The same beards, shoulders, backs, and bellies, the same skinny nags and dingy coaches with ripped plush seats, the same short stovepipe hats with buckles, shiny caftans, greenish belts – yet such a difference in fares!

'Nice,' said Hurban, as Sršeň and I piled into the coach.

Hurban went off to a lecture by Mrs Pankhurst.

The rains ended. The sun shone down on the wet streets of cobbles inlaid with wood. It seemed to me that it was cool

....

[159]   Russian: Porter and cabby.

out. The wind was blowing straight in our faces, pushing before it garbage, tatters of paper and newsprint along the filthy streets. Hoardings, bills, lampposts, the windows of the buildings, all were dirty, buried in dust. The rain must've been very short-lived as it didn't wash any of this grime away. There were also very few people about. It was obvious that here people stayed at home and didn't throng the streets as in Kiev. Most of them were soldiers with their greatcoats draped over their shoulders.

We went off to Liteiny Prospekt. Nevsky flashed, intersecting it: a straight, broad, big-city street, but naked, without any trees. I had been expecting something awesome, wide, beautiful, with side-paths shaded by trees and pavements of devil knows what sort of material; sparkle, flamboyance, luxury, and here – nothing of the sort. No different from a hundred other big-city streets. A so-so effect. But Pushkin himself strolled about here! Gogol writes about the Nevsky Prospekt! Here Lermontov strutted... Has my heart grown so hard?

After setting my things in order and washing up at Sršeň's place, we went out into the streets again. Slowly, we approached the Neva. A dirty, grey river with rotting, blackened boats. And all around it, buildings, buildings, buildings. Everything but greenery. A vacuum.

'There're supposed to be granite embankments somewhere around here,' I thought. 'The Neva's supposed to beat against them.'

But I saw none, and so I asked Sršeň. He pointed across to the other side... I saw there masonry, walls of rock, bastions. At the very riverbank. Behind them a tall tower, with a thin, pointy summit. Nearly the whole thing was shining in the sun.

'The Peter and Paul Fortress,' Sršeň explained. 'Stürmer's being held there, as are Protopopov and company. The dungeons are below water level.'

'Horrible!'

'And here's Shlisselburg's Tavern.'

I looked there and saw a boat upon which a wooden shack was set, with little windows and some scraggy white curtains.

'Let's not go there,' and he takes me by the arm. 'There you pay for a piece of ham – look, my hands are small, but not even for a piece as large as that – five roubles.'

And he shows me his hand. It is tiny.

'And for a miniature piece of veal,' he continues, almost in a whisper, 'ditto.'

So he pulls me off to the Summer Garden, to the left past a high green fence with granite poles. We walk through a sparse orchard with birch, ash, lindens, etc. People in overcoats are sitting on the benches. It's cool and wet out.

There are rows of statues left and right. Goddesses and muses in *déshabillé*, with broken noses, and soiled, armless gods. Here too there aren't many people strolling about. You don't see any of the smartly dressed, ethereal beauties you meet with in Kiev. No laughter. Even those who are out parading aren't ethereal, but subdued rather, weighed down, pale, sort of 'grounded.' Not a spark of beauty or loveliness among them.

We exit the park.

'The Field of Mars.'

A dull, broad *ploshchad*[160] with a wooden shack and little mounds with low, green palings. Very thin, green, ragged ribbons of grass on the mounds. Here lie those who 'laid a sacrifice' at the feet of the Revolution. Graves on the army's parade ground... The army as cemetery. Some idiotic thoughts tumble through my mind.

We wandered through the unfamiliar black streets for quite a while. Around nine in the evening, we arrived at the

....

[160] Russian: Square.

Restaurant Prague, where we supped meagrely and expensively. Bouillon without any egg, veal and three still infant potatoes, seven and a half strawberries: three roubles fifty kopecks. A bottle of something tasting like cat's piss and liquorice for a rouble twenty. Tea and cloakroom at your discretion – but just so as not to get 'that look!' A person so fears 'that look.' It's clear you're not at home here. And before you turn around, six roubles are gone. I sat there a moment with my jaw on the floor. Without coffee, without a cigar – and famished. I was never an ace at math, but as I summed it all up in my mind, it turned out that even though I'm a government official, so to speak, I won't be able to make ends meet. A month of such suppers would cost a person one hundred eighty roubles! …But then the jet of golden tea flashed, and I calmed down. That's what tea is for, you know. To help fill out breakfasts and suppers and dinners, too.

We went out onto Nevsky. All I could see before my eyes were the dowdy and ragged trousers of an old gallant.

Ten o'clock and it's still twilight. The white nights of Petrograd. No moon or stars to be seen. A bright, ash-coloured sky. A canvas of grey. The streetlights are unlit and still you might read the evening news. From quite a distance you could make out an unshaven face or blushing cheeks. A large crowd of people was milling about in front of the editorial offices of the *Evening Times.* They were reading the news from the battlefield, which was hung up there, and debating. Learning how to be free.

'The Anichkov Bridge,' Janko Sršeň explained. 'And here's the Fontanka.'

Four bronze horses and a bronze man at each of the four corners of the bridge. The horses are rearing and the men are trying to control them. They depict a process of pulling them under control from the very start, and the struggle gets more and more heated. The man is struggling more and more strenuously, until he's straining with all he's got.

Involuntarily, the battle with the Bolsheviks came to my mind.

To the right, the Anichkov Palace. The building was flush with red, like all government buildings. The old colour of the old regime and the new colour of freedom. They're about the same. Old infirmity and new freedom. Don't they kind of bleed into one another?

The colonnade of the palace gives onto the Fontanka River and Nevsky Prospekt. Beyond the bridge another palace festooned with red. Even the air has a pinkish tint to it. The bloody water ripples. There are no waves on the river's surface, but it almost seems to be goose-pimpled.

Sršeň points out some of the scars of the revolution to me. Pockmarks of machine-gun rounds on the Anichkov Palace. It had been shot up from armoured vehicles. The shattered windows are pasted over with paper.

'It was interesting,' he said, 'how all the people vanished when the shooting started. Suddenly, no one was to be seen. But the path and trottoirs were covered with winter coats – expensive furs, caps, women's overcoats. High heels, rubbers, hobnailed boots, triangular galoshes… Everything lay there as if on command.'

We turned into Liteiny. Here and there a tardy citizen could be seen hastening home. It was cold. I had a glance at my watch. Eleven o'clock. This was the hour when all the taverns and cafés were closing up.

We had some tea at home. Without tea you can't even say your evening prayers. Before my evening sighs I read a bit more in the *Petrograd Pravda.* But it just lit a fire under me. I tossed it aside and went over to have a look out the window. Bare, yellow walls. Eighty-seven windows and forty-two smoke-pipes. The chimney, the black stones of the yard. A clump of trees and a clump of garbage. Filth. Disorder. And above it all the ashen block of the sky still shining with the Petrograd white night. Should you wake up at this hour you wouldn't know if it was dawn or dusk.

And so I find myself in this grand city. Like a person waking up in the middle of the Petrograd white night I don't know if the sun is rising or setting over the great land of Russia. It's neither night nor day. A bastardised darkness and a bastardised light.

It's like when beef is just on the boil and the 'foam' from the meat floats to the top. Back home, the housewives skim it off as a kind of offscouring. Here too the scum floats to the top. Who's going to skim it off?

I felt as if I were beginning to hate Petrograd.

*

Slovak Voices ceased to be just a tail pinned on to the *Čechoslovan* – two or three pages, sometimes even less, like when they needed more space, which Jožko Gregor and I used to always get upset about. It began to come out as a periodical in its own right in large format, with beautiful print, on good paper, quite a serious undertaking, once a week. The machinery was huge. From typesetter, Vladimír Hurban advanced to editor-in-chief. He'd only show up at important moments with his pearls of wisdom, which usually wound up on page one. There were a lot of important moments, but he began to run out of pearls. And so Janko Sršeň had to leap to his aid with his fiery columns, which often fired me up as well. A bit later, Milo Gavora was also assigned to us; with our scissors, he and I looked like a couple of tailors. Jožko Gergor got tired of being a hero in the rear, so he went out among the soldiers in search of impressions and laurels, trying to become an *udarnik*[161] on the battlefield against the Germans and the Austrians.

....

[161] Russian: Shock-worker.

We had all the American periodicals at our disposal, and now and then a packet of the *Národnie noviny*[162] from Martin would arrive. It was as if you were over-wafted with the clean air of home blowing in from all sides, as if gazing out the windows you could see Lysec, the Blatnické Hills, the mountain summits above Vrútky, bald, with the Považská cavern, and here the whistle of the furniture factory in Veľké Uherce and the cellulose factory in Martin. But when you searched for tongues of fire among the type of these papers, at least a so-so puff of smoke beneath which some sparks and embers were smouldering, you found only silence, cemetery, rows like little graves one after another: in Slovakia, all was dead… Besides this we also had Czech papers, Klecanda would lend us the *Slovenské pohľady*.[163] One also came across Pietor's *Nápor a odpor*.[164] So there were enough wells from which to draw examples of wrongs to incite the peaceful Slovak soul to 'arise like a man and dash the yoke to the ground…'

The editorial offices were located in a little room on Basseinaya Street. When I say a 'little room,' I understand it in the Russian sense of *izbička*. In comparison to our current conceptions of buildings it was an immense hall. It looked out upon a side street. It's also true that when I think of that 'side street' being set somewhere in Prague, it becomes one of the biggest and broadest streets in this capital city of ours.

The locale, as I recall it, was meagrely furnished. Bare walls with no pictures, planed tables, a dirty floor, and, as is the custom in editorial offices, a huge disorder of papers. We would sit here nearly all day long from ten in the morning until nine at night with one short break for an inexpensive,

....

[162] Slovak: *National News.*

[163] Slovak: *Slovak Views.*

[164] *Attack and Resistance* (1905). Actually, the original Slovak title is *Nápor-odpor.*

true, but all the same bad dinner, and just as it had been in Kiev, we talked here a lot more than we wrote. The news from the front and the unrest here in Russia lay heavy on our souls.

Here though, even Professor Masaryk visited us. We were introduced to him by Bohdan Pavlů. Masaryk, smiling, shook hands with each one of us, and without once sitting down, engaged us in a chat.

I had seen him before from time to time at meetings of the collaborators of the Union of Czechoslovak Associations in Kiev; I had seen him both grave and laughing. He would sit there in our midst during various consultations, as chairman, with a sheet of white paper on the table before him. He would listen to each point of view, hear through all our arguments on individual questions, and was always the last to speak, recapitulating all that was said, the pros and cons that were raised, thereupon adding his own view of the matter, which he never imposed on anyone and always expressed as a reflection, admitting debate. I saw how he would laugh whenever anyone put forth his information with good humour, jocularly. At times like that we all became gay, cheerful, closer to our leader. But when he peered intently through his pince-nez, the person at whom he directed his gaze felt as if he had no meat or skin on his bones at all, but was as it were made of clear glass and those grave eyes could see all of the imperfections, faults, and mistakes he has within him, and that no thought whatsoever might be concealed from his sight. As if those eyes were the very conscience of him upon whom they were fixed. After all, in the soul of every human being there is a little cache of baseness, which a person does his best to keep hidden, and every person also has such thoughts which he reserves for himself alone, and of which he would be ashamed if he betrayed them to others. And here all at once someone else's eyes are staring at you, eyes which behold that villainous little soul of yours and read through all those hidden thoughts.

You'd like to run from those eyes, to hide yourself from them, and here you have to stand and look right back into them. At least that's how I felt, all cramped and pathetic, small, empty and stupid, and in order to prove that I'm not like that at all, before that gaze I was ready to carry out any order, only so as to prove myself just the opposite of what I felt myself to be; only to be found pleasing in the eyes of that man. 'Command me,' I would think to myself, 'and I will not be the mean-spirited coward you take me for.' Something similar must have gone on in the soul of that French general who once said of Napoléon, 'I fear neither demon nor god, and yet, whenever I approach him (Napoléon) I feel myself about to quake in my boots like a little boy. He could have made me crawl through the eye of a needle only so as to throw myself into the fire.'

In the editorial offices of the *Slovak Voices*, as I've said, the Professor smiled upon us with an intimate, fatherly – I'd almost say comradely – smile, and judging by myself and the others, all of us who were there at the time had to feel cheerful and bold, as if we'd been enjoying a good wine. We were able to be open with him about everything, barring those most secret villainies and base thoughts; we were ready even to lend one another twenty roubles for dinner.

At such a pleasant moment it crossed my mind – but perhaps it would be over-bold – to ask the Professor for a little allowance for the *Slovak Voices*. As I later learned, the same thought flashed through the mind of Ján Janč*ek.

I thought about Vlado Hurban, that through him perhaps we might ask our guest for the subsidy we desired. Vlado Hurban was the cheekiest journalist of us all, I thought to myself, although Ján Janč*ek is lacking in no journalistic 'impertinence' either. They both are of the younger generation, with sharp elbows, and will always know how to make their way ahead. The world belongs to them, not us, graduates of that old school no longer worth our respect, that stupid school of modesty, which taught us that the beautiful thing was to hang back and stand quietly in the corner, or at the door waiting to be waved in closer.

'In any event, I won't be crawling into any mouse-hole,' I summed up my thoughts, 'If Hurban and Jančேk decline to approach him, I'll ask the Professor myself. After all, how fatherly he's smiling!'

And yet something inside me began to protest. 'Won't it be just like the case of that gentleman, who once extended his hand to his servant, after which the latter plopped himself down at the gentleman's desk and from that time on considered himself to be his good buddy, treating him familiarly, addressing him in informal style?'

The issue of the leaders in Kiev came up. Pavlů pointed at me and said that I feel bad for them and a little dejected at their defeat. This wasn't quite true, and Pavlů's comment irked me. I was offended that Pavlů wanted to smear and shame me in front of our chief. I also wasn't too pleased at the ignobility of a winner who crows over the loser.

But even that comment didn't wipe the smile from the Professor's face. And the apparent insult slid right over me, like a bolt down a lightning rod, to bury itself immediately and harmlessly somewhere in the ground beneath my feet.

'There's no need to laugh at the fallen,' I said, turning to Pavlů.

He also smiled good-naturedly, but this only convinced me the more that to begin a quarrel about the Kiev issues would be out of place and unjustified. But after that comment, as a former Kievan myself, I didn't feel entitled enough to direct a request for funding to the Professor, smiling or not. I decided to tell Jančேk and Hurban to make such a request on behalf of us all when the proper occasion should present itself. They're fighting Petrograders and should be received with more favour.

The visit lasted some three hours. At its conclusion, I accompanied our honoured guest back to the Hotel Europa, it seems, along with Pavlů and someone else I can no longer remember. On the way back, the Professor's demeanour turned serious. What I mean to say is that he was no longer smiling; indeed, to the best of my recollection, he hardly said a word. Others did the talking, and my intention, which I had buried back in the editorial offices, did not resurrect from the dead.

A few days later, Janček informed me with a radiant face that a chatty piece by Professor Masaryk was to be printed in the *Slovak Voices.* Supposedly, it was to consist of recollections of his youth.

He kissed the tips of his fingers in his exultation, in testimony to how excellent a piece it was.

'Do you have it already?' I asked him.

'No, but I will,'

'Jano, you cheeky bastard! How dare you? A man so swamped with important matters as he is, a world-renowned philosopher, politician, writer, and you ask him to scribble something for our wretched *Voices*? Good heavens, have you any idea who Professor Masaryk is!'

'What wretched *Voices*? What ideas? We're making, and writing, history close on Masaryk's heels!'

'For two hundred roubles a month,' I added (such was our monthly salary). 'But tell me, how did the idea of the piece come about, and do you have a firm promise that it will actually be written?'

'Well, you know, the other day in the office, he was smiling so paternally…'

'And you just went over and sat yourself down on Daddy's lap?'

'I'm a journalist!' he snapped haughtily, lifting his chin and pointing with a stiff finger at his own chest.

And those recollections of Masaryk's youth actually did appear.

*

Once, we were summoned from Petrograd to Moscow for a plenary meeting of the Branch. It was while Professor Masaryk was there. It was a legendary conference, that Moscow plenary meeting in August 1917. Not because all of the political and apolitical agents and non-agents were there gathered; or that manifold committees presented their reports, such as the Military Committee, the POW Committee, the Recruitment Committee and the Propaganda Committee; or that the debates were long, or that our Leader presented us with a comprehensive picture of the European situation and our own, indicating the directions according to which it was to develop; or that he gave an important speech in the Moscow theatre, at which he was greeted in the name of all Slovaks by Dr Markovič; not because everything was first-rate, but because of the Slovak council that preceded the meeting, at which for the first time the Slovaks revolted against the Czechs.

One of the speakers claimed, 'The Czechs don't want to have anything to do with us Slovaks. They're constantly talking about the Czech army, the Czech struggle, Czech politics, Czech independence, the Czech state, Czech culture, Czech history, as if we Slovaks didn't even exist!'

Another one said, 'I must express my uneasy suspicions that we Slovaks are merely to be fodder for the Czech lion. Wait and see – we'll just find ourselves in his stomach.'

'Just so they don't kick us away,' a third speaker offered. 'We have to be grateful that they're stretching out a hand to us from firm ground, to pull us out of the swamp...'

'Out of the frying pan into the fire!'

'It makes no difference who devours us!' some of them shouted.

'We can't do anything without the Czechs. We're nothing but grumblers, fantasist, sloths, waiting with open mouths for roasted chickens to fly right in... Just have a look at some of our Slovak "intelligentsia." At home they were considered

"Pan-Slavs," and here they lie low, cash cheques, watch their bellies grow and do nothing but intrigue against our army, crying "Help, help! Save us from the Czechs…!" And if such is the case, what can we expect from the simpler folk…? It's scandalous, shameful… Whoever won't enlist in the army, let's cover him with shame. Let such a one not dare show his face back in our liberated fatherland!'

We resolved to send a deputation to the president of the National Council, Professor Masaryk, requesting him to more frequently use the word 'Czechoslovak.'

This resolution was also presented at the plenary session of the Branch by Ján Országh.

The Professor laughed again pleasantly and said that, after all, that was his entire programme. It's self-evident that he'll be using that word. It's just that he's grown used to saying 'Czech' in his language, so if he happens to omit 'Slovak' from time to time, he begged us to pardon it as an oversight.

During his speech at the theatre, he nearly exclusively said 'the Czechs and the Slovaks, the Czechs and the Slovaks,' and hearing this again and again put the Slovaks at ease.

For all that, Miloš Ruppeldt couldn't forego demanding autonomy for the Slovaks, even though the Republic hadn't even come into existence yet, and some Slovak grabbed me by the sleeve to draw my attention to the fact that the Professor still hadn't taken the trouble to correct his seal, which still read in French: 'Conseil National des pays Tschéques.' As he saw it, that should read 'Tschéquoslovak.' I thrust him away from me with a thump to his chest.

So that I wouldn't have anything evil to worry about once I returned to the liberated fatherland, I hurried off to Dr Daxner, a member of the Recruitment Committee, and had myself enlisted as a soldier. I received from him, thank God, an ID card which proclaimed: 'I swear upon my honour as a citizen, that Dr J.J. has enlisted as a volunteer, and merits full confidence, both patriotically and politically. Dr Vladimír Daxner, *by his own hand.*'

The plenary conference ended and we Petrograders, edified, instructed, and refreshed, returned to drizzly Petrograd. I, on top of it all, was proud as punch of my newest ID.

*

The white nights of Petrograd had come to an end. Like a mortally ill patient, the day barely opened its eyes before closing them again. The weather grew foul. It was threefold: rain coming on, rain, and the sogginess following rain. The aspergillum of the skies was forever sprinkling. Rain came down in buckets, rivers of water in the sky, rivers flowing through the streets. People became amphibious, like frogs, now on dry land, now in water. The Neva seemed angry, but still kept within her banks. The wind galloped through the streets, whistling, but still it caused no harm. The lanterns swung from their wires like comedians, but still they hung on. The same was not true of events, however. They overflowed their banks, flooding the area, and measureless human stupidity bobbed on their surface.

The more time passed the more shooting went on. The second act of the Kornilov epic thundered past. We waited upon that general in our editorial offices in vain. He didn't come. Kerensky betrayed him. That one danced for a while yet and filled the lulls in the action with speeches, but now a second, horrible storm broke. The Bolshevik Revolution of November.[165] The cholera, invisible up until now, became manifest in the Mongoloid skull of Lenin. A skull with hammer and sickle, no star. Over the space of one week of con-

....

[165] Also known as the October Revolution; it broke out on 25 October 1917 (Old Style; 7 November, following the adoption of the Gregorian Calendar by the Russians).

tinuous shooting, the most powerful Slavic state crumbled into ruin. Kerensky, that romantic, dressed himself up in women's clothing and escaped.

We in our editorial offices were nearly shot up as well. Some cries and shots resounded in the street below us. Curious to see what was going on, we rushed to the windows, threw them open and stuck our heads out – to be shouted at by one of the retreating Bolsheviks, rifle in hand, ordering us to close those windows, before he shoots. He thought, perhaps, that we intended to shoot at the revolutionaries from our windows. But our weapon was the pen, after all. And so, we closed the windows with dignified solemnity and sat back down at our desks. Ján Janček again took Pietor's *Attack and Resistance* in hand, looking to extract some more wrongs therefrom, and I submerged myself once more in the papers from Hungary, Slovakia and America, to whittle from them some news.

It wasn't long before the chaos and anarchy of the revolution spread. The Germans took Riga, then Jakobstadt, and the Russian army was nowhere to be seen. The armies at home did not march upon the Germans, but upon one another. They thumped and slaughtered each other, looting and rebelling.

The teeth of all Petrograd were chattering. In terror of the Bolsheviks. In terror of the Germans. In Viborg, the workers' quarter of the city, it wasn't people swarming the streets, but famished, bloodthirsty beasts. Hunting down the bourgeois. Such things occurred during that time as only the crown of God's creation, man, is capable of thinking up. For example:

A captain was seized and dragged before a kangaroo court. They tore him away from his little boy, who kept reaching out his arms toward him and crying 'Papa, papochka! Daite mne moyego papochku!'[166] The father reached out his hand

....

[166] Russian: 'Dad! Daddy! Give me my daddy!'

to his son, and when he grasped it, a sabre flashed, the stroke lopped off the man's arm, and the little boy fell backwards, clutching the severed limb.

Murder and looting were the order of the day – and the night. There was no police, the militia was incompetent. Passers-by were stripped of all their clothing. Bandits broke into peoples' homes. One thought to oneself that it would be enough to equip oneself in ration cards for bread, sugar, and everything one could eat, drink, or wear. The bitter truth was that one needed a paper even to pass into one's own flat. Otherwise one might spend the night strolling up and down the Nevsky Prospekt. This was the so-called *samozashchita*[167] in the face of bandits and burglars. Every citizen had to keep watch over his own home. Usually, it is true, these had nothing of their own anyway. At first men, then women, the bolder and more mature ones. When a stranger came along and looked suspicious, a *trevoga* (alarm) was immediately raised at such a pitch that one's blood ran cold, and everybody came running to the door to see what was going on.

I stood watch there myself every second or third day, now until midnight, now for a two-hour shift after midnight, in a dimly lit entranceway, without a coat, without felt boots, without a gun.

It wasn't enough that the constant Petrograd rain soaked into my boots and squished about my feet, or the fact that my spirit was weeping for Russia. My right eye kept tearing up, as if a cinder or something had made its way in there. It teared up whenever I opened it. My right ear began to ring and to the *trevoga* and *samozashchita* was added purblindness, which kept me from falling asleep. Poisoned in soul and body, I went off to see the doctor, with my eye bandaged, which he then flushed with atropine.

....

[167] Russian: Self-defence.

At the same time, Vlado Hurban broke his arm and Janček fell ill with malaria. Only Gavor was as ruddy and full-cheeked as a young unmarried butcher. If not for him, our entire editorial office would have been battered, half-blind, and feverish, like all the rest of Russia.

I went to visit Hurban in hospital. Thin and dry, with his arm all bound up, he sat on his bed sharp and in good humour. Lady nurses were bustling round him. With a wave of his hand, he motioned them to leave us alone. They made a bow and left. I figured, well, here's a milord for you! or if not a milord, at least an Important Person whose word is gospel. But in those days it was dangerous to be a big shot. Although the dictatorship of the proletariat aimed at being a grand state, it wouldn't suffer grandees.[168] So I deduced that this was no milord on the bed at my side, but rather an Important Person.

'You're going to have to get yourself to Moscow. The Germans will be here any day now.'

'What do you mean "you?" What about yourself?'

'Both me and Janček have other important tasks in hand. We've got to stir up America. My task is diplomatic-political; Janček's is organisational.'

And in his stuttering, high-pitched and raucous voice he began to tell me about the tasks that were awaiting him.

'Well then,' I thought to myself. 'this Vlado is an Important Person. Diplomat, politician, organiser.'

And then I said aloud, 'But won't it be like rats abandoning a sinking ship? There's enough people in America, while here there's only a handful of us Slovaks, and the best of us are departing... Who in hell is at the wheel here?' I asked in the end, flush with regret and envy.

....

[168] In the original Slovak: *Diktatúra proletariátu, hoci chcela byť panstvom, pánov netrpela.* The pun in the original turns on the similarity of the word 'state' *panstvo* and *pán,* 'lord,' 'gentleman.'

Regret for losing two significant people, envy that it wasn't me who'd be going to America.

'Our ship isn't sinking. It's just headed for the open sea. Once the front gets to Russia, it'll all be up for us. We have to make our own way to France. To sail for France.'

'Via Vladivostok?'

'Da.'

'Hmmm.'

Worried, with a heavy heart, I extended my hand to him in farewell.

'One more thing,' he said, as if casually. 'If you come see me again, get yourself shaved, will you?'

He tapped me on my unshaven face with a lordly gesture.

'So, an Important Person *and* a milord,' I thought to myself, heading down the stairs to get myself a shave.

And once again, a journey – into the unknown.

The first snow of November was falling. Petrograd turned white. The heavens brightened. The sun came out, and we began our wandering in the direction of Moscow. My right eye was no longer weeping, but my spirit could use some atropine, for it was quite cramped, tight, and weepy.

XI. MOSCOW – KIEV – MOSCOW

The heart of Russia was cold. The stokers of furnaces stopped their stoking. 'Cold-blooded Britishers,' their employers called them. 'Let the big shots take care of their big shot houses by themselves,' the furnace-stokers said. The turn of the wheel was a cruel one, and all those who used to sit up on top were suddenly hurled down. Those who had been the masters up until then became servants, and those who had been servants up until then, masters. Cooks and maids sat themselves down at the white-spread tables in the dining rooms, and their *vysokoprevoskhoditelstva*[169] found themselves in the kitchen. Old, bearded generals and high-ranking officials now stood on the street corners with bundles of newspapers under their arms, selling them quietly, shyly – the most brazen they got would be to extend fresh copy, timidly, in the direction of a passer-by. One saw intelligent faces, wearing eyeglasses, faces criss-crossed with wrinkles like cages, clearing away the snow and sweeping the streets. Your heart constricted at the sight, and you'd have liked to give them a hand. But 'We stoked their furnaces? Let them stoke them themselves, let them heat their own houses!'

And it was cold everywhere. In our room the thermometer never rose above eight degrees Celsius. We sat there in high felt boots and mantles, with sheepskin hats upon our heads. In the editorial offices, those beautiful 'private'

....

[169] Russian: Excellencies.

apartments of a Czech named Šimúnek, there remained but the tall, wallpapered, magnificent rooms with their elegant furniture; salons with smooth parquet floors, a gigantic library with gilt-edged books in leather bindings, carpets everywhere, and tall, porcelain-tile stoves, clean, white, but without any heat, standing like corpses all drained of blood, cold monuments to warmth from which we turned to freeze elsewhere. In the cafeterias where we went to eat, both soup and tea were steaming while they were being carried to our table, yet they cooled down completely before we had a chance to take a sip.

The stores were full of hams, bacon, sausages, fish both in oil and smoked, conserves and all sorts of delicacies; bottles of expensive wine and champagne glittered enticingly in the electric light, like beautiful girls. There was money; you might stock up, but what was it all worth since bread was not to be had, a hunk of cheerful bread was even out of one's reach. You couldn't eat your ham or your sausage without bread, and if you couldn't eat, why, there was no sense in drinking, either. The bread they gave us made your whiskers stand on end – black it was and as hard as a frozen clod. Only furtively, somewhere at a tram stop or a train station, could you perhaps get some real bread for 100–200 roubles, but you had to be careful lest they grab you and toss you in the slammer along with the peddler.

I myself didn't dare leave the house. I once lost my way so in the tangle of *pereuloks*[170] that I couldn't find my way home. From that moment on, I only went out in the company of those who were familiar with the streets of Moscow.

The wonder of it all was that we didn't stay too long in that *bolshaya derevnya*[171] as the Russians call Moscow. We

....

[170] Russian: Lanes.

[171] Russian: Big village.

JANKO JESENSKÝ

looked around for some cosier region, where we would find more warmth, more bread, and less volcanic earth, which was constantly rumbling beneath our feet there.

So we transferred ourselves to Kiev, which at the time was the capital of the Ukrainian Republic. Here there was bread enough and almost too much heat. We had no sooner sat down to supper than already the clouds began to moil over the hilltops and the cannon began to roar. It was Muravyov's Soviet Army beginning their encirclement of the city.

I was taken in by Živocký – the same one who had earlier loaned me that fox-fur jacket. The windows of his large, bright, and warm room on the first story of a wooden building rattled like chains and shrapnel began whistling and screaming over my head. At first, I was afraid lest an artillery barrage strike the roof and send the whole thing crashing down in a heap along with me, but then I became accustomed to it. I pulled the covers up over my head to deaden the sounds and thought to myself: 'Whatever's supposed to happen, well, let it be.' At which I would fall asleep at once.

Amidst that siege, among the clatter of arms and clouds of gunpowder, explosions, dust, smoke, and fire, in the halls of the 'Hôtel de France,' our leader, Professor Masaryk, solemnly vowed to us that, 'just as he has progressed from the very start according to our national, Slavic programme, so will he continue to march on, in the hopes of enduring in service to our nation to the very end.'

'I swear this to you, our army, our emigration, our nation... And I ask in return such a vow from you, which will mean that in the coming days when the fate of the world is being decided, we must all increase our determination and strengthen the ties that bind us to one another... We demand an independent Czechoslovak state. The independent Czechoslovak nation will be at the forefront of the democratic and progressive nations of the world. Following the example of our Hussite and Taborite forefathers, we shall carry out pervasive changes to our social order. Every Czech – is our brother. Every Czech – is a Slav. Every Czech – is a man. (If only the Slovaks in Moscow had heard that!)

Meanwhile we, standing near him, vowed unto him: 'We wish faithfully to serve our nation in its great, historical struggle, as long as such will be our nation's will, as we are bound to do by honour and our loyalty to our people and our homeland.'

And each of us shook his hand.

'To strengthen the ties that bind us, with all our strength.' Those words kept circling through my mind as I left the hotel with the others and entered that artillery storm, beneath the pyrotechnics in the sky above. 'And here – Slav against Slav...'

The Bolsheviks took Kiev in the first days of February. The Ukrainian government left to appeal to the Germans for aid, and to return along with them.

In the meantime, our nation too began to crumble. The Kiev Soviet announced the formation of a Czechoslovak Red Guard. The Czech periodical *Svoboda*[172] reprinted this decree, along with a call to all who wished to enlist in the socialist army to report to their headquarters, armed.

A socialist army! Hail, O first Czech Bolsheviks. Hail, O first traitors.

The engineer Král arrived along with Němeček with the news that they were organising Czechoslovak units for the volunteer army of General Alekseyev on the Don.

Then our soldiers themselves began to speak of some of the members of the National Council Branch as 'typical bourgeois.' The Branch had to be reorganised, with the addition of members who were not 'typical bourgeois.' They proceeded to add some dissatisfied people.

....

[172] Freedom.

But our seed was heavy, and golden. What blew away was only chaff. What set the golden grain in motion were the Germans. As they drew near Kiev, we all scattered, everyone in his own direction, wherever it was most convenient. The Bolsheviks hoofed it, as did the Czechoslovak Revolutionary Council of Workers and Soldiers, which had succeeded in being called to life with a counterfeit T.G. Masaryk at its head (so as to seduce as many men as possible), and the Professor, and the Branch fled too. Damned Germans! They drove us out of Petrograd, they drove us out of Kiev, they'll expel us from Moscow and from all of Russia in the end.

I myself returned to Moscow. I'll never forget that journey. First, I latched onto a freight train, where I paced the *ploshchadka*[173] until I slipped and fell in the snow, which fell in thick clumps. When I began to freeze from the wet and the wind, I hopped out at some station or other, and waited upon the next passenger train heading in the direction of Moscow. I waited all night long, and when it arrived, I squeezed my way into the corridor and there I stood and stood and stood until I slumped down on the floor among all the rubbish, the dirt, the husks of sunflower seeds that were spit out there, and fell asleep, my back resting against a compartment partition. Upon arriving in Moscow, my legs were so swollen from long standing that I could hardly set one foot in front of the other.

It was a cold Moscow February morning. I spent a moment in thought as to where to direct my steps, whom to honour with my gracious presence. 'Janko Korman, he's a good chap,' crossed my mind. And so I went off to find him...

....

[173] Russian: Platform.

XII. MOSCOW –

OMSK – IRKUTSK

On 11 March we pushed on to Omsk. The Germans were at our heels. It's a stone's throw from Kiev to Moscow. If only they wanted, with a hop, skip, and a jump, the Germans could be in Moscow. 'Anywhere, but further on from here!' was the order of the day, and we were off. The morning was all done up in white, like a cottage in Slovakia before the Christmas holidays. The sun was winking behind some thick organdie and objects cast barely perceptible shadows.

Milk was being sold at the station for fifty kopecks a cup. Three roubles got you a hunk of bread and a sausage as thick as your finger. They were also offering some sort of little black *pagáčiky*,[174] kind of like *bliny*; cigarettes and the *Iskra*[175] newspaper.

There were six of us together: Dr Girsa, Dr Markovič, me, and three invalids. The wagon was unnumbered, proper,[176]

....

[174] Slovak: *pagáčik*, a diminutive of *pagáč*. Pagáč is a Slovak folk delicacy, consisting of thin bread filled with a stuffing of mashed potatoes and sharp cheese and then baked, often served buttered. The best, crispy *pagáč* is rolled very thin, about half the thickness of a slice of Neapolitan pizza or flatbread. It is golden brown, never 'black,' which suggests that whatever was on offer at the Moscow station was burnt to a crisp or made from very poor-quality flour.

[175] Russian: *The Spark*.

[176] Jesenský uses the Slovak adjective *panský* – at the root of which is

quite clean. It was lit by gas, and even had facilities where you could wash. I was pleasantly surprised to find no travellers standing about in the corridors with no room to sit; there were no bundles, baskets, or crates to be seen. Guards with rifles and bayonets stopped the comrades from entering our wagons, which otherwise they would have taken by storm. They thickly occupied the roofs like swarms of bees. They walked, and ran, and thumped around above our heads whenever the train halted, so as to warm up a little. I felt bad for them. The wind was whipping along the snow-covered plains, chasing devil only knows whom, rather than sitting down calmly somewhere in a corner and hushing up.

The uncleanliness of the stations was astonishing – a real sewer, wherever one turned. No one cleaned up or swept. For such was considered the vilest job of all in liberated, revolutionary Russia. Everyone wanted to be a commissar at least. We kept order ourselves.

The news that fell into our hands in the form of *Utro Rossii*, *Novoye slovo*, or *Russkiye vedomosti*[177] wrote always of two things: the speech of Balfour, who sought to aid Russia with a Japanese occupation of Siberia, which signified a great danger for Russia, for such an occupation would mean the same thing as the loss of that rich land. We don't want any friend who seeks to devour us... There was that, and the need of strict discipline in the army; they cited Trotsky's speech, in which this was stressed... What a curious nation. First, they subvert their army and its discipline, and next they 'podi sozidat novuyu armiyu.'[178]

....

the idea of 'gentlemanliness,' 'nobility,' or 'lordliness,' and thus possibly ironic in the context of revolutionary Russia, as above, during his hospital visit.

[177] Russian: *The Russian Morning*; *The New Word*; *Russian News*.

[178] Russian: 'Move on to the creation of a new army.'

In Syzran I was given to read a transcript of the meeting of the Czechoslovak national councillors – Čermák, Klecanda, Dr Markovič, Miškóci and Dr Girsa – in which they addressed the question of who was to go to France with the army, and who was to remain in Russia. These men indicated that they themselves would remain in Russia while the other members of the Council would travel to France as a 'separate division of the branch.' From the agitation-propaganda department, to which I belonged, Pavlů and Kudela were to remain, while Hurban and I were to depart with the army; Hurban with the rank of colonel as the leader of the 'crystal-gazers.'[179]

All right. And so it's France we're off to. The only thing that worried me was that this was hardly certain. Wherever the old saying fit back then, it surely fit amongst us: Man proposes, but God disposes.

The further on we went, the more bread there was to be found, and butter, and milk. In Ufa we got the first hot meal we'd had since the time when Paulíny funded us cooked cabbage for the road. We took cabbage soup, a fillet, and two portions of coffee with cream. Whole towers of bread were stacked on tables spread with unwashed *Wichsleinwand*[180] and you could fit out your wrists and ankles in as many *bubliks*[181] as you might carry like bracelets. But the spoons were wooden and the tinplates all banged up; dinner was a chaotic rattle.

Nourishment for the flesh abounded, but there was none for the soul. No news was to be had. After a long wait, *Zemlya i volya*[182] arrived with old news about Kiev being cut off

....

[179] In Slovak: *rozviedčik*, which can also be translated 'snoop' or 'spy.'

[180] German: Oilcloth.

[181] Russian: A round roll, like a bagel; in Kraków, they are known as *obwarzanki*, as the dough is boiled (*warzone*) before it is baked.

[182] Russian: *Land and Freedom.*

from Moscow and about the Germans in Revel; about peace overtures, and about Trotsky's speech again, and once more the need for an army. In Chelyabinsk they gave us the *Izvestiya chelyabinskogo soveta krestyanskikh, rabochikh i soldatskikh deputatov*; in Kurgan *Izvestiya kurganskogo soveta krestyanskikh, rabochikh i soldatskikh deputatov*.[183] Nothing but *obyavleniya, zayavleniya*,[184] and Trotsky once again with that speech of his about the need for a revolutionary army.

After a journey of nineteen days we arrived, at last, in Omsk, where we were greeted with the news that the city was full up, and it would be difficult to find a place. We didn't even bother getting off the train. At last, late in the evening, brother Glos announced that there was one empty classroom in the *yeparkhialnoye uchilishche*,[185] and, if we liked, it was ours to occupy, but if so, quick, before someone beat us to it.

And so, off we went, racing.

We found a large, unswept hall with smudged whitewashed walls. We slept on the floor. Whoever was able to, made a bed and covered himself with whatever he had to hand. I lay down on my Siberian comforter, put a little bundle beneath my head and covered myself up with the winter coat that Ország had given me in Moscow. I had to return the fox fur that Živocký had loaned me in Kiev, though he liked how it looked on me so much. In its place, he gave me a raincoat, but that proved too thin in Moscow, and so I felt the need to use Mr Ország's coat. As I was falling asleep I thought about Beryozovka-za-Baikalom, how

....

183 Russian: The News of the Chelyabinsk Soviet of Peasants', Workers', and Soldiers' Deputies; The News of the Kurgan Soviet of Peasants', Workers', and Soldiers' Deputies.

184 Russian: announcements; statements.

185 Russian: Eparchial school.

it had been to sleep there. That had been a different thing altogether, and so my thoughts here were more pleasant, and my sleep better.

The next day we went off to have a look around the town. It was still the middle of winter here, even though it was already April. The morning was foggy and grey. Rime encased the trees. The thatched roofs were covered with frost. We had fresh snow underfoot: hard, powdery, and cold. A sharp wind was blowing from the north. The sun shone in the white heavens; later, toward dinner time, it made the walls glow with warmth. The little houses that met our eyes were pretty, wooden structures painted white, with window trimmings of red. Here and there one came across a larger structure of stone; the city centre had a very European air to it, with wide stone pavements. On the side streets, stone gave way to wooden paving. The stores were empty; there was little on display, but lots of people. There were *izvozchiks* with beautiful, large horses and fancy switches.

We took our dinner at the Svoboda restaurant. There were a lot of people here, too, as if dinner were being given away for free. We hardly found ourselves a place. A confusion of tongues. You heard Russian spoken, and German, Czech, Magyar, Lettish, Polish, Plattdeutsch. There were POWs, deserters, soldiers, women, girls, and children. We were served by lazy waitresses. Before anything substantial arrived, you'd have already consumed the two pyramids of white bread that had been set on the table before you, and your eyes began to slide towards the third, set on the table next to yours. A two-course dinner cost two roubles forty kopecks, a three-course meal cost a rouble twenty more, and you paid just as much again for a fourth course. If a person was bent on committing suicide by eating, he could fill himself to bursting for ten roubles. We starvelings savoured the bread the most.

After dinner, I lit up a Virginian that brother Jaroš had given me, and I turned to Otomar Houdek:

'Are we going to stay in the eparchial school?'

'That's all I need! I've gone to school so long in my life that now I can't abide a classroom! I could hardly bear a day in school as a boy, and now as a grown man I'm supposed to sleep in one? Pah!'

'So we'll have to look for a flat.'

'We'll have to.'

The Bolshevik regime had been installed in the city. The attitude of the city authorities towards us was hostile. They didn't trust Czechoslovaks. We were in danger of having to leave Omsk. The German orientation that prevailed there bit into us like a cold, bitter wind. No wonder: some of our Magyars and Germans were on the city Soviet – POWs, who easily influenced the Russian Jews. They were afraid of the Semyonov regiments,[186] which were threatening from the east, and the Bolsheviks were unsure whether our army might join up with them. Telegrams were already flying in from the Moscow Central with orders to disarm us. Our couriers arrived from Penza confirming the rumours. They said that some of our men had already had their weapons confiscated. Each of our echelons was to be left with only one armed platoon –one machine gun and one cannon. The news brought word of broad realignments in the west. They wrote of the Germans bombarding Paris. The local *Izvestiya* fomented anger against us in Russian, as did *Wahrheit* in German and *Forradalom* in Magyar.[187] The *Omsky vestnik*,[188] which still employed old Russian orthography, was not *blagonadyozhny*[189] in the eyes of

....

[186]   The regiments of Grigory Mikhailovich Semyonov (1890–1946), who fought on the White side during the Russian Civil War, in the Trans-Baikal Region.

[187]   Russian: *News*. German: *Truth*. Magyar: *The Revolution*.

[188]   Russian: *The Omsk Herald*.

[189]   Russian: Trustworthy.

the authorities, and was afraid of speaking up on our behalf. We published our own *Informatsionny listok*[190] in Russian, but it wasn't capable of drowning out the hostile voices and influencing the behaviour of any sort of Red commissar.

The Czech and Slovak POWs wanted to call an assembly at the Cadet School, but the Magyar Red Guards – former Magyar POWs – threatened to disperse the meeting with bayonets as an assembly of bourgeois and counter-revolutionaries. Thus we lived to see old Hungary raise its head in Russia, only instead of *nemzetellenes* they said *forradalomellenes* and *népellenes*.[191]

All lodgings had been socialised. Two persons per room. Everyone was afraid of taking in tenants and worried that some would be forced upon them. It was difficult to find a place to stay. Doors were closed in our faces followed by the rattling of keys in locks; they wouldn't even let you say a word.

After a long search we found two rooms, each costing sixty roubles. Bare walls, no furnishings, not even a bed. The young lady of the house interrogated us:

'And when will you be coming home?'

'We'll never go out.'

'You won't be bringing any girls here?'

'No.'

'Or drinking or singing or hollering here at home?'

'We'll be as silent as fish.'

'And you won't be doing any soveshchaniye[192] here?'

'No.'

'You're not Russians?'

....

190   Russian: Informational sheet.

191   Magyar: Counter-national; counter-revolutionary; counter-popular.

192   Russian: Conferences.

'No.'

'Czechoslovaki?'

'Tak tochno.'[193]

I found it funny. The lady was as thoroughly curious as the parish priest at confession. She held out her hand for us to count out one hundred twenty roubles, then glanced around the room to make sure she hadn't left anything anywhere. I pointed through the window at a windmill turning lazily outside.

'Will you be taking that, too?'

She shook her head.

'Thank God!'

Four of us took the room: Otomar Houdek, his brother Zdenko, Dr Dušan Makovický the younger, and I. We had cots made, we organised a table from somewhere and we moved in with our treasures.

We did absolutely nothing but eat, drink, and walk about. We had some time to read, too. Makovický gave me Tolstoy's *Christianity and Patriotism* to read. As much as I had held that 'veliky pisatel zemli russkoi'[194] in honour before reading that book, after I'd finished, I resented him.

'Well, what do you think?' Makovický asked me when I returned the book to him.

'Tolstoy rejects nationalism and patriotism? You can only reject what's actually on offer. In Russia, neither of those things exist. If they did, everything wouldn't be falling to pieces here. There would be no defeat, there would be no Brest-Litovsk. Tolstoy's like a hooligan who plunders what belongs to others, burning and destroying, killing – but the very virtues that his poor nation needs to learn from him, these he won't teach them.'

....

[193] Russian: 'Yessir!'

[194] Russian: Great writer of the Russian land.

'So, read *Odumaites*.'[195]

Tolstoy rejects war. He goes to such an extreme that leads him to the position that Russia means nothing to him; all he wants is for people to sit at home, sow and reap and pray just as Christ commanded them. He would be ready to sell the whole great Slavic empire for one devout Our Father.

'This philosopher of yours won't suit us,' I said to Makovický. 'At least not now. It's beautiful what he says, really, but only on paper. Practical reality is a different matter altogether and has been such since the beginning of the world – and so it shall be until the end.'

'You see, the Russians "came to their senses!"'

'Beautiful! The Germans are at the gates of Petrograd and Moscow, the Bolsheviks don't want any Lord's Prayers – they want an army!'

The bells were still ringing in the church steeples, but there was gunpowder in the air. All that was needed was a spark, and all the peace-loving philosophers would be blown sky-high along with their theories.

Spring came at the end of April. The frosts were over. Instead of snow, the roads were full of black Siberian mud, a thin flow with the consistency of porridge. Rumbling streams. It was nearly impossible to cross from one side to another; where you could cross you had to take a head-start to leap over the stream. Some streets were already dust-covered, while others still had banks of filthy snow. A wind was blowing and drying things, but it made your eyes tear up.

I strolled to the Irtysh. Here the sun baked the wooden wall beneath which I would sit. It was quiet here; nothing but the ice floes continually rushing along the river, colliding, breaking, creaking. The floes would gather together in heaps,

....

[195]   Russian: 'Come to your senses.' A temperance pamphlet written by Tolstoy in 1888.

pause, and then break apart and flow on further. Crows and pigeons fluttered in the air above them. The air seemed to tremble. Crowds of people gathered at the wooden railings. With long poles, they fished out logs bobbing near the river banks. At a yellow gate, the remnants of the gaol where Dostoevsky had been held, were whole piles of dirty snow. The white walls were scribbled over and spattered with clods of mud. Far past the river was a little hill, and beyond it a broad meadow already free of snow.

It was here that I took the sun and chased the rheumatism from my bones, pondering what was to become of us. In the Branch offices a sheet of paper was set out with two columns. The one was to list the names of those who wanted to go to France, and the other – those who would rather remain in Russia. We were to set our names in one column or the other. So, which one? I decided on France, but with a heavy heart. Another long road, at least a month's journey, via Vladivostok and then by sea to America or India.

And so I dressed myself up in greenish military togs and sold all my mufti for four hundred roubles. The army was passing through Omsk. 'I'll latch onto some echelon or other,' I thought. Added encouragement was given me by our Slovak officers in the 7th Regiment: Viest, Čipka, Daxner, Manica, who visited us on the way. We treated them to a Paulíny feast of noodles and cheese, beer, and black coffee.

The days alternated between happy and sad. The trains did not only arrive with living passengers. One day it brought us the remains of Juraj Klecanda, a member of the Branch. He died at twenty-seven, it seems, of typhus. We buried him with military honours. Špačak spoke at his graveside in Czech, and Major Vergé in French. We concluded with the singing of 'Kde domov můj.'[196] It was far away indeed.

....

[196] Czech: 'Where is my homeland?' The Czech national anthem.

I also met up with Jožek Országh, our fellow reveller from the days of the Kiev *Slovenské hlasy*. He was quartermaster to a portion of the army, and immediately invited us into his heated wagon for some vodka. He offered it spiced with some herbs. The clean and unadulterated version tasted better to me.

The other Jožo (Gregor) also showed up. He was – tentatively – wearing a French cap.

'I'm writing an article,' he told me.

'About what?'

He gave me it to read. In it, he attacked Vajanský's politics and praised that of the Young Slovaks.

'What do you say?'

'You're shredding a good old thousand-crown note, of which we have so few, and pressing a new ten-heller coin into our hands with enthusiasm, just because it's shiny. Just as many ten-heller coins as go into a thousand-crown note, that many Young Slovaks you'd need to make up one Vajanský. The significance of Vajanský, my dear brother, is not in politics, but in the sustenance and spread of Slovak culture. It's a bad critic who searches through a work for something that's simply not there, that's not supposed to be there. The Young Slovaks, for example, didn't invent gunpowder. Should I crush them beneath my heel for that? Nor did they invent the Czechoslovak orientation. You can find that in Kollár's writings and those of old Hurban. Nor was organic work their invention. Back in the 1860s every parish priest established temperance societies and spread the word. Nor did the Young Slovaks go to the people to make their appeal. They went to the press so as to malign their elders – and their elders paid them back for it. But the nation, it's true, thank God, didn't read one paper or the other...'

'But that Tsarophile politics! To wait with folded arms for Russia to come to our salvation and to ignore our neighbours the Czechs...'

'Tsarophile? What are you talking about? Have a glance at his poetic works. You'll find there one poem on the death of Alexander II the Liberator. And that's all. Never another mention of the Tsar. And Russian salvation? Who else have we to thank for this army of ours in Russia? The Russians. He ignored his Czech neighbours? You don't even believe that yourself. You've never read his "Epistle to the Czechs?" He calls to them there, saying "There's a place for you beneath snow-capped Tatra." Vajanský was a Slav, and that nation includes the Czechs.'

Our conversation was interrupted by May Day celebrations.

A parade of men, women, and children in long, broad, disordered ranks was processing down the street, waving red banners, to the accompaniment of music and song, just as in Kiev when the first revolution broke out. They were singing the Marseillaise. The majority of the men were our POWs dressed up in Russian uniforms, some on foot, some on horseback or riding cannon. Music behind them and behind the musicians more on foot and horseback. I heard a Magyar parade song and Magyar exclamations: 'Éljen az orosz köztársaság!' And immediately thereafter: 'Doloi Vilgelma!'[197]

But the German envoy was already in Moscow, and the whole Moscow Soviet was in bondage to him. Among other things, the Brest-Litovsk peace accord contained this point, too: that the Germans would not permit any agitation against the German government, state, or army on the territory of Russia. This constituted a real threat to our army. The farther away from Russia we were, the better.

On 25 May, I boarded a train once more, along with Marendiak, Janko Korman, Otoman Houdek, and Dušan

....

[197] Magyar: 'Long live the Russian Republic!' Russian: 'Down with [German Emperor] Wilhelm!'

Makovický (Jr.). We were all to head east to France, as the slogan went, reporting to our military units upon our arrival in Vladivostok.

We were given places in a second-class carriage with red plush benches, cleaned to a sparkle. There were women on the train who kept everything in order. The days were beautiful. Spring breathed in through the open windows. The plains were covered in new grassland, the birches in fresh green leaves. Little wooden stations set amidst cheerful little copses of trees flashed past our gaze. The sun set like glowing iron in the misty west, which it lit up in hues of flaming red. Above, the sky was violet, whitish, greenish. When evening fell, a huge moon arose in the southeast. It was pink at first, then yellow, and then silver. Its light reflected from the marshes and followed us as we rolled on. Little puffs of steam hung above the fields, as if the earth were breathing. Without puffing or snorting, the train just rattled on along the endless rails through the endless plains.

The pleasant and comfortable voyage with a small number of fellow travellers lifted our mood. Korman, Marendiak and Makovický played chess. Houdek, usually, lay on the cot above me and generally didn't go out at all; I read, and, when it was possible, I slept.

But our smooth progress forward didn't last long. In Novonikolayevsk our army was waiting for us. The station was like a hive: buzzing, seething, running about. Some soldiers of ours came onto the train and asked us for our papers.

What happened?

Nothing. Except that all of our orders and plans have gone tits up.

The order: Eastward to France; the order: No getting mixed up in Russian quarrels; the order: No relinquishing of weapons to anyone; the order: No splitting up – all fell to pieces. Antipathies, like mountain streams in springtime, grew and grew. You couldn't tell what bridge they would carry away, what road they would flood, what forest they would uproot. The waters roared, howled, boomed… Until at last a bloody flood covered the land. In Kiev, Muravyov had allowed our armies to depart unmolested. In March, the Bolsheviks were still chivalric, at least on paper. Then Antonov-Ovseyenko, the chief leader of the southern Russian republics, sent the following order to his armies: 'Our comrades of the Czechoslovak military corps, who famously and boldly fought at Zhitomir in defence of Kiev, and at Grebyonka and Bakhmach, defending the road to Poltava and Kharkov, are now about to depart Ukraine. They will relinquish to us a portion of their weaponry. Our revolutionary armies will never forget the fraternal aid with which the Czechoslovak military corps assisted us in the struggle of the working peoples of Ukraine against the rapacious bands of imperialism. The weaponry relinquished by the Czechoslovaks will be accepted by the revolutionary armies as a brotherly gift.'

At the command of the Centre, that is, the Soviet of National Commissars in Moscow, Stalin sent a telegram directly to the representatives of our corps staff, which read:

'The Soviet of National Commissars considers the proposal of the Czechoslovak army staff just and acceptable, in its entirety, under the condition that it transport its echelons immediately to Vladivostok, and swiftly eliminate all counter-revolutionary elements.

'The Czechoslovaks are understood to be journeying, not as combat units, but as free, private citizens, taking along with themselves a certain amount of weapons for their self-defence from the attacks of counter-revolutionary forces.

'The Soviet of National Commissars commands the Soviet in Penza – Comrade Kurayev – to replace all the former commissars with new, trustworthy ones, such as will lead the Czs. army to Vladivostok, directly assuring their progress to the intended goal, and submitting reports to the Soviet of National Commissars concerning all events transpiring during the transport of the Czechoslovaks.

'For this purpose, telegrams will be sent to all Soviet deputies concerned.

'Please inform the Czechoslovaks that the Soviet of National Commissars is prepared to provide them with assistance on the territory of Russia under the condition of their honourable and ardent loyalty. By order of the Soviet of National Commissars – Stalin.'

Our corps staff commanded that each of our echelons should have, for its defence, one armed company consisting of eighty-four double columns, including non-commissioned officers, and besides this, one heavy machine gun. Three hundred rounds per rifle, twelve hundred rounds per machine gun. All weaponry above that number was to be returned. Each echelon with an air unit was to be assured of one armed company, and one such company was to be provided for the corps staff itself.

The relinquishing of arms was to begin on 27 March, at noon. It was to be carried out as the echelons were passing through Penza. The echelons were to be permitted to continue on to Samara only after the arms had been handed over.

The army began to grumble,

'That's Mirbach's idea!'

'It's a provocation of the Czech Communists.'

'Dr Růžička, Strombach, Heizel, Brabec, Knoflíček, Beneš, Hain, Muna. The louses!'

'And that Hašek in Samara.'

These were the Czech Bolsheviks who informed on us to the Russians, and fought against us.

And immediately it was no longer clear where we'd be off to.

The *Československý deník*[198] posed the question: East or West?

....

[198] Czech: *The Czechoslovak Daily.*

And then a third destination surfaced: to Arkhangelsk.

'One more plot!' the army worried. 'They want to divide us, weaken us, herd us into the open gullet of the Germans. We're not going to Arkhangelsk!' people shouted. 'We'll die of hunger there.'

'But that's what the Allies want,' they tried to calm us. 'Look – even Major Vergé wants that – the French attaché to our army staff. That's what our embassy in Moscow's been telegraphing, too – those we sent there: Maxa, Markovič, Janík...'

'We won't believe it. We want nothing to do with that. We won't go.'

Then, a spark fell into that atmosphere heavy with gunpowder, and an explosion erupted.

Some of our echelons were at the station in Chelyabinsk. They were supposed to head east. There were also some trains there with Austro-Hungarian POWs, the majority of whom were Magyars and Germans; these were heading west. One of these POW trains was already speeding away, when one of the POWs threw a piece of iron at one of our volunteers and hit him right in the head, as a result of which he fell down, stunned. Our men stopped that train and made the POWs hand over the guilty party – whom they killed on the spot in their anger. The Chelyabinsk Soviet determined to investigate the matter and summoned some of our volunteers to give evidence as witnesses. They went – and were imprisoned. We sent out a special deputation to the Soviet demanding that the imprisoned men be released. And this deputation was imprisoned as well. So we sent an armed unit to the city, demanding that the arrested men be released, otherwise things would get ugly. The local Soviet took fright at this, and complied with the demand. The armed unit returned with the men they liberated. The army was satisfied and calmed down. Not so the Bolsheviks.

A telegram from the Chelyabinsk Soviet to Yekaterinburg was intercepted, with which they requested reinforcements for the disarming of our men entrained at the Chelyabinsk station. Some telegrams from Aralov also fell into our hands – the head of the operational unit of the People's Commissariat of War, which called for the immediate disarming and dismantling of the Czechoslovak Army Corps, 'the remnants of an old, actual army.' Then the most extreme telegram of all came to light, in which Trotsky himself commanded 'all Soviets along the railway line, under the threat of dire consequences, to disarm the Czechoslovaks. Every Czechoslovak discovered with arms on the railway line is to be shot on the spot. Every echelon, in which one armed man is found, is to be loaded off the wagons and imprisoned in POW camps. It is the responsibility of the local military commissariats to carry out this order immediately. Each case of default in this matter will be interpreted as dishonourable and treasonous, and the guilty party will be punished mercilessly. Simultaneous with this telegram I am dispatching forces to the rear of the Czechoslovak echelons, and these have been instructed to teach the rebels order. As for the honourable Czechoslovaks, who relinquish their weapons and subject themselves to the Soviet government, we will treat them as brothers and they will receive all possible assistance from us. We hereby inform all railway officials that no single wagon carrying Czechoslovaks is to be permitted to travel eastward. Whoever gives in to force in this regard and in so doing aids and abets the Czechoslovaks in their eastward progress shall be punished mercilessly.'

During this time, the Czechoslovak Revolutionary Convention, summoned by the Branch, met in Chelyabinsk. Immediately, at the first sitting, the delegates unanimously resolved that any negotiations with the Bolsheviks concerning our transport is a futile waste of time, and that our echelons are to move on as far as possible, entirely on their own. The question of the transport of the army was transferred

JANKO JESENSKÝ

from the competence of the Czechoslovak National Council Branch (OČSNR) to the Temporary Executive Committee, which was entrusted with the management of the movement of the army along the route to Vladivostok. During the transport of the troops, this committee was to be the sole organ authorised to give orders. Any regulations of the OČSNR were to be considered invalid.

After those intercepted telegrams, the council decided to bat away those malicious attacks of Trotsky's with weapon in hand.

News arrived that in Zlatoust and Maryanovka the Bolsheviks had already fallen upon our echelons, so the two-thousand man garrison in Chelyabinsk wasn't to be allowed reinforcements from Yekaterinburg. Even before they were quite awake in the early morning of 27 May, at 4 a.m., precisely, it was they who were disarmed, and the city was in our hands. Almost without a shot having been fired, all of their weapons, ammunitions, and kit were loaded onto our carts.

We took the stations at Palatayevo, Miass, Argayash, Troitsk, Zlatoust, Petropavlovsk, Kurgan – and so it went along the main Siberian railway line, like a spark running down a fuse. And thus began our so-called Siberian 'anabasis.'

We learned of all this in Novonikolayevsk. Captain Gajda advised us not to go any farther, for the road was uncertain and all the stations weren't in our hands.

'Further! Further!' we resolved after a short discussion, If no farther, at least to Mariinsk, of which we had reliable news that it had been taken by Captain Kadlec.

But we didn't get to Mariinsk. We were held up in Taiga the station south of Tomsk. Taiga was in the hands of the Red Army. We'd fallen into a trap and now we worried what would become of us. Marendiak tore the ribbon from his cap, Makovický changed into civilian clothes, and the rest of us sat in our wagon on pins and needles. If the Bolsheviks should decide to have a look at the train, we'd be right in the palm of their hand – and in the best possible case, we'd find ourselves locked upon the nearest POW camp.

I was amazed at the fact that there was no traitor among the other travellers who would spill the beans to the Bolsheviks about there being Czechoslovak soldiers on the train, even if unarmed.

We sat like that for a whole week, waiting on what would happen next. It was here we learned that Čipka, with whom we'd drunk Paulíny beer in Omsk, had died in the Tomsk hospital. He'd fallen off the train and lost an arm. Marendiak and Makovický went to his funeral in Tomsk, but couldn't find it. We started to talk about what we feared. An *obysk*[199] was in the offing. Then – as if on cue – our soldiers showed up in Taiga and we let out our breath. Makovický changed back into this French uniform, and Marendiak sewed his ribbon back on his cap.

We went on. We didn't get too far; just to Izhmorskaya station. Here they unhooked our locomotive and ran it in the direction of Taiga. One night, our soldiers came checking through the wagons, agitated. They told us that past Mariinsk there'd still be fighting for twenty-five versts.

Izhmorsky is a little village. A station, like all others; yellow, wooden, set in a little copse of birches and blooming elders. There was a great meadow to one side of the line, and past it, the taiga and aspens. We'd walk on that meadow when we left our wagon and light bonfires against the mosquitos and take our tea sprawling about on the grass or sitting on logs. We lived on eggs, milk, tea, and bread. You couldn't stand it in the wagons on account of the heat and the flies.

The name of Captain Gajda buzzed along the line. He'd published a manifesto declaring that all he wanted was free

....

[199] Russian: Search.

passage to Vladivostok and from there to France, for Russia's deprived us of the possibility of fighting against the Germans here in Russia, and now the Bolshevik government's impeding us in our journey. They want to hand us over to the Germans. They've already gone and imprisoned three members of the Branch. And so, we're coming out armed, though we have no intentions of mixing ourselves up in the internal affairs of Russia. We'll be off, and then you go and do whatever you like, etc.

'We too should reach for the sword,' said Marendiak once, bent over the chessboard. 'It won't do for us to travel along like some general staff, far to the rear of the battlefield.'

'I'd like to liquidate my assets first,' said Korman. 'As soon as I sell my furs, I'm off for the army.'

'Who cares about furs when it's our own skin at stake?' Marendiak shamed him.

'But we're off to France, after all,' replied Houdek.

'Check!' exclaimed Makovický, and Marendiak shook his head.

I extracted the document I held along with Janko Korman, and read aloud: "'Ekstrenny otzyv:[200] Please accept for transport from station Omsk to station Vladivostok, in second-class wagon, two volunteers of the reserve battalions of the Czechoslovak Revolutionary Army, travelling under orders to their division in Vladivostok, which I confirm by signature and seal. Reserve Battalion of the Czechoslovak Revolutionary Armies, Omsk..." That not enough for you? Well then, if you please – here's a second document: "Certificate presented by the Omsk Reserve Battalion of the Revolutionary Czechoslovak Army to Comrade... in confirmation of the fact that the bearer is travelling under orders to the city of Vladivostok, where he is to report to the commander

....

[200]   Russian: An urgent recall to duty.

of the 12th Reserve Battalion, Comrade V. Rappl, which by this signature…" etc.'

'That was fine in times of peace, but now it's war. They'll go on and say that we're loafers,' said Marendiak, recalling to mind his chess game.

'Who would have thought it? Now that we've got orders to head to Vladivostok and report to the 12th Reserve Battalion, we must get there, later to continue on to the struggle in France, as Gajda wrote, even though the sky be raining axes, as Luther said…' Makovický boomed in his bass, grabbing the knight by the horse's head and circling with it above the chessboard.

'You, as a Tolstoyan, even so daren't resist evil with evil, or even postpone it to France, if it can't be done immediately,' Houdak teased Makovický, watching the game. 'Watch out! He'll take him there,' he warned, and Makovický picked up the knight again, pondering deeply and *hmmm*ing.

Marendiak couldn't take it. He'd lost his way. That is, he'd joined the army, somewhere, to put it bluntly, to do his part – and according to his *ekstrenny otzyv* – as soon as he came across it. Korman turned melancholy. He philosophised about the army once having had a purpose, which now it had lost.

'Our army hasn't lost anything,' I argued. 'It has its purpose – such as few others have. And right now it's heading out on the road so as to fulfil it.'

'A long road.'

'True.'

'And uncertain.'

'True.'

'It'd be more certain if we were with the army. Duty…'

In a word: our consciences had awakened. Out there soldiers are fighting, shedding their blood, and here we are, travelling second class – now, God only knows where and what for. We're going to have to clarify our situation when we get to Irkutsk. Exchange chess for something more serious. Toss away pen and paper, give away our furs.

It took about a month before we moved farther on. We passed through Achinsk and Krasnoyarsk. Following a leg of three days, they held us up again in Kansk-Yeniseisky. They pulled our train onto the last siding, which was a sign that our farther journey wasn't to be an easy task, and that we could carry on with our carefree vacationing. We exchanged the village of Izhmorsky for a little town of two or three streets, wooden houses and wooden pavements. All around it stretched that same flat steppe; only to the south could you see some low mounds. The only life to be found was at the station. We received news that our army was pushing forward triumphantly in the war of the echelons; one after another, the stations were falling into our hands. Instead of a German front in France, we had the Russian front at home. But that too was a German front after all, for the Bolshevik guards were in good part recruited from amongst the German and Magyar POWs, and their headquarters command in Moscow was also German – Mirbach's. Hatred of those POWs grew and grew. Whether they were fighting against us or not, they were seen as our chief enemies.

I myself witnessed a cruel execution.

One day, an echelon of German prisoners was passing through the station. Our boys threw themselves upon them, stripping them of their money, their clothes, their bedclothes and coverings, their underclothes, packages and crates – whatever they had – all the way down to shaving mirrors and leather straps. There was a haggard, bony officer in command of our echelon. He himself strutted about with a pouch slung round his neck and urged on the looting. Some of the Germans tore their banknotes to pieces before his eyes; if they weren't to keep them, he wouldn't get them either. He had these men taken away and shot, not far from the station. I saw their bodies and was ashamed of this bestiality. But I said nothing; I didn't dare get mixed up in that, or they would have shot me, too.

We passed through Taishet and came to Nizhneudinsk. Our papers were examined – first by a Russian, then by a Czech officer. We showed them our documents. They sufficed, but you can never be too cautious. It was touch and go, and Dr Vladimír Daxner, a Slovak officer, nearly had us arrested.

His salon-wagon had been coupled to an echelon of bakers. In it, he had a little room with a table, chairs, and a divan, rugs; a separate bedroom, kitchen, and toilet, and there he lived with his servant. He visited us around dinnertime. We went off for a beer, and then to a hill (amongst swarms of flies) and after this to his wagon, where he treated us to tea and butter.

'I've got a hell of a lot of work,' he told us. 'I'd like to join the army. I reported to Gajda, and he told me to work up a programme I intend to carry out for some individual all-Slovak regiments. I'm to wait for some of the members of the Branch, with whom I'm to iron out the details of the proposal.'

'That'd be separatism. And here you are a supporter of mixing the Slovaks and Czechs together. At least that's what you said at the plenary meeting back in Kiev, and Professor Masaryk approved it all, so that the Slovaks should stop fearing the Czechs,' I reminded him.

'That's right... But we still have heaps of Slovak POWs who'd be more attracted to a Slovak regiment than a Czech one – with Slovak colours, Slovak command, Slovak officers.'

'I don't think that our brothers would cotton on to it, as beautiful and encouraging as it sounds. People talk about the Slovak fear of the Czechs, but there's also Czechs who fear the Slovaks. This fear must be overcome on both sides. Unity can't be founded on fear, or, if you prefer, distrust. And this fear can only be overcome when we have a good look at the bogeyman, straight in the eyes, and ascertain that he doesn't exist. So mix, mix, mix in the Czechs with the Slovaks, and vice versa.'

'You're not taking characters and psychology into consideration. Your Czech is quick, your Slovak slow. Czechs are loud, Slovaks quiet. Czechs are practical, Slovaks dreamers. Czechs aren't too concerned with God and priest, Slovaks are pious. Czechs are nationally conscious, the Slovaks aren't quite there yet. The Czech is bold, the Slovak tongue-tied, and so on. Differences ad infinitum.'

'All the more reason why they should be mixed together.'

'It's all about luring them in. To give the stick-in-the-muds the prod they need to join the army.'

A little later, Korman told me how Daxner had chided him.

'You're causing scandal. Four Slovaks who aren't entering the army. I'm going to send a telegram off to Gajda to have you arrested.'

'What? Didn't you show him your documents?'

'No. I told him that we're on our way to France. And he says that nothing's going to come of France. Five Anglo-French corps are to invade from Murmansk. That's supposed to be the core around which a new Russian Army is to form. And we're going to join it too, and open up a front in Russia against the Germans. We're going to sweep the Germans out of Russia and Ukraine. The front'll be here. You don't have to go chasing off to France in search of it.'

'Five corps?… I'll believe that when I see it. You'd sell your furs ten times over and liquidate your goods a full twenty before they get here… And here he goes looking to arrest people! In short order!'

I rummaged around in my documents for my *Legitimačný lístok* which Daxner gave me in Moscow, when I reported to him, as a member of the recruitment commission, to become a soldier. I showed this to Korman.

'Look – if you had a document like this, they wouldn't be able to grab you.'

'I don't have anything like that.'

'See? I've got nothing to fear – they won't lock me up again like back then in Hungary. There it was Lieutenant Šír, and here it's Daxner.'

'It'd be best to return to Omsk.'

'Go ahead.'

In Tulun, where we stopped for twelve days, at the baths in Uda, Korman's idea of 'liquidating his goods' and selling his furs matured like a well-watered flower, until it fell off the stem. Our Janko returned to Omsk. We gave him a letter with the question: What'll become of us if the wheels come off the plans to go to France? Besides that, we telegraphed concerning where we were to lay down our careworn heads. Are we to return, or to continue our travels according to the *ekstrenny otzyv*? The answer was not forthcoming before our train headed on. Now, we were just three musketeers.

On 29 July we crawled into Irkutsk station from Inno-kentyevskaya. It took us two months and three days to get from Omsk to Irkutsk. Our jolly little summer outing lasted all summer long.

We left our wagon, luggage in hand, to set up shop at a table in the waiting room. We had dinner, and after dinner a confab – what now? We found no solution to the question before a youngster with a green and white band on his sleeve approached us.

'Documents, please,' he said in Russian.

We handed them over.

'Eto Chekhi,'[201] he said, turning round to another young-ster standing behind him.

That one glanced at the papers and nodded.

....

[201] Russian: 'They're Czechs.'

'Ochen izvinyayus. Ya dumal Madiari.'[202]

We didn't dare hang around much longer at the station or in the waiting room. We went to the station master and requested places in a heated wagon in any train heading to Vladivostok. He replied that there were no trains going to Vladivostok, and he informed us of his having given out a circular letter to the effect that all persons were to take themselves off from the waiting rooms, because waiting rooms weren't meant for people to lounge around in.

We could respect that – indeed, we even praised the introduction of such order, but now we had to go off in search of lodgings in town. The evening was coming on. We reached the town, which lies on the other side of the river Angara, by way of a wooden pontoon bridge. I was captivated by the green, smooth, transparent and swiftly-flowing river. You could also see the Irkut, which joins the Angara here. There was a great circulation of people on the bridge, so that we could hardly push our way through. How many lodgings have I inspected in Russia! When a person is away from home, he is ceaselessly in search of someplace to be at home. We went to the Hotel Metropol. There, a dirty little Jew with a greasy face and flakes of dandruff on his threadbare, dark coat showed us two rooms at twelve and nine roubles per day. Everywhere it stank of mould. Old, dowdy, torn furniture with greasy stains. Feathers and clumps of horsehair stuck out of the armchairs. The couch gave out a yelp when Houdek sat down on it. We didn't take the room. We had a look through six hotels, all with names like 'Modern,' 'Grand,' and 'Central,' as well as various 'furnished rooms.' At last, in a hotel called 'The Star,' we were shown a small, dark chamber for eight roubles a day. Everything that makes a lodging comfortable... was located on some far-off

....

[202] Russian: 'My deepest apologies. I thought you were Magyars.'

star, as the name suggests, while all that we found therein were bare mattresses on creaky bed-frames, one table with a colourful cloth thrown over it, decorated with the evidence of past meals, pale reddish wallpaper, strips of which were dangling unglued here and there, and a metal washbasin in an iron base, from which the paint and enamel had chipped off long ago, leaving behind nothing but rusty stains. The room seemed to be a collection point for all mauled and mutilated things that were found in the hotel – a sort of rubbish heap. You couldn't close the door if your life depended on it. Only by pressing our combined weight against it were we able to insert the latch into the bent metal loops. Nor was the door really necessary, as the wall that separated us from the corridor didn't quite reach the ceiling – just as it should be in all proper homes. Anyone at all might slip into the room through that gap if the fancy took him. On the other hand, they did a fine job those days of ringing up the hotel constantly, which precipitated a busy trampling of boots outside in the corridor and loud, concerned inquiries: 'Who's calling? Who's calling?' And also: heavy Russian boots stomping, coughing, and loud conversations, huge flies always buzzing about, well-fed bedbugs who didn't bother nibbling... In short, a room of one's dreams.

Whenever possible, we would gladly leave it behind to wander about the main street, which was called Bolshaya,[203] pebble-strewn, along which beautiful houses stood. Or we would go to the park on the banks of the Angara, where there was a spruce wood, without any great wide-spreading trees, without shade, but with benches, kiosks, clean, well-swept paths and a statue of Alexander III, who survived the Revolution, I reckon, only because someone had stuck a red banner into his hand.

....

[203] Russian: Great.

JANKO JESENSKÝ

Life there was an expensive proposition. A cup of tea cost a rouble; a slice of pastry to go with it almost two. You couldn't get dinner for less than four roubles; in the better establishments, it went for as high as ten. By chance, we met Ivan Daxner, an artillery officer, and shared a bottle of wine with him. They charged us sixty roubles for it; a bottle of champagne cost two hundred sixty. Carried away with enthusiasm, Ivan nearly had them bring us a second bottle, but I discouraged him. For all that he promised me ten pounds of sugar, a leather belt, cheap boots worth one hundred roubles, and a whole wagon to ourselves when we'd need it.

He explained the situation to me, and what had happened in Irkutsk. The Red Army – most of them Germans and Magyars, were in control of the Irkutsk station. Our artillery rolled in, and the Reds demanded their weapons. Without waiting for an answer, they opened fire on our boys with machine guns. Our lads leapt out of the wagons, unarmed, and, with bare hands, captured the machine guns and chased off the enemy. More than one of our poor wretches bit the dust there. They immediately informed the echelons of the 7th Regiment about what had happened, and these set off in the direction of Irkutsk under the command of Staff Captain Hoblík. These echelons took the station in Batareinaya. Armed with their cannons and rifles, they moved on to Innokentyevskaya station and prepared an assault on Irkutsk. And here some Allied emissaries came, with Major Vergé at their head, demanding that we relinquish the weapons. Our men refused, indicating how our artillerymen had been attacked at Irkutsk, and expressing worry at the possibility of a repeat performance. Major Vergé stood firm and insisted upon the immediate handing over of the weaponry. At this, the commander obeyed, and the echelons departed Irkutsk for the east.

'The bastards,'[204] Ivan spat, bitterly.

....

[204] In Slovak *kone* literally means 'the horses.' It might also be trans-

'The bastards,' I concurred.

That we were correct in our assessment was later proved by the fact that Irkutsk was lost, as well as thirty-nine tunnels to the east, near Baikal – and all of that had to be retaken. If the Bolsheviks succeeded in taking out the tunnels, the transport would be stymied for at least a year – and a great amount of money would be needed to clear them.

'So then, we're going to Vladivostok?' I asked.

'Yes. So?'

'Because Vlado was saying that we were to remain here.'

'Rumours. We're not going to give the Russians a hand ourselves...'

Gajda was the hero of those times. His health was toasted by speakers at banquets; he was feted, greeted, praised to the skies and carried about on shoulders, as it were. Everyone was looking to him as some sort of political oracle, but he kept his lips sealed. And our soldiers too were bathed in nimbus and aureole. They could bathe for free – not in the Angara, that was too cold – but at the baths, where they were given linen for free. When they went for a shave, the barber would bow low to them, thanking them for the honour of shaving them, and taking no fee in return. The girls went wild for them. More than one soldier got himself entangled here. The political parties fought amongst themselves for the honour of giving them banquets, evening teas with vodka, wine, and champagne, at which the officers found themselves rubbing shoulders with big shots, and squiring beautiful and sweet Russian ladies. Balls were held, and parties, at which our boys were treated first and best. Donations were collected: funds and other things for the army, to which even the Chinese contributed fivers and tenners.

....

lated 'the beasts,' but that word doesn't seem to have the requisite bitterness.

Vaňo promised to introduce us to Russian society. But that didn't come about. I bought *Telegramy* and read in there that I had been chosen vice-president of the OČSNR[205] at a meeting in Chelyabinsk. There were to be three of us: the first was Pavlů, I, for the Slovaks, was the second, and the third – Dr Patejdl.

I was so astounded at the news that sweat broke out upon my brow.

I was moved at the honour and trust that was conferred on me, but the thought of the twenty-day return trip to Chelyabinsk also had its effect on my feelings. What had I done to deserve this? That's Jožo Gregor's doing again! What a strange fellow. Every other person he wants on the wheelbarrow that he's pushing, and he's always racing about, shoving it along. He's probably thinking: 'Why should I climb on the cart? I'll be noticed here behind it anyway. It's not the position that makes the man, but the man that makes the position. Fame, like the grass of the fields...'

It took me a whole hour to calm down. Meditating on how politics is done, and who amongst us Slovaks might do it well, I arrived at the conviction that it was rather natural for me to become one of the vice presidents. Vlado Hurban and Janček went off to America as politicians: one as a diplomat and the other an organiser. Markovič was in Paris wearing both hats. Dr Vladimír Daxner is going to be a colonel of the Slovak regiment in Irkutsk; Orísek was elected Slovak 'minister' in the Branch, Jožo Gregor was chief of Slovak publishing in the 'ministry' of education, the head of which was Dr Jozef Kudela – so I too had to get myself some sort of high position, since it so chanced that I was still in Russia, thanks to my joining up with the army, and the fact of my

....

[205] Odbočka Československej Národnej Rady (Czechoslovak National Council Branch).

rather advanced age, having rheumatism – that comes and goes – only in my arms and neck. I'm not sick in the head yet. Why should I not become a politician? Bohdan Pavlů and Dr Patejdl are smart enough. They'll be able to fix it if something jumps the tracks in my brain.

So politics ceased to trouble me. It only complicated my return. Twenty days for sure, if the trains would be running well and if we didn't come across any fighting on the way. It's possible that I'll be working like a pendulum: going now to the west, now to the east. That's the way it was at the time with our government in Siberia: it was on wheels and travelled around, stopping here and there, now and then, pausing at one station before setting off farther down the line, or going back. And so it would be no different with me, as a part of the state and the government. Vajs, the commandant of the Irkutsk station, a Moravian, provided me and Houdek with a private compartment. Gavora, my erstwhile editorial comrade from the *Slovenské hlasy* in Petrograd and now a soldier, fixed us up with sugar, cheese, and vodka, wishing us a happy journey. Daxner forgot all about those cheap boots and leather belt, but he brought along with him cordial wishes of good fortune.

But despite these pleasant wishes and kind words, we were all but killed on the way. Our train was derailed. A couple of people lost their lives, many were injured, but we were only tossed from one side of the wagon to the other for a few minutes, and our coffers fell down on our heads from the racks above us. And yet, at the time, while the jostling and tossing were going on, it seemed as if this would be the end of us, too. Thanks be to God, we emerged unscathed, and with us, Slovakia was safe and sound. She was forced to disembark, of course, and wait for a long time in the field for another train to arrive, but then, sitting in the *teplushka*[206]

....

[206] Russian: Freight car.

on our crates and coffers, we travelled on to Omsk and from there to Chelyabinsk.

I was off on my calculations by only one day: the trip took not twenty days, but nineteen.

XIII. CHELYABINSK

In Chelyabinsk, I took myself to a Finnish wagon, where there was first and second class. I had my own compartment there, and slept on the upper berth.

I'd never had it so nice and comfortable. I reminisced about the time I passed this way from Beryozovka-za-Baika-lom to Voronezh, under Russian guard, and bought myself a Jewish cap and ate in some cafeteria or other where I paid a rouble for two, including a tip. A year or so had passed since then. The cafeteria was still there, but what an im-mense change! That 'Austrian' POW had 'just about, nearly, little was lacking for it' become little less than a ministerial president, although my humble title was Vice-President of the OČSNR, and in Russian: 'Tovarishch predsedatel Chek-hoslovatskogo natsionalnogo Soveta Otdeleniya v Rossii.' It all sounded fantastically elevated; it had a striking ring to it. It all seemed – like a prelude. Even though it's true that, instead of one rouble for dinner for two, I had to pay between ten and fifteen for supper for one, still I went to the park, the theatre, and political meetings in an automo-bile or by *izvozchik*. As I said, I was living in a first- and second-class Finnish wagon, in all possible comfort, as an important politician who busies himself only with important things – while others take care of the petty details. From time to time I gazed sadly upon the pale and thin POWs still in their Austrian caps and mantles as they swept the stations clean. Just about a year ago I had the same sort of broom in my own two hands.

The other 'ministers' or, as we more modestly referred to them the 'administrators' of the individual departments, had gone off to Yekaterinburg. We had to remain, along with Medek, 'minister' – pardon me – *administrator* of the Ministry of the Army, so as to determine the fate of the Russian government, of which there were several in Chelyabinsk at the time.

There was that of the Bolsheviks, that is, the Soviet government, against whom we were fighting. Besides this there was the Siberian government with its seat in Omsk, the Samara government with its seat in that city, the Ural government with its capital in Yekaterinburg; somewhere far afield near Chita was the Cossack government with Ataman Semyonov, and even farther afield the Vladivostok government – and ours, of course.

A Russian government of unity was supposed to be formed.

At first, each of the governments took counsel with itself, then later with us, then together, and then at last with us one more time. When we consider how great a jealousy existed between these governments, each one vying for leadership, duelling over turf to such an extent as to establish customs points on the borders between their various spheres of influence; that questions of irredentism arose amongst them; when we think that there were at those councils members of the Constituent Assembly living in the liberated areas, the central committees of the political parties, the representatives of the Cossack armies, the Bashkirs, Tatars, Turkmens; the envoys of the Allies and us – and therefore, people and politicians of extreme right-wing orientations, moderately right-wing ones, Germanophiles, leftists and extreme leftists, and when we add to all this the loquacity native to the Russians, their eternal philosophising, even when the roof is aflame above their heads and the floor collapsing beneath their feet, it isn't hard to see that it was tough going – that the consultations were endless, and finished... not by finishing, but 'to be continued.' But when? That was one of the tough nuts to crack – so that none of the governments should win out over the others... and the debate was renewed.

The representatives of national unity cast a jaundiced eye upon the Socialists. These in turn looked askance at the nationalists. For example, before it was quite clear whether or not Milyukov was pursuing a German policy, two hours passed, and still we knew not where the truth lay.

We were greeted with just as much sumptuousness as Gajda in Irkutsk. We were met with applause when we were led into the council chambers. Pavlů accepted it all in our name, his aides. The president of the assembly first addressed us as 'liberators.' Pavlů thanked him. Then we were seated in places of honour, which we assumed with serious expressions of silent wisdom upon our faces. I was quite shocked by what had been said; I didn't feel like a liberator at all, although I too was heart and soul behind the 'resurrection of Russia,' as the saying went at the time.

While these conferences were going on, the real liberators – our army – were standing firm, bravely, at the Volga. The front was just a hundred versts away.

The bloody progression eastward to France had developed into war in all four corners of Russia. After the taking of Penza our echelons moved in the direction of Kuznetsk and Syzran. Samara was taken after a huge battle at Lipyagi. From Samara they went on further. The Kinel station was taken; a crossroads on the tract leading to Ufa and Orenburg. Buzuluk was taken. After its fall, the Cossacks took Orenburg. Our units hastened in the direction of Ufa, which they took, and then the forward echelons set off in the direction of Zlatoust. The Samara and Chelyabinsk groups joined together on 6 July at the Minyar station between Ufa and Zlatoust. The integration with the Omsk group had been effected following the taking of Omsk, which had happened as early as 6 June.

The assault on Yekaterinburg also succeeded.

Now it was necessary to consider whether we should abandon these liberated territories and head onwards toward Vladivostok, or hold the Volga line. Jeanot, the French consul in Samara, and Guinet, the deputy of the French military mission, officially declared to our executive committee the Allies' desideratum: that our army should hold the line at the Volga as the avant-corps of the Allied armies, who would come to our aid shortly. An encrypted telegram from the French consulate in Vologda, with the same contents, was presented. Following this declaration our executive committee resolved – with the agreement of our revolutionary convention – to hold the Volga line until the Allies should arrive. Meanwhile, Syzran and Kuznetsk were occupied once again and the road to Simbirsk and Orenburg secured.

Our commander, Syrový, blared a blast on the war trumpet: 'I send my greetings to our bold warriors, who in tormented and dying Russia first arose to face the Bolshevik mercenaries of the Germans... It is to your credit that the damnable stain of the Brest-Litovsk Peace has been washed away. Once again, Russians are taking their place on the global front to do battle, in firm unity with the Allied nations, against Austro-German imperialism, for the liberation and unification of Russia, for the Constituent Assembly, for the rights of the nations, for self-determination. It is to your credit that new volunteer units are being formed from the oppressed nations of Central Europe to fight for the liberation of Russia and that of their own lands. With united effort, with common sacrifice, we shall know how to forge the victory of our colours! Forward, warriors, to liberty!'

But help from the Allies never arrived. We read about nothing but their respect, their sincere greetings, their promises.

'The Allies acknowledged the Czechoslovak National Council to be the legitimate governmental organ of the Czechoslovak State.'

'The Allies have determined to support the Czechoslovaks in Russia with their might, disembarking, with that aim in mind, British, French, Japanese and American troops.'

While still in Irkutsk, Gajda telegraphed the news that the American consul general informed him that he would take all necessary steps to ensure that the aid of the American forces arrive in time.

Later, he announced that the representative of the Japanese government had arrived to present him with a Japanese manifesto, declaring that Japan wished to effectively renew the front against Germany. He assured him of a great army being mobilised in Japan, which was to be sent to Russia.

Etc.

But genuine aid was nowhere to be found. The Russian armies, sent here and there by turns, weren't quite functional and our army began to get nervous, wondering whether they were not enduring all their hardship in vain. The road to Vladivostok had been taken and was now clear. We were supposed to go to France by way of Vladivostok. We didn't have anything to look for here. Let the Russians put everything in order with that promised aid.

'Hold on!' the Branch soothed. 'Help is on the way!'

'They're rocking us like babies!' the wags said.

'They're treating us like babies!' the Branch might also have said.

'And us!' the press might have added.

These were days of great rocking and swaying, back and forth.

Like us, the political leadership of the OČSNR urged the Russians to form an all-Russian government as soon possible, or our army would stop fighting.

Slowly, we came to know all of the Russian big shots that there were in Chelyabinsk in those days. And there were quite a few of them. Avksentyev stands out in my memory, gesticulating temperamentally while speaking:

'Czechs and Slovaks, themselves oppressed in far-off Austria–Hungary, are spilling their precious blood on behalf of oppressed Russia, helping us. I greet them cordially here amongst us, with emotions of deep gratitude and a sense of obligation towards them, in hopes that we Russians too, united, might help them in turn, those dear brothers of ours, in their struggle against their own oppressors...'

He had great sympathy of us, and, at least on the face of things, supported us.

Grishin-Almazov was contemptuous and acrimonious. He mocked: 'Why don't we head off to France for a rest, since we're laying down our weapons?' We replied to his mockery by not showing up at the dinner he invited us to.

Maslov was a patriarchal, good-natured gentleman with sad eyes.

Here too I saw Kolchak with his thin, clean-shaven, steady, sun-burnt and pleasant face, a man of medium height; an honest and noble admiral – the future dictator who would come to a tragic end in the prison in Irkutsk.

One day, Patejdl grabbed me by the button of my coat and said:

'This won't work, Jáno. It's all supposed to be collegial, you know.'

He was complaining to me about Pavlů doing everything by himself, negotiating with the Russians, not conferring with us on anything, presenting nothing to us, treating us as if we were nothing but his acolytes, altar boys without censers. Absolutist tendencies, for sure.

'At gatherings only his name is mentioned, ours not,' he went on. 'He wanted Father Golitsyn's head to roll – the one who's running things in Yekaterinburg. What's he getting mixed up in that for? Let the Russians look after their own heads themselves. No, it can't go on like this...'

'We can't start snapping at one another now like the Russians,' I warned him. 'You're supposed to be the third vice president, right? And yet you always precede me. What is it you're after?'

'I'm not going to let myself be pushed aside.'

'We'd need a really wide door frame for us to enter a room shoulder to shoulder. And anyway, he'd still have to be in the centre, as the first vice president.'

It was good that the Russian consultations finally came to an end. We were nearly wearing holes in the seats of our pants from sitting there. They resolved... to resume meeting on 8 September in Ufa.

XIV. YEKATERINBURG

We headed off to Yekaterinburg on a passenger train that crept along like a slug. It also had two horns like one: two smoke-boxes and two chimneys. We felt insulted – the engineer must not be aware of whom he's transporting, otherwise he'd've got a move on. Medek, the administrator of the war department, an advocate of the strong personality, got angry and had them uncouple some grain wagons so that they wouldn't be a drag on us, but that was no help. How might it be, since we ourselves were such heavy grain, intended both for sowing, and at the same time the sowers, who were to make fertile the fields?

The little valley through which we were riding was narrow, set amidst low hills – a landscape like ours, mountainous, billowy. We were told that there were rich deposits of iron here, and coal, salt, amethyst, topaz, gold, platinum, and copper. They mine a lot, but extract little.

Yekaterinburg itself is a beautiful European city with brick buildings, streets paved with stone, as well as stone pavements. The pearl of the Urals, still spattered with the fresh blood of the recently murdered Tsar and his family. The front was close, and, accordingly, there seemed to be few people about. The citizenry was said to be of hostile mind, thanks to the strong Bolshevik element in many of the area factories, and on account of the large number of German POWs here. Supposedly, the place was full of spies. The British consul himself had a German wife and his daughters were Germanophiles.

The Branch offices were located among the 'American numbers' in a hotel with dark corridors and many rooms to the left and right of them.

I was assigned a large, furnished chamber with armchairs, carpets, heavy, impenetrable drapes on the large windows, a writing table, and a little alcove with a bed behind thick partitioning drapes. Due to these drapes, the sun never shone into the room, inside which it was dark, gloomy, dreary.

On the other hand, my private apartment was pleasant. Four windows, sun, palms, it was good that there was no fountain splashing water in the middle of the large room. The owner was German, an engineer. Quiet, unassuming, fond of peace at the hearthside and felt boots. The lady of the house was a robust forty-year-old, I guess, but unusually youthful, fitful, now sad, now stormy-cheerful – she seemed somewhat hysterical to me. At first she begged us not to *rugat*[207] them, but later, when she warmed up to us, she was all jokes and laughter. What didn't suit her was her constant interest in 'young people.' When the conversation turned to someone she didn't know, her first question was:

'Interesny?'

'Konechno, interesny.'

'A vy menya poznakomili by...'[208]

She called us in for tea and evening gatherings at which the cream of Russian society in Yekaterinburg was found.

Three of us rented from her: Otomar Houdek, Jožo Gregor, and I. Each of us had a room to himself. Each one of these was different, and each of us paid at a different rate. I, as a 'just about, nearly, little was lacking for it' ministerial chief was assessed one hundred fifty roubles; Houdek, as a

....

[207] Russian: To scold.

[208] Russian: 'Interesting?'; 'For sure, interesting.'; 'And you perhaps could introduce me...'

gentleman of much more humble status, eighty-five, and Jožo Gregor, the *Slovatsky pisatel*,[209] as he began introducing himself as long ago as in Kiev, fifty.

And so I was informed that it was no trifle to sport a band on one's arm embroidered with the gold letters ČSNR, as the vice presidents and administrators of the individual Branch departments wore; I must 'represent' as well, it seemed. And this I took literally. I paid for the flat. Other representatives took a practical attitude towards the issue: they requisitioned their flats so that they paid nothing at all for them, or very little, if anything.

And further, I was marked by one more natural feature of the Slovaks: impractical noblesse, on account of which we will appear for a long time yet as lordly, undemocratic, and, accordingly, less estimable, stupider. Other brothers of ours were more level-headed; through some of these heads even Bolshevik winds had already whistled.

'Look there, look there!' they said. 'He wants to *represent*, doesn't he? There's a toff for you; there's that Magyar culture reflecting back from him...'

Magyar culture? Hell! It's only right that I pay for what I take!

'Look at that Pavlů – there's a nobleman for you, there's elegance!'

Even Pavlů wasn't much to their liking.

'He wants to be a dictator, he does. By himself, always by himself. He negotiates with consuls, rides around in a train all to himself while the others travel in *teplushkas*; he's got an adjutant, a servant, an automobile, while the rest of us have to go about on foot, versts at a time...'

'What about Medek? He's a young fellow you can't say a word against, I reckon.'

....

209 Russian: Slovak writer.

'Medek lives in a palace, rides in a motorcar too, while he's looking to set up his co-workers in barracks... He goes about in pyjamas at home, sits in his armchair in front of a mirror popping pimples. He's in love with himself...'

'The Lord God pay you back for your pettiness.'

'What "Lord" God? God wants to lord it over us too?'

These were those 'atypical bourgeois' who as early as back in Kiev labelled Pavlů, Hess, and Špaček 'typical bourgeois' and demanded that it be 'red' blood circulating in the veins of the Branch. I reckon that they'd never seen a real bourgeois or aristocrat in their life, and so every person they came across who was clean-shaven, with well-combed hair, they took for a bourgeois, an aristocrat, an opponent of democracy. They themselves constituted an opposition at the plenary sessions of the Branch and were always opposed to everything that stank to them of old, lordly mould. For example: the officers of the new Russian army began wearing *pogony*[210] again, as they had during the Tsarist days. Horrors. They demanded the government intervene. We wanted to organise a club where we might gather, read, share our thoughts – whatever occurred to us. 'A club? A club?!' O, that sounds lordly. We don't want any club...! We should visit each other now and then, so as to get to know one another. Blood and thunder! We're here to go around paying visits? Whoever needs us will visit us soon enough... We don't need any committees in our army; our officers all come of the people; they've grown into the nation, all 'peasant' sons... But please, let's not insult the majesty of the nation. There will be no army without committees, we can guarantee that.

I trained my attention upon some of those 'atypical bourgeois.' They were worthy lads, but – like everyone else – vain and envious.

....

[210] Russian: Shoulder straps.

But were they *new*? No. All familiar types. On account of grand politics and care for the nation's destiny, busied on all sides, they were often unable to distinguish what is foreign from what is one's own; all of them, small-minded and calculating, forgot that debts must be repaid. They always knew where to get their *kerosin*,[211] their good wine cheap, spirits for vodka, tobacco, leather for parade-quality boots, cloth for proper clothing. They were beyond all competition in such matters, and the Russians themselves turned to them whenever they needed anything.

I can be petty, too. Once, at a Branch plenary, there was a discussion concerning a promotion for bravery and loyal service. One of those calculating politicians bristled:

'I protest. He's a reactionary.'

'But even a reactionary can be brave and loyal,' someone said.

'Not in our army. Our army has been formed on democratic bases...'

'Whoever's with us is our brother,' someone else said. 'A brother's a brother.'

'You have to be able to make distinctions among people...'

I trained my eyes on him. He was in a French coat, a well-pressed striped shirt and thin tie. They seemed familiar. I moved over closer to him. Indeed!

'Future Bolsheviks,' I thought to myself, want to make distinctions among people, but they aren't able to do so among things. Who would take care of little things like that? That's what servants are for.

Not only Russian men, but Russian ladies too thought that, as 'conquerors,' we have everything and can do everything.

....

[211] Russian: Kerosene. In the original Jesenský translates it as 'oil' in the brackets.

Our landlady used to be visited by Nina Ivanovna, a pretty blonde thing with a thin, tender face and large eyes; tall, slender, interesting – the wife of an engineer who supposedly was at the front. Sometimes she held evenings that were attended by our boys as well as the Russians.

'If you'd like to be invited to one of her parties,' our landlady advised us, 'you need to pay her a visit.'

'She's a beautiful woman,' I said.

'Captivating,' said Houdek.

So away we went, well-brushed and clean-shaven, in shining boots, in an auto, so as to impress her all the more. With visiting card on which were listed all of our former, and current, titles.

Nina Ivanovna greeted us and led us into the salon. We sat down. I went off into a spiel about the Beautiful, art, and Russian literature, here and there dropping the names of poets, novelists, philosophers, and critics, so she would know that this was no bumpkin sitting of front of her, but a well-read person.

Houdek entered the lists with me, turning the conversation to the great wealth of the Urals, citing fragments of his article, which he had published in *Slovenské hlasy*.

The young lady listened to us with a charming smile on her lips. Then, at the first opportune pause, she asked me:

'Ivan Ivanovich, a kerasinu u vas net?'[212]

I still don't know how we arrived at kerosene. But I do remember that suddenly, everything began to reek. Even Nina Ivanovna, that gorgeous girl, with so gentle a profile, was like a rose plunged into petroleum. And here I wanted to treat my sense of smell to the natural, inebriating fragrance of a rose, and smelled nothing in her vicinity but oil.

I shot a glance at Houdek.

....

[212]   Russian: 'You can't get your hands on any oil, can you?'

'We can get you some,' he said.

'And spirits?' she asked, inclining sweetly in his direction.

'And spirits.'

We left there deflated.

It was all to be chalked up to the rumour that all the petroleum wells, distilleries and vineyards were in our hands. But it would be unjust of me if I were to suggest that this was the only reason we were invited into Yekaterinburg society. The people there were altruistic souls. When we gave them spirits, we too enjoyed the vodka they distilled from it. Some of us were so inflamed by it that, not being satisfied with their own fire, they would shoot off their revolvers into the dark sky as they made their way home through the streets.

Oríšek, the 'representative' of the Slovaks in Russia, as he referred to himself in official notices, also frequented a young lady, another wife of an older, bearded, honest gentleman. We liked to go there ourselves. In general, they were typical Slavic evenings – *halušky* with sheep's cheese, and vodka.

What a strange beverage, that vodka! It made a person sad, though there was nothing to be sad about: our affairs were going along nicely, both in Russia and in France, and above all at home, but – God knows why – a fellow became somehow glum, agitated, perhaps on account of that rose thrust into the petroleum, and here they're pushing vodka at you. You inhale one shot, another, a third, as if you were downing headache pills, and – the curtain rises, all is clear! One young lady you now behold in a rosy glow, another light-haired lass in an orange nimbus, and a third dark-haired girl, in a purple aura. And now you've lifted a fourth glass in toast. And so you recall a certain white face, sky-blue eyes and red lips; white, blue, red – our national colours – how can you not love them?

'Long live our hostess, Maria Sergeyevna!'

The light-haired young miss with pale cheeks, dressed in red, was like the moon glowing golden above the coming dawn... 'The moon it glows, the moon it glows, hey! But it gives no warmth at all...' The words of the old song flitted through one's head. If only it heated a little, like the sun... And that third one, the most beautiful one, in the dark dress, is like the night, in which two stars nestle: her two eyes. And these in turn see their lights dimmed by the mists of her thick eyelashes...

'Ivan Ivanovich, ne uvlekaites!'

'Voskhititelna!'

'Ne dlya vas!'

'"Ne dlya menya vzoidyot zarya..."'[213] the light-haired girl intoned.

At which the rest of them picked up the melody and joined in:

'Ne dlya menya Vag razolyotsya
i serdtse radostyu zabyotsya
ne dlya menya
ne dlya menya...'[214]

About Russian women it is said that they are magnificent, but only for fun and games, parties. This is not true. In Voronezh I came to know some housewives who worked from sunrise to sunset and certainly had been great at parties in their younger years. What is it that makes Russian women so captivating? The fact that they are unaffected, they put on no airs, are always cordial and warm; I'd say that their souls are like open bottles of a wondrous liquor, that bend forward on their own to pour out their wonderful nectar fearlessly. Our ladies too are full of sweet juice, but in a stoppered bottle

....

[213] Russian: 'Ivan Ivanovich, don't get carried away!'; '[She's] sublime!'; 'Not for you!'; 'Not for me the dawn breaks...'

[214] Russian: 'Not for me the Váh spills wide / And the heart beats with joy / Not for me / Not for me...'

you need to open with a *Stoppelzieher*.[215] At which you must be very careful not to break them and cut yourself on the sharp edges!

It was easy enough to 'get carried away.' This had nothing in common with love – it was an exaltation. It bound no one, it was not a serious thing like *lyubov*[216] – on the contrary: it was light, gay, ephemeral. 'Lovi minutu vdokhnovenya!'[217] A minute, an hour, a week. Some 'got carried away' for the rest of their lives. They hadn't been careful, playing with fire, and fell right in love. I'm convinced that they never regretted it, and that they now have splendid wives.

Otherwise, an enduring, serious emotion might undermine the seriousness of our position, the fact that we were only passing through.

Although everything looked as if we were setting ourselves up for an extended stay.

The Branch instituted a draft.

It claimed all Czechs and Slovaks who were still POWs, invoking its 'supreme authority' to do so. It commanded that they report at gathering points for a census. Whoever refused to so report would face a court-martial.

The *Slovenské hlasy* wrote very charmingly that 'our army is the only firm rock in this Russian bog, upon which might be raised a redoubt to defend us from the swelter, the rain, and inclement weather. In the Russian darkness, it is the only torch that gives light, and warmth, and reveals our path to our eyes. In the enslaved Russian land, it is the only free nation that will take on all comers in its fight for liberty. But it is too small yet to dry all the marshes, disperse all the gloom,

....

215 German: Corkscrew.

216 Russian: Love.

217 Russian: 'Catch minutes of inspiration.' A line from Aleksei Khomyakov's poem 'Vdokhnoveniye' [Inspiration, 1831].

and liberate all from the enemies of freedom. The Bolsheviks, the Germans, and the Magyars are rushing upon it from all sides... Many, too many of our brothers cling to the rags in which they once served foreigners. Thousands of them wallow in POW camps when we are spreading wide before them the door leading to freedom, so that they too might become free warriors, fighting on behalf of goals so great... An animal in a menagerie will exit his cage as soon as the door to it is opened. A dog let loose from his chain will frisk about in joy. Are only people to be such as wish to remain prisoners when their own friends are spreading wide the door before them, so that they might exit their gaol for freedom? Are only people to beg for the chains that have been removed from them by those who call to them, urging them to become the same as all who wear our uniform...?'

So Jožo Gregor compared freedom to a shirt, and was not about to stop: 'So you're going to be like stone? Well, we're going to chisel that stone into conscious people, Slovaks... There will be schooling. We're going to teach you to read and write in Slovak. Numbers, geography, history, and all the necessary skills and crafts. We're going to teach you how to think like Slovaks, not Magyars or Austrians, as you've been thinking up until now. And when you become of one mind with us, you'll set out on the same road with us in search of your own shirt to wear, which is called freedom...'

We began to compose schoolbooks. *A Pictorial Atlas of Slovakia, A Short Sketch of Slovak Orthography, War and Peace, or a Short History of the Revolution.* Dr Hojo translated *Counsels and Resolutions of the I Revolutionary Congress.* Dr Daxner wrote *Commands.* An instructional camp was set up in Irkutsk for Slovak POWs. Geryk was placed in charge of it, and as instructors they appointed Manica, Slézak, Čatloš, Ledník, Zachar, Štefanovič, Jahn, Houdek, Ruman, Hrivnák, etc. Gavora was the superintendent. Dr Makovický was entrusted with the health service.

The cheery news that Slovaks were now flooding into the army arrived. 373 joined up in Novonikolayevsk, 1200 in Irkutsk, 1000 at Omsk. We now had at least one volunteer from just about every village. There were whole platoons from some towns. Every day brought dozens of new recruits, if not hundreds. The Branch authorised some anthems, too: 'Hej, Slováci,' Kde domov môj,' 'Kdo za pravdu horí.' The Slovaks by now made up a single electoral district, and we were to elect ten representatives to the future Diet.

It was now common knowledge that nothing would be coming of France. And the politics of 'not meddling' had been tossed out onto the scrap heap long ago. The new Russian army fought alongside ours, and as our bloods mixed on the various fronts, so did our political aims begin to merge. There was to be no acknowledgement of the Brest-Litovsk Peace; new military units were to be called into existence from among us and the Russians; the struggle against the Germans and Bolsheviks was confirmed, as was the aim of resurrecting a mighty Russia according to the notions of Syrový.

During the Ufa conference the agreement of all the governments to all of these points was unanimous, but as far as the question of the responsibility of the future government of unity was concerned, opinions differed. The possibility of a dictatorship loomed ominously over them. The democratic plan was for the government to be responsible to a fraction of the Diet, which would consist of former members of the Constituent Assembly, until such time as elections to the permanent Diet had taken place.

The democratic plan was a beautiful one, but reality proved stronger. The democrats began slyly retreating from their positions once it became clear that slowly, everything that had been won was being lost again, slowly: Kazan, Simbirsk, and, before long, Samara too.

A five-member Directorate was then formed, which was to be responsible to the Diet. This Directorate remained in

Ufa for a while. Then it moved on to Chelyabinsk. It chose Yekaterinburg as its seat of power, but then, when the front got too near, it took itself off to Omsk. Omsk was the last straw. Here, except for us, there was no one to greet it; they could hardly find office space. The Omsk government sniffed out that their liquidation was imminent, and so began to intrigue. The apparatus of the old Omsk government wormed its way into the Directorate, and all of the Siberian ministers, it seemed, got into the new ministries – nothing but reactionaries, as the democrats put it. Certainly they were the stronger individuals, since they imposed their will upon others. And so – in this fashion, the Omsk government became the de facto government of Russia.

Then, on the night of 16–17 November, Directors Avksentyev and Rogovsky, along with Deputy Director Zenzinov, were arrested by a military unit loyal to Ataman Krasilnikov.

Their colleagues in the council of ministers did not demand their release or the punishment of the guilty. Rather, they resolved to dissolve the Directorate and assume all governmental powers themselves, which they proceeded to entrust to one member: Admiral Kolchak.

And so – a seizure of power. From Directorate to Dictator. Just as it had been with the French Revolution.

The rumour spread that the *coup d'état* had taken place with the approval of the Czechoslovaks.

Now, this was too strong a pinch of tobacco for the innocent Branch. The rumour struck like a thunderbolt, and singed the members of our political leadership. They feared that the army would be aggravated that, fighting against the Bolshevik dictatorship, they were actually fighting *for* a dictator – which is much the same sort of devil, whatever name you give him.

Ministerial Chairman Pavlů and Cabinet Secretary Richter travelled to see General Štefánik in Vladivostok. The remainder of the Branch members, after long consultations, resolved to meddle with Russian politics once more, and condemned the Omsk *coup d'état*.

They declared:

'Brothers! We have addressed the following declaration to the Russian people, and to the representatives of the Allied governments:

'In order to counteract and limit the spread of various rumours concerning the attitude of the Czechoslovak National Council Branch in Russia to the recent events, we hereby declare that the Czechoslovak Army, which is fighting on behalf of liberty and government by the people, cannot, nor will it, support or approve of any violent seizure of power such as contravene these principles. The *coup d'état* that took place in Omsk on 18 November of the present year has done violence to the rule of law and the respect upon which all states, including the Russian, must be founded. We, the representatives of the Czechoslovak Army, upon whom up until the present day, the main burden of the struggle against the Bolsheviks has rested, express our concern and disappointment at the fact that, to the rear of our army in active combat, violent seizures of power are being carried out, with the use of forces that are rather needed at the front. This cannot continue. The Czechoslovak National Council Branch in Russia trusts that the present governmental crisis, elicited by the arrest of members of the current all-Russian government of unity, will be brought to a conclusion by legal means. For this reason, we do not consider the matter of said crisis closed.

'In bringing our determination to your attention, we request that you remain calm, assured of your security, with which we are ourselves concerned, and carry on, effectively solving your crisis in a peaceful manner.'

With this we guaranteed ourselves the decided hostility of the Siberians. The Russian news media began to speak of us in ugly terms. The former 'victors' and 'liberators' were now termed prisoners of war, who dared to interfere in the international affairs of Russia; foreigners grasping for power here. Censorship of our newspapers was called for, so as to put an end to our 'seditious' writing.

Just as a good thermometer displays both how warm and how cool it is, so our hearts, in regard to the Russians, and theirs in regard to ours, sank towards zero from the warmth they had recorded up until now.

The injection that was the declaration of the Branch did not encourage perseverance. As time passed, the army grew weaker from exhaustion. The units in Vladivostok, which were already at the sea-shore from which they were to be transferred to the Western Front, were in absolutely no mood for another war. The draft mobilisation of Czechs and Slovaks had introduced many unreliable elements into the army. Some units mutinied. Gajda attacked Perm, it is true, but there he ground to a halt. The Russian army – now the army of Kolchak, was weak, poorly clothed, poorly equipped, and only showed enthusiasm when it had the chance to surrender to the Bolsheviks or desert to them. The promised Allied aid never arrived. The only Allies to show up were individual envoys, consuls, and representatives, but without armies. To the rear, members of the Constituent Assembly were hunted down and locked up so that they would cause no discomfort to the Omsk dictatorship. Members of the Branch aided them, hiding them, while the disobedient Gajda used our units to capture them.

Amidst all of this, the most joyous news arrived from home: a Czechoslovak government had been formed. That being the case, the army could no longer see any sense in remaining in Russia, or what it would be fighting for there any more. It was said that for lack of any such idea, an idea had to be invented.

The Bolsheviks themselves, as if knowing what was going on in the thoughts and hearts of our soldiers, were enticing us with the promise of allowing us to leave Russia for home. In the name of the Soviet government, Chicherin sent a telegram to Prague by way of Berlin, which announced that 'despite our victories, we regret the bloodshed and thereby declare to the provisional Czechoslovak government our will to allow the Czechoslovaks to return to their homeland through Russia. The Soviet government is willing to enter into negotiations with the government in Prague with a view toward establishing the conditions for the passage through.'

Our political leadership declined the offer, but an old – hardly new! – thought began to spread through the army: to get home, as far as possible, without any more fighting.

An armistice was declared between the Germans and the French. The Germans were required to withdraw all of their armies both west and east to the borders as they existed on 1 August 1914. They were to abandon the conquered territories of France and Belgium, the occupied territories of Russia, the Ukraine, Poland, Romania and Alsace-Lorraine; the Brest-Litovsk Pact was to be considered null and void, as was the Romanian accord.

All of this as proof that they would no longer fight.

We also learned of Kramář's first note to the Magyars from the newspapers. Such were the contents of the note sent to Graf Károlyi by Dr Kramář, the chairman of the Czechoslovak National Council:

'All of the Allied states have acknowledged all lands occupied by Slovaks to form an integral, indivisible part of the one Czechoslovak state. This being the case, the Hungarian government had no right to declare any such armistice as would bind the Slovak regions. The borders of the Czechoslovak and Magyar states shall be determined at the peace conference.'

There you go! And here we are, stuck here, instead of settling our accounts at home with the Magyars. A peace conference has been called for the beginning of the new year, and here we are spilling our blood!

We thought up no new idea such as would enflame our army with the will to continue the fight against the Bolsheviks, on behalf of Greater Russia.

In vain did Medek write in his appeals: 'We demand that you hold out... You, the heroes of a war now lasting nearly five years. You, the heroes of Zborov; you, the liberators of Siberia and the Urals; you, the engineers of a great renaissance of Russia and all Slavdom, who have pride of place amongst all the glorious armies in this great struggle for the freedom of oppressed nations and better days for all mankind... We demand that this army of independent Czechoslovakia not cease, not weaken, not sag on its grand and glorious road to our liberated fatherland...'

Such was his injection against ceasing, weakening, and sagging on the road to glory.

In vain did the Branch plead: 'We've got to tense all our strength; endure in the struggle... Many a difficult battle yet awaits us on our road home... We must make firm our fighting strength, heighten our capabilities of attack and defence, so that we should achieve the greatest success in these battles and suffer the least damage; so that the army that enters our fatherland be such as our nation will be proud of, an army such as will be the dependable support of our young state at the difficult outset of its life. We, your representatives and your leaders, summon you to labour, to discipline, to the strict execution of your duty and the fulfilment of the commands you receive in this service. We call upon you to foster reciprocal trust and fraternal devotion, to preserve your old faith in one another. For above all, we have always relied on one another, on our own strength, on our labour, our arms, our nation.'

The injection for reciprocal trust, self-trust, discipline, the execution of orders.

Whatever was appealed to, that was already tottering in our army. Hang on! There was no more hanging on. Discipline! There was no more discipline. Reciprocal trust! Nope. Self-confidence! Vanished. Fight! No strength was left.

The universal desire was for rest. And then came the questions: When are we going home? What way, home? Nothing but home, home, home!

And still one more injection: the gala official presentation of the colours to the 5th, 6th, 7th, and 8th regiments of II Division. Syrový, Gajda, the members of the Branch. Fiery speeches. And in Slovak, to the Slovaks:

'Dear brothers! Every idea has its own symbol. Just as the Christian idea has the Cross, the Socialist idea the red banner, the idea of the state its crown, so too the army, fighting for its own particular idea, has its colours.

'Now, what is the idea behind these colours of ours?

'The ideas of liberation and unity.

'Beneath these colours stand all those who desire the liberation and unification of the Czech lands and Slovakia. Beneath them stand all of those who wish to liberate and unify Russia. Beneath them stand all those who hold in their hearts the desire that all the Slavic lands should be liberated and join together in one strong union.

'These ideas have led us so far in our common struggle against the Germans and the Magyars on the old fronts, then on the Eastern Front, and now on all the present fronts. These ideas lead us in the battle against the Bolsheviks, those base servants of the Germans. These ideas press us westward to our home, that we might fight for our fatherland. These ideas urge us to get for ourselves a good neighbour, one who should not be hostile toward us, but one on whom we may rely. And that neighbour is none other than great, Slavic Russia, for only alongside a great, united, Slavic Russia will we ourselves be worth anything. Without Russia there can be no Slovak rebirth, liberation, unification.

'This is the message that our colours bring us.

'And this is the message that must be foremost in our thoughts; this is what we must feel; this must be our conviction.

'Whoever has any convictions other than these, let him not dare join us beneath these banners!

'With such convictions, and with a willingness to fight for them, we head westward for home!'

Anthems. Defilades in front of the officers and members of the Branch, so that everyone's eyes might gaze their fill upon our beautiful regimental ranks.

We were ready to weep our hearts out over that Slavdom of ours. Old Uncle Hurban would've liked to kiss us all on both cheeks if he were among us then, and not rotting away in the cemetery at Martin. After all, what was this save his own frightful politics?

On 8 December, at last, General Štefánik himself arrived at Yekaterinburg. He didn't even pay a courtesy visit to Kolchak, the dictator at Omsk, for fear of embarrassing the Branch members on account of their protest against the Omsk *coup d'état*. We greeted him with a full parade. Without a greatcoat, lightly dressed, with Sam Browne belt and the ribbons of various medals on his breast, he emerged from his vehicle gingerly and slowly. He made no reply to the speech with which we greeted him. Someone else read his speech for him. Following the anthem he passed down the ranks of those greeting him, his hand stiffly at his general's cap in salute.

'I can't speak,' he whispered to me at our second meeting at the 'American numbers' where the Branch offices were located, as I went up the staircase with him.

His carriage was serious, but fresh.

In Pavlů's grand reception hall we all gathered round him.

We had been waiting for him as if he were Moses, who would lead his Siberian nation home. But both Moses and his nation were a little disappointed: Moses in the nation, and the nation in Moses.

He brought President Masaryk's order with him:

'Hang on...! A heavy burden weighs upon you, brothers in Russia and Siberia; for you can't return home as quickly as you would wish... But your sacrifice will make our nation's position all the stronger at the peace conference. In Russia, you will receive the aid of the Allies...'

Štefánik himself directed an appeal in his own name as a 'member of the Czechoslovak government, appointed Minister of National Defence by the will of the liberated nation,' in which he noted that honour and Allied solidarity oblige our army to remain at its labours in the field... Warmest thanks to those faithful sons who have raised aloft the banner of freedom... Tasks await us. When these tasks have been discharged, we shall set out together on the road to our free fatherland... We must complete the work of selfless Slavs and loyal allies...

'We need Great Russia,' he said. 'We are fighting against the Bolsheviks. We are not going to ask any favours of them; we must fight our way to Archangelsk and Murman ourselves. By ourselves, with the Russians...! No Allied help will arrive. I'll find out who was dispensing such rubbish your way and see that he is punished...'

'But you know, that was the President himself in his Order of the Day for 14 November: "You will be aided by the Allies in Russia,"' someone noted.

'No help will come here. But great preparations are being made, which I can reveal to you only in the strictest confidence, because as a minister I can't just take a swing at an offensive against Moscow. Some French divisions are concentrating in Romania, with tanks, ready to enter Russia. Berthellot, with five divisions... and the Allied armies in Murman are going to be reinforced... We must take Kungur... The seizing of Perm would clear the road to Archangelsk for us... Then we'll draw down the army from the front. We'll have a rest then. The army will be restored, reorganised, and we'll go home... We'll slash our way home, with me at the head of the troops. I'll either go back with you all, or remain here with you all. I won't go back without you... Without too much to-do, we'll go home, through Russia, in glory...'

So, homeward, fighting our way, without any direct Allied aid. A promised rest. But first fighting. And then, more fighting. The nation was a little agitated.

The nation condemned the dictatorship of Kolchak, the minister condemned the Branch for protesting the Omsk *coup d'état*.

'That was village politicking. Only the government in Prague has the right to concern itself with such things.'

The nation wanted Diets and politicking, the minister wanted to fight.

'The only Diet is the National Assembly in Prague.'

The nation had elected members to the Branch as their political leadership and government. The minister disbanded the Branch.

'There's only one government – in Prague.'

A few days after his arrival he summoned us to his salon wagon and there, in a long speech, he laid out his position. Every member of the Branch was to submit his 'resignation.'

In mine I wrote:

'With the creation of the Czechoslovak Government in our Fatherland and the liquidation of the Czechoslovak National Council and its Branches in America and Italy, which was announced to the official Branch of the National Council in Russia by a member of the Czechoslovak Government, the Minister of National Defence General Milan Štefánik, I acknowledge the functioning of the Branch of the Czechoslovak National Council in Russia, as the governing organ of the Czechoslovak Revolution in Russia, to have been legally terminated.

'In consequence of the above, I hereby resign from membership in the Branch of the Czechoslovak National Council in Russia, at the same time declaring my readiness to present an account of my activities as a member of the presidium whenever such be required of me.

'I hereby request a transfer to the army.

'Given in Yekaterinburg, 10 December 1918. Signed.'

But it all didn't go so smoothly. The Socialist wing of the Branch: Dávid, Janík, Král, Kysela, and Polák, emphasised that they had been elected to their positions by the military-revolutionary Diet, and only a new Diet would be authorised to deprive them of their mandate and to liquidate the Branch.

'Nonsense,' Štefánik repeated. 'One government. One Diet.'

'Prague is a long way away from here,' the Socialists stated. 'The situation here is divided. It won't be so easy to consult with that Diet or that government. We need an organ here that will take care of things here and now.'

'That's what I'm here for. The Minister of War. The plenipotentiary of the government.'

'That's called a dictatorship.'

'That's called an order from the President.'

It wasn't advisable to poke the bear that was Štefánik. And anyway, the majority of the members of the Branch: Dr Kudela, Dr Patejdl, Oríšek, and Richter also composed and submitted their resignations, acknowledging Štefánik as the sole representative of the government and the Branch of the National Council in Russia to be irrelevant. Willingly or not, the Socialists also signed their 'abdication' papers, but never ceased shaking their heads as a sign of their opposition to it. For them, Štefánik had become an unsympathetic, undemocratic, bourgeois, western general of the old system, who enters all places with his sabre drawn.

'Kolchak's dictatorship in its Czechoslovak edition.'

Item: that which came to be two years ago in Petrograd, with such difficulty – the Branch of the National Council – was annihilated in Yekaterinburg in the wink of an eye by Brother Minister-General.

Poof! went my 'just about, nearly, little was lacking for it' ministerial chairmanship; poof! went my authority. I became a common soldier.

The General did appoint me to the delegation that was to travel home and inform the President and the government about the condition of our army in Siberia. Along with me there was Dr Patejdl, the vice-chairman (ret.), and, to my great surprise, those who had snapped back at Brother Minister: Janík, Dávid, Dr Polák, all 'ministers (ret.).' Another of their number was Maisner, former vice-president of the former military-revolutionary Diet.

'And you'll write a little poem for us, when we come back to Slovakia,' Brother Minister said to me.

Now, I always put the writing of verse on the back burner, when there was other work to do, as a plaything of sorts, as a good cup of wine in pleasant company. Žd'ársky used to say that the writing of poetry was a luxury, especially when you can say the same thing in prose, and that in a more understandable and natural way.

'What?' I thought. 'Am I not good for anything else, except the writing of "little poems"?'

I was so mortified I couldn't even speak. I looked around the place. The General and the other brothers were smiling. None of them said:

'Brother General, don't send him; he's needed here.'

I lowered my gaze and mumbled:

'Thank you. I'm honoured.'

But I didn't feel so bad immediately. I had the feeling that they only send inconvenient ones on such delegations. But I wasn't inconvenient; I could only be unnecessary. And at that moment, I wasn't looking forward to going home. I wanted to remain with everyone else, in Russia, to the end.

Meanwhile Štefánik went off to Omsk. I sent a telegram there, requesting that, instead of me, Jožo Gregor be sent, he being my superior. The answer I received in return from Pavlů read: 'The General understands your request as testimony to your amicable desire to remain in solidarity with your comrades at this difficult juncture. However, the reasons that determined the sending of the working commission have not changed. Dr J. will perform an important service in going along. The General awaits him, along with the others, in Omsk, in the near future. Let none lag behind. Pavlů.'

'He's a hard man, a hard man,' passed through my mind. 'What would happen if I decided not to obey him?'

So I didn't go along with the other members of the 'working commission' – as it was called in the telegram, instead of 'delegation' or 'deputation' – on the day indicated. Had I been bitten by the Bolshevik bug myself? Or what? Quite simply: I didn't want to go. But the other members of the commission were even bigger Bolsheviks. When I arrived at my office, it all looked as if the office had been tossed. Papers were scattered all over the floor. All the drawers had been picked through. The large crate, which they had prepared for us for the long journey: gone. They even took the tobacco and the cigarettes. It was this that saved me from disobeying the General's order.

So I chased off after my things to Omsk so as to catch up with the delegates. It was hard to find them among the crowd of so many wagons that cluttered the station. They were just getting ready for their audience with the minister when I found them.

Štefánik had taken one of his turns[218] and we were made to wait a long, long time on him in his train. At last, they let us

....

[218] In Slovak: *mal záchvat.* He seems to have had health problems; this

into his salon, where he was waiting for us. There we received our commissions. Dr Patejdl, who was supposed to head us, as the wisest one among us, was commissioned a first lieutenant, and the rest of us second lieutenants. Dr Patejdl stood at attention like a soldier while receiving his instructions from the General – as did we all. Later, when freely conversing with Štefánik, and I reminded the General that the Slovaks demanded that their orders be read to them in Slovak, he said:

'There is to be one language in the army,' at which he looked at me with such tired and annoyed eyes, that I clammed up.

He presented me with the Legionary Emblem of our state with some hesitancy.

'I don't have many left.'

As I was leaving, he grabbed me and gave me a quick kiss on the cheeks.

'Till we meet again,' I said to him.

'I'm not so sure we will.'

At the time, I took this as a passing mood, following his recent fit. After such a sudden turn of illness, we're readier to believe in death than life.[219]

We were in despair as to what sort of emblems we needed to sew onto our clothes so that it would be evident that we were officers. We found some yellow bands in a store, and with these we decorated our sleeves. Patejdl, as the highest in rank, got three, and the rest of us two. We couldn't be certain that this was correct, but the main thing was that we felt like generals.

It's all one now. Let it be however one wishes: from *szakaszvezető*[220] to 'just about, nearly, little was lacking for it'

....

means a sort of (unspecified) seizure.

[219] Štefánik, an aviator, was to die in an air catastrophe on 4 May 1919.

[220] Magyar: Sergeant.

ministerial chairman promoting major generals to lieutenant generals, to, in the end, being myself promoted by a general to second lieutenant with two yellow stripes and told to go home.

That's what a revolution is like.

All sorts of things happen on the road to freedom.

XV. HOME

We arrived in Yokohama on 17 January, around four in the afternoon. It was warm and sunny. It had taken us three days to get there from Vladivostok. It took about an hour for the paperwork to be completed before our old, Italian boat *Roma* was allowed into port. But then we passed the jetty and lowered anchor. The gangways were lowered. The captain came out onto the deck, forwards, and greeted the Italians who were waiting on shore. Then they came aboard, and along with them, a whole brood of agents, tailors, merchants and peddlers with all sorts of fandangles, postcards, little boxes, patterned cloth and albums. They set up shop and began hawking their wares.

Until they let us disembark, we walked around, gazing at these and at the shore. The port was a model of cleanliness. Rows of delivery vans constantly rolled up. Japanese with some sort of loops on their backs, in blue caftans, unloaded the goods with a fantastic alacrity. Japanese women stood near the sacks with needle and thread in hand to stitch up any that had been torn. Others, dressed in brighter colours, with high hair-dos, in wooden clogs, most of them carrying children, strolled about the shore. They kept their hands plunged into their broad sleeves and seemed unapproachable. But they looked at us, and we looked at them, both with curiosity.

Soon enough we went down the gangplank ourselves. In our Russian uniforms, with our gigantic *papakhas* on our heads, we made quite a sensation. Some people laughed at us; others smiled. We caused a panic among the children. At each step a rickshaw blocked our path, offering its services. These are Japanese fiacres, with which we'd already become familiar in Harbin. They are carts with two large wheels, with rubber tyres. You sit on the cart and the Japanese chap trots in front of you, wearing a hat that looks like a mushroom, dressed in short pants and – usually black – socks with rubber soles. At first, we were taken aback by the arrangement, thinking it demeaning for one man to pull around another like that, taking orders from him, dragging him wherever he pleased, and all for twenty sen an hour. On principle, we went about on foot most of the time, so as not to debase in this way the crown of creation, until we came to see that, in this way, we were depriving him of his meagre, hard-earned pay. Everyone was doing it, and here the five of us were being so sentimental…

We had a look around the Japanese mercantile quarter. After big, big Russia everything here seemed small: the Japanese, their little shops, their little homes. But there were a lot of goods, and everything inexpensive. Bright colours everywhere. The colours screamed at you, especially from the women and children's clothes. In the evening, when the lamps were lit, the streets look like they do back home when decorated for the holidays. In the pauses of the street traffic, all you heard was the constant rattle of those wooden sandals. Klep, klep, klep…

We found the Japanese women beautiful, but only the younger and prettier ones, with their slanted brows, their dark, doe-like eyes and yellowish cheeks. Although they loved dressing up, I never saw any wearing earrings. Yet there was hardly a single one without gold fillings. It was clear that their kimonos were their luxury items, as were the broad obis they wore wrapped around their kimonos as belts, and the satchels they carried on their backs. All of this was silk, and silk-embroidered. Their wooden sandals could also be parade-quality: here and there one saw toes of dark leather or lacquer and the straps that held them on were also of colourful silk. We were especially impressed with their towering coiffeurs and great hair-pins.

We wandered about for a long time on the following day too. We took ourselves up the hill into the European quarter. The streets here were narrow too. Free-standing houses in the Japanese style. Two small Gothic churches. Cold, proud, European ladies in rickshaws or automobiles. Quickly, we went back down among the smiling, polite Japanese. We were amused with them, and they with us, and we got along, even though we couldn't really communicate.

We also dared try out a Japanese restaurant. We were served by sixteen-year-old Eiko, who had a beautiful, narrow face. She accepted an apple from us and thanked us in English. She also accepted a half yen as a tip. Then she sat down with us at our invitation and drank the cup of coffee we offered her. Janík pulled out his camera and Eiko, all in a fluster of excitement that she was to be photographed, tore off the rose-coloured tape that gathered fast her sleeves, adjusted the obi that wrapped around her kimono, and fixed her hair in the mirror.

In the evening we went off to Yoshiwara. This is the red-light district. Two streets fully lined with shotgun barracks filled with Japanese girls. You enter through the gate and there, behind a lattice, just like in a shop window, crouch Japanese girls, undressed for all the world to see, keeping themselves warm around coal stoves. If you're not afraid, you can pick one out for yourself from among them. Although we were soldiers, we satisfied ourselves with just a look.

From Yokohama we took the train to Tokyo, the capital of Japan, a twenty-minute journey by rail. Only here and there along the short route were fields with vegetables, flowers, and trees to be seen. The cities themselves, with their buildings, are like one great city of two grown together. Arable land occupies only 25% of the country, it seems. Wheat is imported in gigantic amounts. Workers earn an average of one yen per day, but this seems to suffice for their modest needs. Their diet consists mainly of rice, with a little bit of meat. There are very few butchers; I saw only one shop with sausages. I also saw only one beggar. And he was singing – lamentably – for his supper.

We walked our legs to the knees in Tokyo. Whatever there was to see, we saw it; whatever there was to smell, we smelled it; whatever was offered as food, we ate it. We also went to a theatrical presentation. The theatre was a European building, with corridors, a cloakroom, and a restaurant, but the play was bizarre. They were putting on a tragedy of some sort. We understood that some great and powerful political lord had demanded a sacrifice from his rival, whom he had already shamefully overcome: his two children were to be beheaded. Off in the wings someone was twanging a single string, and that was supposed to be music; someone else was yowling, and that was supposed to be song. On the stage, the sorrowing family was lamenting, striking their foreheads upon the ground. Nearly all of the actors played their roles seated on the ground, and whenever they moved, they moved about on their knees. Only in the third scene did some of them sit on little stools. The actors left the stage over a plank. Some sort of knight arrived on horseback – a prop, of course. When he slid off his horse, he moved about just like our tragedians, in dactyls (one long, and two short steps). During changes of scene no curtain was lowered; the stage was rotated, mechanically. It must have been a sad story, for the audience wept, especially the Japanese ladies, who were gripping their handkerchiefs, with which they wiped away their tears.

We braved it out for three acts. When the hangman refused to behead the children, the audience sighed with relief, as did we.

Following the classical tragedy, it seems that they performed a comedy. According to Patejdl, it was quite in the European style, modern.

'I couldn't understand a thing, but my sides were splitting from laughter. It was a wonderful play. Very artistic' he said. And so we were sorry that we had been so impatient.

Between acts, the Japanese took supper in a great dining hall filled with flowers. Pink cherry-blossoms dominated.

We gave the Japanese cloakroom attendant half a yen for taking care of our wraps. She pushed the money away as a sign that she didn't want it. Somebody said that the Japanese don't steal, and that you can't give a person any more than he's asking. Strange nation.

One evening we were visited by our plenipotentiary, or ambassador, to Japan, Dr Němec. He told us all sorts of things. For example, that in Vladivostok Dr Girsa didn't take Štefánik's illness seriously. Štefánik was returning to France. He'd already reserved two cabins, it seemed, on a French ship.

'One dictator squeezing out another,' said someone from our delegation.

'Pavlů?' someone asked.

'Running away?' asked another.

A discussion ensued.

'He's leaving Pavlů behind in Russia, as the political plenipotentiary!'

'Pavlů's going to be leading our politics there, instead of the Branch!'

'Impossible!'

'Horrid!'

'Our entire mission is nothing but humbug!' cried Polák, the most left-leaning member of our delegation. 'Štefánik will beat us to it.'

'Indeed the information will be varied...' I thought to myself amidst the uproar.

A week or so after our arrival we found ourselves rocking on the open sea again. I felt dizzy; my head wasn't in great pain, but my stomach was fluttering.

JANKO JESENSKÝ

At the start of the journey, almost all of us showed up for dinner. Dávid had hardly touched the noodles he'd ladled out on his plate before he rose all of a sudden and went off even faster. A moment after him, it was Polák's turn. Maisner said he had to loosen his leather belt – it was too constraining. Since he didn't want to do that at table, he too went out…

'Where's Janík?' Patejdl asked me.

'He was here just now.'

Janík had vanished like a ghost, fork and all, I reckon.

'How's it with you?' I asked Patejdl.

'I took care of all that in the afternoon already.'

The dining room was half empty. None of the ladies were present. The waves calmed down when we arrived at the harbour in Kobe. There was less rolling, but more jerking and shaking, like on the Manchurian Railway. The queasy began to reappear and sit down at the laid tables.

We dropped anchor at sea, as we weren't permitted to enter the harbour. Supposedly, measles were raging in the city. We went on through the narrows, with mountain summits on both sides already free of snow. Little villages on the slopes of the hills. Sailboats were spread over the surface of the sea, along with three or four large ships. The arc light of the lighthouse swept near, and then away again. The ship rolled heavily. It was cold out on deck. On the deck chairs, the ladies shrank inside great fur coats. A group of newly-arrived passengers circled among them. Our attention was especially drawn to a fat man with a round stomach, wearing a monocle. He strutted up and down proudly, his cheeks spilling over his soft, clean collar. He would take off his monocle, spin it round his fingers by the band, and then place it back on his eye, just to take it off once more and repeat the procedure. It was as if he were practicing something. A blonde woman with a big nose laughed aloud and unnaturally. A heavy young lady sat there, lips trembling as she tried not to laugh, but the gentleman paid them no mind, and kept on with his production.

No one took any note of us, either, the *zavoyevateli*[221] of Siberia. In vain did Janík search his face in the mirror – thrice – to see if all was in order before he went out on deck; in vain did he parade about with camera, binoculars, Sam Brownes, *papakha*; it was all to no effect. Nor were linguistic gymnastics, loud, wise, important pronouncements, of any help.

'Alas for Russia! Alas for Verochka!' someone sighed.

All of us felt a little chilled at soul among these cultured, western, buttoned-up folks, the Italians and the French. We missed real Russians and, even more, 'nastoyashchaya russkaya devushka'[222] – with her gaiety, directness, modesty and beauty, such as those we would meet with from time to time in Russia. Such a girl would lift our spirits, a piece of Russia, a piece of Slavdom on the boat. We wouldn't be shaving ourselves in vain if such were the case!

Oftentimes, we were seized by a *toska*[223] for Russia. Everyone who leaves Russia, feels it sometime.

We then arrived at the harbour of Moji. We saw pleasing hills there, set in a semicircle, like a half-finished wreath. A big city at the foot of the hills. Factories were belching smoke; the smokestacks of ships were puffing too; the awnings of the barges flashed in the sun. Motorboats were speeding here and there, slicing the waves with their prows and leaving behind them long white wakes. The clever Japanese conducted trade with our ship from their boats, delivering their goods in baskets on long bamboo poles.

The ship took on coal. Just as at a construction site back home bricks are passed from hand to hand, so here, the Japanese men and women passed on coal in straw baskets. They also constructed scaffolding for this purpose. The work was

....

[221]   Russian: Conquerors.

[222]   Russian: A real Russian girl.

[223]   Russian: Yearning.

carried out with speed. The baskets were passed aboard our boat in bucket-brigade fashion.

I gazed for a long while at the crackling pace of the job they were doing.

Then Patejdl came up.

'Shall we go into the city?' I asked him.

'They won't let us.'

'Stupidity!'

'Some kind of cholera, everywhere.'

And still and all our Socialist comrades, along with the chief of our delegation, Patejdl, went.

'Why didn't you tell me you were going?' I asked our leader, grabbing hold of him. 'Weren't you afraid of cholera?'

'What for! And who had time to go looking for you? Stick by me.'

And thus the relations between us had become very relaxed. Kind of wild. Social manners and drawing room customs were jettisoned long ago as antediluvian rubbish. Everyone did what he wanted to do, and how he wanted to do it. I too cast off all my old manners that I'd accumulated over the space of forty years. No greetings when meeting in the morning. At dinner, I plunged right into the bowl of noodles; I'd even order sevenths, though the waiter's hands were trembling with fatigue. That's what servants are for, right? He could've been born a baron... I wiped my nose and my nape with my napkin. I constructed towers of roast, pyramids of apples, log cabins of bananas; I poured Italian wine into me from the bottle and sipped black coffee from tea saucers, with dozens of sugar cubes between my teeth. I'm not going to eat my fill when the State's paying the bill? I never went back to my berth without first filling my pockets before getting up from the table. It was all so beautiful, natural, and exhilarating! I trampled the fetters of social falsity beneath my heels. Bourgeois custom squirmed in pain beneath my feet.

'What's that there stupid wop steaming about over there?' Maisner once asked me.

'He can kiss my arse,' Dávid answered on my behalf.

It wasn't advisable to touch dry land. After each such foray, after each stop, seasickness might return. A person might think that seasickness comes along only once, and when you're past it, it's gone for good. Wrong. You can get seasick even twenty times over.

After leaving Moji the Roma swung like a dancing girl. Nose up, backside up, from right to left and left to right, five or six metres each time. The waves rushed and crashed at the windows of the first class cabins, and across the deck. We were now sailing the most agitated sea – the China Sea. Brother Janík was overcome at once and fled to his berth. There were only two of us at dinner. Maisner wanted at least to have a sniff at the first course. So he sniffed, and then he left. Polák and Dávid were moaning somewhere out of sight. In a word, history was repeating itself. My head was spinning. I slept poorly and had nightmares: I was constantly getting married, yet I already had a wife! This caused me great fear: had my wife died? I kept asking everyone about this. Few of those I queried gave me a straight answer, and those who did said straight out: She's dead. I cried as if my heart were breaking until Štěpán woke me and asked me what the matter was. But then I fell asleep again, and in my dreams I was visited by dead people.

All of this was due to the rolling of the ship. I gazed out the window. Now they were full of the sea, and a moment later, the sky. The wind whistled and the waves were foaming. Whole lines of dolphins were cutting through the water, arching again and again their black backs above the waves before diving down once more into the depths. The farther away we were from land, the fewer and fewer were the gulls. The sailboats had disappeared long ago. Fujiyama and the other Japanese summits, which had accompanied us for a long while, were gone now, too. The only things to be seen were sea, sky, and the few people on the boat. Sea-boredom settled in. When I was already sick of lying in my berth I went out on deck. Time dragged on as slowly as the Roma. One ate, slept, gaped, read, smoked cigars and cigarettes, slurped at cognac now and again, ate one's fill of mandarins, swallowed a few almonds, a few clusters of Malaga grapes, broke off a slice of chocolate. One sat and listened to the piano. You knew it was a thin, pale, agreeable Italian woman playing, the wife of some officer, with two children, a boy and a girl. The officer would sing, or rather growl, to her accompaniment. He was miffed at us; we should be ashamed of ourselves that none of us savages played any instrument, and we from a nation so famed for its musicians! Sometimes, Patejdl would try to sing in a tenor voice as thin as a thread, but no one knew how to accompany him, either by vocal harmony, or at the piano. Janík sang a lot, whenever he wasn't seasick. Maisner buzzed along in vague, weak accompaniment, while I aided with my shoemaker's bass. Dávid and Polák sat quietly and listened:

> She was all rosy and white;
> She kissed me all through the night;
> She was all rosy and white;
> She to me some troth did plight,
> My sweet and lovely Báruška...

We played cards to kill time. I pulled out my French grammar and began learning French for the ninth or tenth time in my life. But just as eight or nine times before, I set it aside again, as soon as I learned that *mais* is pronounced *mé*, which means something totally different in Slovak than it does in French.[224] Too big a contrast.

....

[224] In Slovak, it is onomatopoetic for bleating ('baa').

We were all in good health. The waves grew small and the ship sailed on silently over a sea as yellow as clay. It rocked us only now and then. The weather changed. Rain and fog. It became unpleasant in the cabins, muggy. We were drawing close to Shanghai.

We didn't even feel it when the ship anchored at the buoy, invisible in the fog. Towards evening the fog lifted, and there appeared to our eyes a city full of lights, and above it a rosy glow, as if of a fire. A light snow was swirling above the sea. It was unpleasantly cold and clammy.

We hurried off into the city, not even waiting for breakfast. We exchanged our yens and roubles. Twenty-five yen got us twelve dollars and fifty Chinese groschen – one thousand roubles got one hundred dollars. Ah, the poor rouble! Clunk! English was spoken in the English and Chinese shops. It was easier for us to communicate using gestures, like the deaf and dumb, than for Patejdl, who walked about with a phrasebook and read out the most important questions. His pronunciation must have sounded Swedish or Scottish.

We searched out the most elegant restaurant, the 'Hotel Palace.' Someone had told us where to go when we cocked our heads like magpies and Janík pointed at his mouth and said:

'Ham, ham, ham!'

And soon we were seated in a lift and, a moment later, in a great dining-room, where we had a dinner both expensive and foul.

Once, in our looking around the Chinese city, we went too far. We wore our eyes out on figures of all sorts – inscriptions, signs, lampposts; we'd lost our way. We tried to communicate with the rickshaw cabbies, to get us back. But which way?

'K more!'[225]

They couldn't understand.

....

[225] Slovak: 'To the sea!'

'Mare.'

Nothing.

'Meer.'

Again, nothing.

'How do you say *more* in English?'

Nobody knew. We tried Magyar. Maybe they're related to the Magyars.

'Tenger.'

They had no idea what that was. Patejdl wasn't with us. We could've used his phrasebook now.

'How stupid are those Chinamen!' Janík growled, angrily.

Then he spit on the pavement and tried to explain, pointing to his spit and swaying with his arms, as if to indicate 'sea,' the great, broad sea.

'They won't get that,' I said. 'Too sublime a style.' And I pulled some postcards out of my wallet.

One of them showed a ship on the ocean. I pointed at the ship and said:

'Fu, fu, fu...'

The Chinese man laughed with joy. He slapped his palm against his forehead. He got it! And he set off at a trot straight for the sea.

When we got to the ship we learned that Štefánik was in Shanghai. He was on his way to France, just as they'd told us in Yokohama. Supposedly, Dr Němec was with him too, having arrived in his wake.

So we went to pay him a visit: Patejdl, Janík and me. He was lying in bed. He said that he was ill, but his movements were fresh and his voice strong. He told us that he was on his way to France and began philosophising about democracy.

'Democracy rests in the nobilitation of man, in his betterment. That he should be the best – aristos. In this sense, democracy means spiritual aristocracy.'

This was the prelude to a dressing-down. He said that someone in our delegation had called him a monarchist.

'When we get back home, and we all gather together, we'll speak straight from the shoulder to one another. We'll have a nice exchange of ideas,' he remarked bitterly.

We all tried to guess who it might be who he was referring to. Janík, Polák, and Maisner certainly spoke against Štefánik from time to time, but I never heard them use that word. I thought back to a conversation on the ship in Yokohama. Who was intriguing here?

Štefánik was angry with Dr Girsa, too. In my heart I asked myself who had riled him up against that splendid man, who so cared for us when we were high and dry without money in Harbin.

After a conversation that lasted about an hour, interrupted three times by visitors, he dismissed us.

That evening we were the guests of a fellow-countryman named Jedlička, who was, or was to be, nominated consul in Shanghai. He set out a diplomatic spread. There was a little of everything – just a little. Wine, but a little. Champagne, but a little. And everything was quick, quick, quick. Official, and cool. We didn't even have a chance to warm up. No one there was cordial or nice.

Here we learned that Dr Hess had been appointed political plenipotentiary for eastern Russia, and was supposed to have his office in Harbin. Supposedly, the Czechs did battle with the Magyars near Bratislava.[226] With what success – no one knew. In Bohemia, the editorial offices of the *Práva lidu*[227] had been demolished.

Late at night, we returned home. On the way back to the boat the Socialists were all in a lather:

'Hess, political plenipotentiary!'

....

[226] Jesenský uses the city-name Prešporok here, which was the Slovak name of the city until 1919.

[227] Czech: People's Right.

'Laughable!'

'Shameful!'

The next day was Chinese New Year (1 February). Shanghai was white with snow. All the stores were closed. The streets were full of holiday revellers; Chinese music could be heard in the streets and spilling out of the houses. Dragons, crawling up to the porches, were chased away with firecrackers. So much banging, it sounded like the front. Chinese lovelies in silk jackets, trousers, and slippers with bows, some on rickshaws, some in broad fiacres, others on foot. Driving and strolling by. The variety of bright colours. Fat bankers, dandies in little hats with a button on the top, in silk caftans and aprons to the ankles. The poorer beggars and labourers weren't in such trousers – only the lordlier ones.

We walked among them, adding to the chaos and the uproar. We went into the 'New World,' which is something like a small Vienna Prater, with all sorts of games, rides, little menageries, museums, a circus, and eating places.

A much more entertaining evening than that spent with Jedlička was awaiting us. Our countryman Engel invited us to a little Chinese banquet. His wife is Chinese. She even dared sit down at table with us, which supposedly real Chinese women never do. Pale, slender, with black hair and eyes, smiling, in a little dress, silk jacket, diamond earrings. She urged us to eat in a very homely manner, seeing to everything, concerned about all, of simple and pleasant manners.

We were given manifold bowls of fish, mushrooms, vegetables, ham, cups filled with rice, and soup in a great Chinese tureen. We took a bit of everything and ate it with rice, sometimes placing it right in the rice cups and eating it, though it wasn't very appealing. They gave us long sticks to eat with, but none of us knew how to work them. So they gave us our plain old forks. At the end of our dinner, we were offered napkins soaked in hot water, with which we were to wipe our face and hands. And then we took coffee in another room, with cognac and a strong Chinese liquor with a strange, unpleasant flavour. It was a happy, warm, family-like evening, and we were in a wonderful mood beside the cheery fireplace with coffee and cigarettes.

Some high-placed Chinese official, in eyeglasses, from some ministry, was also there. Conversation was carried out in English, Chinese, and Czech.

We saw no one but policemen on our way back to our ship. Those Indians in their red turbans are the ornaments of the city. Their beards are red, too; all of them are tall, well-built, good-looking chaps. Poor fellows, freezing outside in the snow, which never stopped falling. It was cold for us, too. The only ones sweating were those pulling the rickshaws, dragging around their clients for pennies. We were taken across the harbour to the ship on little boats. The boatmen had all been waiting on their fares, drowsing in their little ferryboats amid the pens. Our teeth were chattering with the cold just like back then in Siberia. But there, the winter is dry, sunny, and there's somewhere to go to get warm. Nothing of the sort on the ship. The sun shone on one side of the deck, it's true, but a cold, sharp wind was always blowing.

The sea changed colour. From clay-yellow it again became dark green. We left the China Sea behind. Ventilating fans were installed. The canaries in the berth of the kitchen mate began singing gaily. They said that before long we'd be passing into the tropics. We celebrated Candlemas on the open sea. Snow never ceased falling into the greenish water.

'How beautiful it must be now, in Russia,' I thought, walking about the deck. Once more, the warm-hearted soul of the Russians came to my mind as I strolled around. The soul glows in the cruellest Siberian winters, to warm you. I reminisced about all that 'ukhazhivaniye, uvlecheniye, lyubov… A ved lyubov ne rassuzhdayet… Zhit tak, kak kho-chetsya…'[228] I sat down in the penumbra of the salon and brooded.

…A cold, bright night. Two of us, at midnight, returning from an evening at Lina Ivanovna's. We felt like students; I like a young, carefree, unattached fellow who kisses the lips of a young woman. Her cap falls to the snow. To hear such words whispered:

'Kak skuchno budet, kak strashno!'[229]

You bend down for the cap, replace it on her dark head; you gaze into those dark eyes and once more the little cap falls to the ground.

'Da, da, skuchno budet. Eto verno…'[230]

And now! Sea-boredom. You've got time enough to brood over what was, and what shall be… We always dread what is to happen, what's waiting on us, for it's unclear, uncertain. A joy that fears, and, added to that fear, regret at what's been lost.

That's what you call love for Russia. And just as all of us individuals feel sadness thinking of Russia, so will our whole nation feel sad, when Russia perishes.

'Yes, boredom. And longing!'

This Candlemas sentimentality of mine was accompanied by the monotonous hum of the engine.

The waves splash, cling to the window, darkening it, before slipping down to spume aloft again, smashing apart and falling in droplets, as if they were snorting in anger at the boat for pressing them down and pushing them aside. Near and far: white trails, white tatters of foam. A March wind.

....

[228] Russian: 'Courtship, infatuation, love… You know, love does not reason… Live the way you want to live.'

[229] Russian: 'How boring it will be, how horrid.'

[230] Russian: 'Yes, yes, boring it shall be. That's for sure…'

Once again the sea changed colour, becoming greyish, as if it were again to turn the shade of clay. Far off to the right we caught sight of some dark blue hills. This told us that we were now past Formosa, the graveyard of the Russian fleet during the Russo-Japanese War. The ship began to rock again, and yet the wind had ceased blowing some time ago. It was like a storm on a clear day. The air had calmed down, but not the sea. The rocking was so strong that things began to slide around and fall. In our cabin, which was below deck, we looked directly out onto the sea through our windows whenever the ship rolled that way. There was a constant banging to be heard.

But we had already grown accustomed to the rolling, and didn't feel dizzy any more. We got our sea-legs too. We didn't have to hold onto railings and posts. When needed, one's leg shortened of its own accord and one kept one's balance. Even the women were up and about. The young governess was laughing now, and the fat Russian woman was waddling over the deck like a duck. Only the blonde with the big nose and the Italian woman with her swaddled head were nowhere to be seen. The dining room was full of children. Chaotic clamour.

The sea became black. Only when the waves rose and thinned did the water turn a beautiful dark green. It started to get close and hot in the cabins. Sweat began to pour down our faces in streams. The fan that had been brought out didn't work. I slept half-naked under a bedsheet. I bathed in a tub, but the water was tepid and the bathroom stuffy, too. The best one could do was to sit in the shade on the highest deck without moving at all, for every movement of your arm brought forth new floods of sweat. We didn't even want to talk. We'd already exhausted all our storehouse of thought concerning Russia, Germany, Bohemia-Moravia, Socialism, western culture, which isn't worth a jot, or hasn't proven itself worth anything, and eastern culture, which is the future. We'd already knocked the Lord God off His throne, declaring Him to be a mere human invention; we'd chased the soul from the body, stating that it's nothing more than the working of the brain and the circulation of the blood, and yet we packed off all of our diplomats to Hell, with Štefánik the dictator at the head of them all. I already understood perfectly what collectivism was, and individualism, party, democracy, demagoguery. I learned the faults of every person, their private lives, who is a bastard, how one fights at meetings, how to pull a chair out from under a person when he rises to speak, how to envy a white collar and a chain of gold on a vest, how to crave the life of a lord. I was convinced as to what constituted progress and what reaction. I now knew that we were the only true progressives, and that all the rest were crooks. None of this rhymed with democracy as expounded by Štefánik in Shanghai, but then again Štefánik was nothing but a bourgeois.

We stopped talking on account of the heat and because we'd already run out of things to say, and still Singapore was nowhere to be seen. Five days passed, six, seven, and all around us there was nothing but water, water, water, and above, a sky with a blistering sun. We were agitated. We drank a lot of red wine. One fine day we exploded again – flaming out at Patejdl.

'Patejdl! Patejdl! What've you gotten us into? We're travelling right around the world, almost; we've been gone for half a year, and still we see nothing, we experience nothing, we learn nothing…'

'That's what happens when some farmer boy takes charge of things! He'd like to get everything for free, or at least cut-rate. Lunch is cheap, but it won't fill your stomach! The skin-flint. A ripped shirt, but three yens in the pocketbook. Baggy trousers, but a belt'd cost money! How he rejoices when he dickers down the price of a piece of silk to fifty cents, after a half hour of haggling! Or when he can wheedle a poor rickshaw-man out of sixpence…'

'O, niggling, small-minded wretches, whose chief idol is a golden calf in a rickety, dirty tabernacle, bitching when hungry, bitching when thirsty. What else have to you jabber at your graven image?'

'Where is Singapore, chief? Damn you!'

'We can't take this swelter any longer!'

'What's up with the fan?'

'What – no vegetables?!'

'How come they don't open the windows to let in a little breeze?'

'It's like a sauna in here.'

'Hotter every day... How long will this continue?'

'You call this boat fit for the tropics? It's hellish...! Was this your idea? To boil us alive...? How come you didn't arrange some sort of fast, express, luxury ship?'

In a word, it was mutiny. Our flesh was melting. To top it all off, the captain ordered that jackets and footwear must be worn in the dining room. Men had begun showing up in shirts unbuttoned to the navel, displaying their hairy chests for all to see, wearing slippers on sockless feet. The ladies, surely, were scandalised. For only they have the privilege of being undressed in public.

I took my Russian bedclothes and roamed at night up to the highest deck. There I made my bed on a bench. You could feel a sort of breeze up here. The nights were beautiful; the moon was waxing. Everything shone in its light, especially the sea. I would fall asleep up there, gazing at the light, with the sound of the benign, soft waves in my ears.

At last, in front of the ship, we caught sight of a narrow defile. To the right were several large ships, and a city stretching at the foot of low, green hills arranged in a semicircle. And above the city, smoke and dust again.

Singapore.

All we did in Singapore was bathe. In the tropical warmth, we wanted to give our warm Russian clothes and *papakhas* a good shake. Little remained in our memories of Singapore except for the huge British mercantile stores. You could walk into one bare, thirsty, and hungry, and leave well-dressed, full, and drunk. Before us there paraded the British, Siamese, and Malayans; whites, chocolate-coloured folk, and blacks, with white streaks painted on their brows and arms, as if someone had smeared them with lime. They had women's hair-dos. We wouldn't have been able to distinguish their sexes if it were not for the nose-pieces, which supposedly only women are allowed to wear. Otherwise, everyone was in togas tossed over their backs and stomachs, in screaming bright colours. Some of them walked along proudly, with a serious mien, like chocolate versions of Roman senators. Half-naked rickshaw-men, boatmen, Japanese, Cathayans. An immense park with tall palms and clean, broad alleys. Enough.

Plantations of rubber trees, bamboo fields, and forests; we hadn't enough time measured out to us to make the rounds of the palace of the King of Siam, the museums, and the churches. We wanted to go to the theatre, and to bathe, but we had to rush, because the boat was to set sail at six that afternoon.

But even so we got a lot done: in one day we all were so transformed from head to toe that we had to introduce ourselves to one another again.

I (donkeys to the front), Janík and Polák all had panama hats, and we were all in white. Patejdl bought himself a huge British pith helmet and bamboo cane. He was dressed up as yellow as a canary. Maisner was now dressed in white, now in yellow, a bourgeois as the day is long. Janík also bought himself a bamboo cane, so that, back on the sea, he could show how he had rushed at the enemy during the war. Only poor Polák had to remain in his military uniform, because he couldn't button his shirt without buttons – and these he had forgotten to buy.

It was only then that I realised how impressive a military uniform can be. Where before I had seen generals, now before me there stood only very simple people, grey, dime-a-dozen civilians. Our leader Patejdl always seemed to have some dirty string dangling out from his pants cuffs or shirt, where none was to be found before, even when he was walking around in slippers.

We were heading to Colombo.

Before us, on a high mountain, our eyes were fooled by a trick of the light. It was as if someone were raising a fiery torch three times, again and again, after short breathers, now in front of us, now to the right, now from behind, and on and on, as long as you didn't tire of looking.

To our left was Sumatra with its tall, active volcano smoking. Otherwise, the hills of Sumatra are not that high; half-bald, with angular summits and slopes, gentle, not so steep. Then, farther on, to the left, in front, there was another range of mountains, and, jutting beyond their saddles, other, paler highlands and mountains.

Again more passengers embarked. There was hardly room to stroll around the deck now. Chairs were set up everywhere and on each some lady or some consul was stretched out. A lot of children. Shrill squalling. I could no longer walk about with Janík, listening to his fiery words, without having to grab that arm of his (with the bamboo cane) so that he shouldn't strike some majesty with it, unawares; without having to watch our step so as not to trip against the lounging women's legs that were stretched out everywhere, as not a single one of them drew their gams out of the way. Finally, we just came across all manner of gooey, disgusting tenderness of petting couples. You don't need seasickness to feel your stomach turn.

Even Patejdl fumed:

'How come they don't require a dress code for the deck as well as the dining room? …Shameless beasts, sprawling around like that… Just look how that goat over there is pawing her… And that one over there with the big behind and her tits flopping about in that light dress of hers! Hemline above the knees, and legs like logs... She got no other way of chafing her cavalier? ...How many abominable skirts everywhere, how many females...'

'The grapes are out of reach, and so they must be sour,' commented Dávid. 'Otherwise you'd be all aflame yourself, if one of those prima donnas, one of those signorinas, turned a tender glance your way.'

'We look shady to them,' said Janík. 'Slavs are as welcome to the Italians, and Italians to Slavs, as the knife is to the goat – and all because of Yugoslavia. What the hell do we care about them? And yet they still think of themselves as Romans.'

At last, a wind began to blow about the deck and births. We caught it in our ventilator fans and all of them began spinning. But the wind wasn't a dry one. Everywhere: mugginess, humidity. You pulled the crate out from underneath your cot – it was hot, as was everything inside it. This was no cabin worthy of former 'ministers.' We got the worst berths, which in proper times would be assigned to servants. But the whole boat was like a veteran, down at the heels, worn seams splitting. And veins. The old pipes of the Roma were knocking all the time, and water was dripping and splashing; now from above, now from below. We were in the lower decks, which were always being flooded. Štěpán was constantly running around with a rag.

Very soon thereafter there appeared on the dark blue, fairly smooth sea, boats, white sails, misty summits. We were approaching Ceylon, and the city of Colombo.

Here we stopped only for the night, leaving the next morning at 10:30. We were ordered to be back on board no later than 9:30. We took a boat across the harbour early in the morning. We had a look at Victory Park, the pagoda with the three Buddhas – large, medium, and small – and each cost a shilling to inspect. The guide stuck out his hand: 'Shilling.'

The Indian children came up and pushed some sort of flowers and twigs into our hands: 'Shilling.'

Polák, of course, bought some little elephants, embroidery, tea, coffee, soap, clothes, cards, and it so happened that when we were returning to the boat the captain already knew from afar who it was approaching. Well, let him think what he likes, let him leave us here on Ceylon collecting elephants and stripping the tea and coffee plantations, as, supposedly, he did in the case of a few invalids, whom he left behind on the island.

In Singapore and Colombo we paraded around so that the invalids who were travelling with us under the care of brother Major Jirásek began to get envious, and griped that we were travelling like barons: we had nice clothes and boots, we ate in the dining room and slept in private berths. They didn't give a thought to who we were once, who we were now, and who we might become. They wanted equality. The brother Socialists began to scratch their heads. All this didn't quite fit their Socialist programme. The invalids were right. But instead of giving up their berths to them, they said that even democracy has bitter pills and these must be swallowed...

The time came for us to divide up the photographs that Patejdl was to distribute, fairly, among us. These were photos of our military and political life from Kiev to Vladivostok. I requested a complete collection for the National Museum in Martin. Maisner, Polák and Dávid were opposed to the idea. Even Maisner sniped at me:

'What is Slovakia, anyway? Does it have its own government, or what?'

I looked closely at him to see if he was serious. He was.

'I can't help you now, if you're so stupid as not to know what Slovakia is. I suppose you've never been to school. You ought to take a little trip from Bratislava to Užhorod, since you don't know... Idiot!' I cut him, speaking to him as we'd grown used to. 'You can shuffle cards, but not ideas. We're talking about pictures, not governments... Blockhead!'

According to the minutes, the division took place mainly out of regard for Slovakia, but all the brothers took their share, although all of them already had complete collections, which they'd received back in Yekaterinburg. Only Patejdl was so decent as to give me his share. The minutes were falsified. But God be with the minutes, and all those greedy brothers as well! For all that, the rather awkward thought occurred to me: if this is what all the divisions and sharing are to be like from now on in our Republic, it doesn't bode very well for us.

The seas provided some fireworks for this quiet quarrel of ours, phosphorescing. Dots of light here and there. Some said this was from fish; others, from bugs.

We went along as if sliding over oil. The sea was smooth, without foam; it was no longer battering the ship as before; it stroked and petted it. You could hardly hear the waves. Fish flew up from time to time, a metre and a half above the surface of the water. Some of these were greyish, others black with a little white belly, like swallows. The purple calixes, with which the sea was decorated, glowed at night, slowly bobbing on the waves. Maybe that's where the phosphorescence was coming from. Nobody knew how to explain it to us. The canaries in their cages veritably exploded with their chirping in the pleasant mornings.

Off to the right, far away in the mist, our eyes were met with a small, roughhewn, rocky shore. Probably the islet of Abdul-Kuli or Sokotra. According to the map, we were about to enter a bay, the narrow straits of which lead to the Red Sea. Then, to the left, was Massawa, the Italian province of Abyssinia.

Towards evening, Africa emerged from the calm surface of the sea. An immense, blocky cliff with slopes falling away abruptly. Behind it, a third headland. The sun was setting behind it. To the right, the steep summits of the islands soared upwards.

The shore grew distant once again. To the right was nothing but sea, and far to the left, the pale silhouettes of the mountains of Africa. Suddenly, as if slit away with a knife, the sea changed colour. From dark to bright green, at once.

We entered the Red Sea.

We anchored at Massawa. The ship was pulled up right at the shore. The port hadn't yet been completed. The buildings were oriental in style, with shutters covering windows without glass panes, flat garrets without sloping roofs. All around, the same sort of rugged mountains. There was hardly any green to be seen anywhere. Although some of the buildings were beautiful, large, everywhere there was a sort of emptiness, a vacuum, poverty. The natives had skinny arms and legs; you could see their ribcages; they went about half naked. They grabbed at the bread we tossed to them from the ship, devouring it greedily. There were Arabs to be seen, dressed in white, and Arab women, with their faces masked, black women with half-covered faces and ornaments in their noses; Abyssinian women with rings on their black fingers and bracelets on their legs.

The Abyssinian quarter was supposedly one big bordello. They lived here only from the sale of their bodies. We were told to be careful – disease was rampant.

I went into the quarter in the forenoon. It was like a ghost town.

We also visited a neighbouring Abyssinian village. Gypsy huts and little houses plastered together, hovels of boards and mud. The whole nation was wretchedly thin and poor. There we also came across some Abyssinian women all dressed up, with more skin on their bones, ornaments in their noses, rings, bracelets on necks, wrists and ankles. They smiled at us, but – careful!

We were delighted at how good the little boys were at swimming. They stayed afloat for hours on the surface of the sea, like corks. They plunged beneath the waves, diving deep to retrieve coins tossed in the ocean.

Walking along the shore we collected a little bag of shells, fossils, and various snail whorls before returning to the ship.

We were still asleep when the ship set out again.

The weather changed. A cool wind was blowing and we put on our military clothes again. The summits of Sinai, Suez – the Suez Canal, through which we travelled some twelve hours to Port Said, between bare sandy hillocks, from which the wind sprayed a thin yellow sand. Here and there we saw rows of palm trees – oases. It was a sad sight. It was good that we more or less stopped at Port Said.

'Aren't we going to see the pyramids, the sphinxes, the obelisks, Cairo, Alexandria?' I asked Patejdl.

'Hell! Pyramids?'

'You're the leader. You have to be such a naysayer?'

'So, go if you want to go. No one's stopping you.'

We didn't go. Janík and I visited the Arab quarter where the Arab women were all dressed in black, with faces covered and pirns on their noses. All you could see were their dark eyes: sparkling, gay, cloudy. It was the eyes told us which of them were old, which young, which beautiful – and which not. Some of them went about barefoot, other were in slippers; here and there we saw dark silk stockings. We saw Arabs wearing red fezzes; outside of that they were dressed like us. We went to a minaret, where they had us place great straw slippers on our feet. And then whatever majolica tile, whatever Koran, whatever old picture of Mecca you wanted to inspect – a shilling each. And then outside again the boys were summoning us to their 'Margarets,' grabbing at our legs, urging a shoeshine, offering cigarettes, little pictures, little trifles. Like a swarm of wasps. We couldn't beat them away.

We visited Lesseps, who dredged the Suez Canal and got a statue in return. He stood there high upon the pier, bewhiskered, half-bald, holding a paper upon which was written: *Aperire terram gentibus.*[231] The water lapped at his pedestal, at the shattered rocks and over the balustrade onto the pier. On the banks, Arabs were netting fish. There were a lot of English soldiers on the pier in their light summer khakis. In the café I saw a lot of them drunk.

Janík bought so many kimonos it was as if he had four wives at home. I supplied myself with enough Egyptian tobacco to last me half a year.

In the news, we read of the Yugoslav-Italian conflict over Trieste and Dalmatia. They wrote that the Yugoslavs were mobilising.

Nathan, an Italian poet, otherwise a Jew, an acquaintance from the ship, asked us where our sympathies lay, with the Serbs or the Italians. His nom-de-plume was Pierro Jacchia.[232] He gave me his *Il Nascituro*[233] to read, but it was all Italian to me. He promised to send me his work. He wrote down my address and promised to keep in touch.

'All beautiful, and all lies,' I thought to myself. 'I know a beautiful mask when I see it. I can wait!'

How many writers have I met who made promises like that. And no one ever sent me anything. There's three possibilities here: either that's a nation that doesn't keep its word, or it's a forgetful nation, or a nation that doesn't keep its word and forgets about everything.

Besides that Italian, we got familiar with a hefty young lady whom we named the 'fat Russian.' She liked to speak

---

[231] Latin: Open the land to the nations.

[232] Or Piero Jacchia. According to the University of Barcelona's International Brigade files, he was born in Trieste in 1883, and died at the rank of Major of the Garibaldi Brigade (Brigada XII) in the Spanish Civil War in 1937. As profession, 'poet' is listed: <https://sidbrint.ub.edu/es/content/jacchia-piero> (accessed 27 November 2021).

[233] Italian: *The Unborn Child.*

JANKO JESENSKÝ

with Dávid, the best-looking young fellow among us. Lately, she had been spending three fourths of the year in Japan.

'There's nothing decent there,' she said of Japan. 'Everything's beautiful, but only on the surface. The beauty fades quickly. The only beautiful views are in March when the cherry blossoms are in bloom. Beautiful petals, but no aroma...'

She was right. The things they sold us were also beautiful, but only skin deep. The tobacco boxes already went black, the chains rusty, the mother of pearl on the albums darkened, and just a couple of weeks before everything had been so beautiful, shiny, gold and opalesque...

'What is it? Why are we turning?'

'We can't go past Messina at night.'

'Why not?'

'Underwater mines.'

'So, late again.'

'Again.'

'Devil take him!'

We'd been cruising the Mediterranean for some time now, at a stately pace, quietly, twelve miles an hour. The days were beautiful. The mornings were cool, spring mornings. We passed by Crete and saw its high, snowy summits, and then they were gone.

When we were near Syracuse we sent a telegram to our political plenipotentiary in Rome, asking him to reserve a 'special' wagon for us and another for our baggage.

The head waiter warned us that travel in Italy was a bad affair.

'Railways are few and crowds are huge,' he said.

'Just as in Russia. There, everybody had his own train, except the Russians.'

A response arrived; our telegram had reached Rome. General Štefánik enquired as to our health and whether we'd arrived in Naples yet. He also enquired about the invalids and Major Jirásek. The General was to be in Marseilles on 12 March, one day after we'd arrived in Naples.

We started packing.

Chests, baskets, boxes, valises, and bales – we had one hundred five pieces of baggage. We'd left Yokohama with a little pile of things, and since then, this had grown into a mountain range. Silk, kimonos, vases, books, atlases, albums, gadgets, leather items, snuff boxes, wallets and purses, bracelets, chains and fobs, bamboo, elephants, coffee, tea, sugar, tobacco, linen. You could hardly squeeze your way into the cabin on account of the crates and bundles. And the funny thing was – the less important the politician, the more stuff he had!

But now we caught sight of some huge snowless summits. We passed Messina without any explosions. Messina is a large town set between the mountains, on the shore. Lots of ruins on account of earthquakes. Etna revealed herself to our eyes, to the waist. Further on, to the left, a city of lighthouses. To the right, a village with a railway station on the very seashore, among caves. The cliff of Scylla soaring aloft. Behind it, the small city half in ruins. Then the straits. The tall funnel of the volcano, with its cap of smoke on its head, rising straight from the sea. At night it emitted fiery clouds. Strombolo...

Naples!

We arrived early on the morning of 11 March.

They didn't let us ashore. Everybody was disembarked except for us. Our cabins were locked shut and we stood there on the deck agape with shock.

'We're not invalids,' we stated.

'We're on a mission. To heads of state.'

'We're former members of the Czechoslovak National Council Branch in Russia.'

'They're Bolsheviks,' the Italians whispered among themselves, as we later learned.

It was Polák who was suspected of Bolshevism, and we along with him.

'That's because of what you jabbered in Yokohama.'

'Remember how bitter Štefánik was in Shanghai?'

'When Dr Němec visited the General...'

Revenge seemed to be circling the ship like a black owl, instead of white gulls. She alighted on the boat and hooted ominously. And so this is why the Italians were so cool to us on the ship... So there you have it! The gloomy owl threw herself upon us mice in the name of the Czechoslovak Republic.

One more insult.

They told us that a telegram arrived saying that Polák was not to proceed to Prague, but to Paris.

'General Štefánik wants to have a word with you,' Patejdl told him.

'I won't go!' Polák shook his head. A search was made of his luggage, and that of Dávid. It was evening before we set foot on dry land and found ourselves in a wagon – a *teplushka* of the medical train that had been sent to Prague for the invalids. Following 'first class' travel, in cabins with all the comforts, we got our 'special' wagon – intended 'for six horses or twelve persons.' There was room enough; we were only five.

Among our leftists the griping resumed:

'We're not invalids.'

'We're part of a mission.'

'We were just about ministers.'

'We need a special wagon, one for us and another for our luggage.'

And thus we made our way to Rome, 'insulted and humiliated.'[234] We were set up in the Parque Hotel and here we demanded to travel by special train. How would it look if we 'grandees' arrived in Prague in a cattle-wagon?

....

[234] The title of an 1861 novel by Fyodor Dostoyevsky.

Then Polák was called before some Roman big shot, where he was told that he was not to leave Rome.

'Greetings, Liberty!'

We started getting angry. We filed a protest with our political plenipotentiary. We categorically stated that Polák won't be going to any Paris. First he was coming to Prague with us, and then, maybe.

'This is what you call democracy? This is spiritual aristocracy? Revenge? "Die Rache ist süss, aber gemein,"'[235] one of us quoted. 'How stupid it is to honour people with martyrdom. Polák is some sort of danger to our republic? The poor wretch!'

We were all disgusted.

We had a hard time getting a coupé for ourselves, then we headed off for home with our heads hanging low. And from Austria on, we were persecuted by poverty. No sugar, tea, coffee, or meat to be had. From Innsbruck on there wasn't even any bread.

At the threshold of the Republic we were told that we wouldn't be taken any farther. We had to telegraph to Budějovice for a locomotive. It arrived.

Not having bathed since Rome, exhausted with lack of sleep, we slipped beneath some colourful eiderdowns in Budějovice, which were narrow and short – if you covered your shoulders, your feet stuck out, if your back, then your knees...

'You fall asleep a great man, and wake up a dwarf. Everything will seem small to a man who's tasted greatness, even a republic,' passed through my head.

There'll be quite a few of us tiny grandees or big dwarves, who will want to keep warm.

We were met in Prague by soldiers. Patejdl greeted them:

....

[235] German: 'Revenge is sweet, but common.'

'Cheers!'

'Cheers!'

And off we went in cars to the Hotel Gráf on Komenského Náměstí, where our lodgings were first-rate.

We had an audience with the President.

Smiling and gracious, he had us sit down. Patejdl began with the memorandum we'd composed on the ship and had all signed, concerning Polák.

'Is this your work, Doctor?'

Patejdl nodded in agreement.

As the conversation progressed, our leftists poured out their gripes concerning all the little insults they'd suffered. They complained of Štefánik for dissolving the Branch, for meeting with Kolchak, for trying to have Polák arrested; they whined that Pavlů was unbearable, just like Dr Němec in Japan and Dr Hess in Harbin; they complained that Dr Girsa was made subordinate to Dr Hess...

'Soldiers are like children,' the President smiled in reply.

'Mr President, what is going to happen with our Siberian Army?' someone asked.

'We're leaving them in Russia until the conclusion of the peace conference and the signing of the pact. Then we'll negotiate with the Bolsheviks for their return through Central Russia.'

All of us were of a different mind, but we didn't dare say so to the President's face.

'How are your finances?'

'Thank you, Mr President, we have all we need,' we responded nobly, as never before.

But how we would respond to such a question in the future, only time would tell. Perhaps we would answer it differently, but the question won't be posed...

Many people told me: 'You, Jáno, are going to be needed in Slovakia.'

At the time there was no bread to be had even in Prague, nor coffee; it was all Lenten fare with lentils, peas, no meat.

'So I'm off,' I said. 'There's a lot of you, and not much bread here.'

POEMS

from Zo zajatia [From Captivity]

WHAT CAN I GIVE TO YOU?

What can I give to you, my dear?
The king's seal's stamped on all my gear.

It's on my cap of greyish-green
along with 'Regiment Fifteen.'

On my shirts and on my tunics:
numbers and *K-und-K* runics.

It's even on my puttees, Love,
and on my boots, and on each glove,

on pack, on linen of each sort,
on trousers (which are somewhat short)

on winter-weave and underwear
(really, they've even stamped it there)

my cartridge-box, buttons, mess-tin,
each bag and pouch, needle and pin,

belt, rifle, bayonet; above
my heart — they'd like to stamp my love!

my mind, my will, my hopes and fears
and all my stolen youthful years.

I've left with nothing of my own:
where his lists, is my spirit blown,

with all that can be humped or worn
I'm whipped into a lead hail-storm.

JANKO JESENSKÝ

What can I give to you, my dear?
The King's seal's stamped on all my gear.

RUSSIA

They would have liked to spit right in my face.
Prodded by bayonets, my both wrists cut
by tight handcuffs, into a dark, wet place
they thrust me, and slammed the cast-iron door shut.

Covered in curses, from the daylight banned,
all that I hold sacred they'd vilify,
because I yearned for You, broad Russian land
as I yearn for the blue and open sky.

Then, my feet trod your dusty roads, it's true;
passing through mountains, woods of birch and larch,
with madly beating heart I rushed to You,
my fetters burst, smashed through the prison bars —
I shall be free!...
                    In a quaint barracks yard,
For you...
            greet me with prison fetters too.

                                    Kharkov, 17 VII 1915

LAND OF PUSHKIN...

Land of Pushkin and Lermontov!
In my cosy room, snug by window
I beheld You in the warm glow
of their words, which stirred me to love.

So I prayed, 'That blessed land trod
by sad Tatyana and Onegin,
the snowy summits of Pechorin,
Vera... O, grant me visit, dear God!'

Well, here I sit, in a brick-walled yard,
with cold flagstones to recline on, dressed
in this soiled Honvéd tunic. Your bards
no longer trill of love confessed
or passions tragic and ill-starred.
Their tongue: the bellows of prison guards.

Kharkov, 18 VII 1915

GO WITH GOD

Hey — 'Go with God,' that was, and not 'Farewell,'
when for the last time we clasped hands

and your face paled — a hanky in the distance
waving me Good Luck on the path to Hell.

No, good luck there'll be none — and our tears fell
helpless, at parting, in empty silence
when all we love was ripped from us by bands
of stupid folk — all but longing eternal...

My thoughts are like a spider's web, unfurled
to catch its prey: one single firefly.
The more it struggles, the more it's tangled, curled
in my heart's prison, where I keep it; I
need its dim flicker on these endless, dry
Russian wastes — to recall our dear, lost world.

Kharkov, 21 VII 1915

JANKO JESENSKÝ

PARTING OF THE WAYS

We've torn the emblem from our caps,
the initialled buttons from our shirts;
the bold state ribbons from our cuffs
lay humbled in the Russian dirt.

The tongues flop sadly from our boots
decaying piece by flimsy piece;
like love to our dear Fatherland
the hobnails hold on yet, at least.

The heels are coming loose, it seems:
they clump and thump with each footfall
like clappers during Lenten Mass
or muffled drum at funeral.

The tobacconist snorts at my change
as if he'd whiffed some filthy smell.
Respect evaporates like mist;
my three stars scatter all to Hell.

As for white rolls and *pirohy* —
where are the snows of yesteryear?
I'll come across such delicacies
only in Villon's verse, I fear.

I smoke *makhorka* — bitter weed!
and sip unsweetened brackish tea.
The wide expanse of Russia holds
no single sugar cube for me.

All that is left is beggar's gruel,
served with the cook's swear words. Perhaps

I'll make a complaint? ...But to whom?
We've torn Franz Joseph from our caps!

Kharkov, 23 VII 1915

30.VII.1909

I

Recalling our anniversary, my heart cries
in pain, my throat constricts, and my eyes grow
misty; I wipe away this flood of woe
but none of the tears I shed ever dries.

I see You, a young girl, before my eyes
waiting with hope upon my train, to throw
in all she has, in hopes that hope will grow
into the blest good fortune of two lives

entwined. Six years ago… Your eyes laugh, clear;
Your face — the only lips I've been so bold
to kiss… your hand slipped in my own — right here!
And love with love along the bright road rolled
into a future bathed in warmth and gold…
The stars — they shine for us! The mountains cheer!

II

The coach-wheels growl. The shaded path glows white;
the left-hand slope slides gently into park,
the right-hand mountain's filled with spruce-woods,
                                                    dark…
Afar the village glitters — candle light

the only lamps to guide our happy flight
along this road of dappled light and stark
shadows, to where the guests gather to mark
our coming, on this joyous wedding night…

which passed... as six full years are vanishing
since that time... full of tears and bitterness
enough... Listen: if you had known all that
which was to come — how I can be a cad,
petty, mean, bringing — more than laughter — sadness,
would you still agree to this your... banishing?

Kharkov, 26 VII 1915

MORNING AND AFTERNOON

Morning and afternoon a spell
my shirt I laundered at the well:
tattered in places, black with grime,
to make sure that the shirt was mine.
The sun beat down as hot as Hell,
the water sloshed, sweat dripped as well;
and since I rinsed it with my tears
it's never been that white in years.
It's white and clean, and now it's dry:
a soft breeze puffs it, with a sigh…

But, black with woe, this soul of mine.
What laundering can make it shine?
Though my heart weeps like pouring rain
It rinses and wrings it in vain.
Futile they rush on like a flood,
leaving behind: mere bleary mud.
If only I could sail that tide
to where one grey-eyed girl abides,
once more those tender hands to see
that washed my filthy shirts for me.

Kharkov, 28 VII 1915

SUPPER

The factory whistle blasts now, to fetch in
The work-day's end; the *plenniki*,[236] like ants
Roil the yard with mess-plates in their hands —
Like hungry beasts for fish-soup from the kitchen.

With famished maws they crouch about the camp;
Among the mob I gulp the thin broth too,
With greed; if not there's nothing left to do
But lay these bones down, light the votive lamp.

My wife — I remember — it was just last year!
Oh how concerned she was with what to fix
For a nice dinner! Nervously she licks
Her lips; I trot out for a mug of beer;
I raise a toast to her first, with a kiss
And sit to table, with no care, no fear...

Kharkov, 28 VII 1915

---

[236] Russian: Captives, prisoners.

THE VISTA SPREADS...

The vista spreads past windows broader, higher.
I gaze upon city and poplar copse;
church abuts church and cross soars next to cross;
everywhere glitters onion-dome and spire.

Nearby a snow-white villa. Smugger, nigher,
a factory. Its chimney fumes aloft
smoke into Heaven, through which falcons toss
their sleek frames after doves against the fire

of sunset. Bloody, burning, the globe rolls
toward the rim, setting the clouds aflame.
The villa glows red, church after church, whole
forests of crosses catching fire, the same
firestorm sweeps roof, yard... At the window frame
I sense something howling deep within my soul.

Kharkov, 29 VII 1915

31.VII.1915

(UPON SELLING MY WEDDING RING)

And now my soul lies bleeding on the sand,
Struck down for the first time in this sad war;
The saddest thing of all: the reason. For
The blow was dealt by my very own hand.

This morning I slipped off the wedding band
You placed there at the altar. Never more
Will it declare to all that this man swore
His faith to you. I sold it for the grand

Sum of a few coins. My dear wife! Will you spare
Me your remorse when I shall see your face
Again, and ring you round in an embrace
Which, stronger than all metal, shall declare
My troth, which even death shall not displace,
Although both of my wretched hands be bare?

Kharkov, 31 VII 1915

JANKO JESENSKÝ

THE LITTLE PICTURE...

The little picture painted on my heart.
From time to time, do you think of it, Dear?
Since time first painted it, a full six years
have passed since when we vowed never to part...

We left the table strewn with bloom and tart,
the joyful chatter, the unfinished beer,
for the outdoors, tempted there by a clear,
mysterious voice only we heard. In the yard

alone, beneath bright stars and spreading trees,
you slipped your hand in mine, and there we vowed,
with faces glowing like pure beams of light
we'd always be together, like that night,
our first, but such was not to be. For now
we know that vows can be shredded by countries.

Kharkov, 31 VII 1915

THE EVENING CHILL

The evening chill spreads even through the barracks.
The dovecote grows still, while some prisoners
mumble some songs from home through their whiskers;
some yowl as though they're screeching to attack.
Among those snoring calmly on their beds
One kicks out — is he dreaming of heroics?
These talk of gruel, and that one speaks of fish...
I think, *if only there were more black bread...*

Then in his heavy boots passes the Russian
turnkey — and all the songs from home go dumb;
the orange disks of fag-ends disappear...

Outside, the breeze sighs, through the poplars hushing;
that little sliver of the moon, bright, clear
now sinks into the clouds, as does the glum
(Russian) song 'not for me, ah, not for me...'[237]

Kharkov, 3 VIII 1915

....

[237] See footnote 212 and 213 in Chapter XIV.

A SIGH

I know, I know that many here will perish.
I know that we must keep them all in mind.
But, God, don't let me die until I find
myself back in the fatherland I cherish

and she, to whom I swore eternal love,
who on my finger slipped her wedding ring,
should one last handful of devotion fling
from brimming heart down on me, from above.

And then let them all gather, everyone, each
of those who love me, in our humble home,
after all my dearest ones a clod have thrown
upon my coffin and its modest wreath.
Light lies the earth upon him who lies near
all those whom during life he held most dear.

Kharkov, 4 VIII 1915

OPEN, GATE...

Open, gate! Hear me! I can't wait
To see instead — another gate.

Ah, to exchange this mud packed hard
for other soil, another yard.

Armed guard, you are dismissed! At ease!
Another guard, other arms, now, please.

Kharkov, 6 VIII 1915

TEA

The scruffy *soldat*[238] from platoon
(Lord, treat him tenderly!)
opens his gummy eyes at dawn
and quickly calls 'Tea!'

He swings his feet down to the floor
and sits there groggy; he
would lay back down, but *yefreitor*'s
already wheeled in tea.

They've sugar-cubes to sip through, rolls
as white as white can be;
they've politics to gripe about
over their morning tea.

A Cossack gallops near, 'Some new
captives have come,' you see —
'The barracks must be readied.' 'Yes,
but first, let's finish tea.'

They've not yet washed, although it's said
a morning bath's healthy;
'Oh, there'll be time enough for that.
First, let's finish our tea.'

All Russia's busy at the brew
as far as eye can see.
It's getting near to dinner time,
but still they're sipping tea.

....

[238] Russian: Soldier, private.

Then, mournful tolls the dinner bell
'Good Lord, not fish, but *shchi*[239]!'
They wave their hands and sit back down
and go on drinking tea.

Tea after borscht, tea after mash,
Oh, life is heavenly!
From early morning till midnight,
Tea, tea, tea, tea, tea, tea.

The 'Tsarist' service is a lark!
God yield 'em generously.
Leave 'em their borscht, leave 'em their mash,
Leave 'em their morning tea.

Kharkov, 9 VIII 1915

....

[239] Russian-style cabbage soup.

JANKO JESENSKÝ

WHEN THE NIGHT FALLS...

When the night falls and all are stilled to rest,
shielding my little candle from the draught,
I pull your letters and your photograph
out of my cartridge box (my treasure chest).

God only knows how many times I read;
God only knows how many times I gaze;
God only knows how many times I raise
this little chapel where, sobbing, I plead

for them to speak with living voice, each line;
for that face to blush warm, draw near with sighs;
for that sweet hand to tremble into mine;
for my soul to drink deep of those blue eyes —
this grateful soul, who now can only pine.

Kharkov, 19 VIII 1915

YULETIDE

A ruined church, the bells down-hurled,
in Hell's throat, cold, God's worship lies.
Darkness, waste. Banished from the skies
the Lord begs alms through a cold world.

The empty board. Our Christmas feast:
tepid salt water in tin bowl.
The fist that sloshes it is cold —
Siberian love. Our sign of peace.

Back home, amid the festive cheer
at table, have they left the place
where I sat at this time last year?
Are they done praying the short grace
and, as they toasted, did a tear
shine for us, who've no holidays?

Beryozovka-za-Baikalom, 24 XII 1915

FOR THE NEW YEAR

Where have you gone? Where have you disappeared,
you love-filled years, ending with kisses, songs,
when with heart dancing through the happy throngs
we wished wife, mother, all: Happy New Year!

Where's your broad smile, amidst the happy feast
ringing in New Year, full of health, and gay?
Years of delight — where are they found today,
your ruddy West, your purple-tinted East?

You have been drowned in blood, stifled in groans,
flooded by tears, consumed like each city
reduced to ash, deafened by cannon booms
thundering forth God's harsh, vengeful decree.
I curse you, New Year, and God's penalty,
and all rulers, from least to Highest throne!

Beryozovka, 1 I 1916

WILL THERE NEVER BE AN END...

Will there never be an end to this?
That hundred-headed, bloody beast
who grows by slaughter, as it feasts
on others' lives and happiness?

When will it be sated at last?
How long until it's fully gorged?
What wit can find the words to urge
it to a strict, enduring fast?

Time drags, although the wheeling year
Brings Easter round again — now, twice
I've spent the bitter season here
waiting for slaughtered peace to rise

again — Vain prattle's all you hear.
O, close your mouths, open your eyes!
Perhaps the beast will disappear!

Voronezh, 21 IV 1916

JANKO JESENSKÝ

WHO SHALL RE-STITCH...

Who shall re-stitch the roads that warring shreds?
Who shall direct our pilgrim feet back home,
where there will be no fists or bayonets
or sadness to squeeze from our hearts a groan?

The shining orb of God's justice now sets,
by man's hot flame of vengeance overgrown;
for no one's found the strength or valour yet
to stem the flood of gore in which we drown.

Liberty, Liberty, O, dearly bought!
Days of repose, and days to swink for bread
our nation shall bestow — for which we've fought.
Emerging from this gory bath blood-red,
we'll show the kings of this world — the whole lot! —
the couch we've joined, where they shall rest their head.

Voronezh, 20 V 1916

TO THE GENERALS

REFLECTIONS

How grand it is — the drums of war,
king, country — all that falderal;
how beautiful it is indeed
as long as you're a general.

The infantrymen rush on, red,
wading through frigid pool and mud.
The general is ruddy too:
it's warm beneath that fur-lined hood.

The battle-storms shatter the oaks,
and once again, the same old story:
the thunder blasts the soldiers' heads;
around the general's shines a glory.

The snow piles on the soldiers' backs
as they lie, to the cold ground pressed;
the general's sheets are white as snow
where he lays his 'tired limbs' to rest.

Upon the rough-hewn, blackened cross
the withered autumn foliage settles.
Meanwhile, the general's bosom blooms
with rows of new, glittering medals.

The general's mounted high on steed,
far to the rear of the reserve groups,
and yet in all the news reports
they say 'The general leads his troops.'

From that rear-end, the general
whips on to war his infantry.

JANKO JESENSKÝ

And when the battle's won, he cries
'It was my splendid victory!'

Only the general can free
us from our fetters and our pain.
But that won't be too soon: he still
drags us along, choker and chain.

It's logical: who's at the head
is snugly set farthest behind.
Away from shrapnel, bomb and shot's
the favourite haunt of the great mind.

How grand it is, the drums, the war,
king, country — ah, how beautiful.
Indeed, it's glorious and great
as long as you're a general.

Kiev, 20 I 1917

BENEATH THE RED BANNER

Once more the scarlet banner flutters, flies,
and is it streams of blood to flow, again,
or towns burnt from the memory of men,
and tears heartbroken that it signifies,

or freedom's dawn that here I see arise…
the frontiers of enslavement to broaden,
the latest in a legion of headsmen —
Hell's lackey, though he comes in gentle guise?

And as on stormy seas loom swelling waves,
so heads on heads multiply in a flood
of anger as they sound their Marseillaise,

beneath that banner scarlet as spilt blood…
I look down — and what is it meets my gaze
but our hymn, and Slavdom, trodden underfoot.

Kiev, 29 II 1917

JANKO JESENSKÝ

RESURRECTION

Let them not speak to me yet of salvation.
Why am I fettered still, and bear the stings
of whip? For love of mother-tongue that sings,
for hatred of the foes throttling my nation,

for shame with which they'd foul my meditations,
for pure words bubbling forth from crystal springs,
for a heart's home to which no grave-mould clings,
for life for centuries, not generations.

The Lord Christ's risen not! No Resurrection!
The Lord Christ's risen not! My vengeance cries.
The Lord Christ's risen not! Tears and dejection...
The Lord Christ's risen not! Suffering and lies.
Nailed to a cross, my humbled nation sighs;
Till they're unpinned — there can be no Redemption.

Kiev, 19 III 1917

ONE PRAYER...

One prayer amongst the suppliant throngs:
to be back home, where we belong!
That God conduct this Slovak band
Safe to our Slovak fatherland.

The clouded eye once more would shine,
the splintered bones once more would bind,
supple would grow the ill-set bone
at the word that we're heading home.
The apathetic to his feet
would spring, the jaded eye would weep
to set out on that winding road
that leads to that distant abode
still hidden from the sight, through glade
and mountain, forest, swelter, shade —
the path that leads to that one gate
at which one person stands, and waits!

At her side, finally, to rest
after ages of bitterness...
after nights sleepless, filled with groans
and longing for that distant home.

Voronezh, 30 III 1917

TO JANISSARY SET A JANISSARY

To janissary — set a janissary.
    Clench tight those eyes of yours that brim with tears;
    set hard your face, however sad and weary;
    stifle your groans with hard, heroic cheers!

Set wolf on wolf — be not like sheep, meek, tame.
    Extend no begging hand — shake a fierce fist!
    Enough sorrow — blaze with a vengeful flame.
    No time for cringing now — threaten! Insist!

He only sees the world who high has soared
    Above the cliffs and summits, on proud wings.
    You want no master? Act then like a lord!
    Only the kingly are treated as kings!

Petrograd, 3 X 1917

ON MY COT

I sit here sunk in gloomy thought
smoking *makhorka* on my cot.
Bitter *makhorka*, bitterly.
Some things I'd much rather not see.

Around the fire some soldiers sit,
smoking *makhorka*, trading wit.
Each young, ruddy-faced, friendly, gay;
each laughs, each has something to say,
each of them is, or so it seems
from the hamlet just 'cross the stream.

And this is why I'm sunk in thought
smoking *makhorka* on my cot.

THROW OFF THOSE RAGS

Shrug those rags off from your bones.
They're only fit for slaves and drones.

Tear away that mark of Cain.
For then you will be free again.

Free as a bird that cuts the air
and not some sheep led… you know where.

That royal seal upon your cap
replace with our tricolour strap:

This ribbon, red and blue and white
will all our injuries requite!

ON THE RUN-DOWN

You're weak and tired, and feel run-down?
You stagger beneath the Magyar crown.

Your thoughts are sluggish, dull as lead?
Tear the king's cap from off your head.

Your heart's as heavy as a stone?
That medal's pierced you to the bone.

You're bent low? Why, upon your back
you lug your own weight in that pack.

Your beggar's legs are numb, unwilling?
It's all that marching, all that drilling.

Your arms hang limply to your boots?
That's what comes of constant salutes.

Look what you've slung there on your shoulder:
that thing can bite, if you be bolder,

and in that cartridge belt there's pills
to cure more than one of your ills

If you would just turn and be done
with your slave-master, with the one

who cares less if you live or die;
who's never cast a caring eye

upon your wounds, your path of thorns,
where sleet chills you and swelter burns,

JANKO JESENSKÝ

who's never suffered hunger, thirst,
who's nothing for the poor but a curse,

strike him! He deserves it like no other,
and we shall greet you like a brother!

GLOSSARY

ADY, Endre (1877–1919). Magyar poet and journalist, influenced by Baudelaire.

ALEKSEYEV, Mikhail Vasilyevich (1857–1918). Tsarist general, who later served in the army of the Provisional Government, and as head of the 'Volunteer Army' fighting the Bolsheviks during the Russian Civil War.

ALEXANDER II (Nikolayevich, 'The Liberator,' 1818–1881). Russian Tsar. His reforms intended to move Russia toward a less authoritarian type of government, modernisation of the economy, and especially his abolishing of serfdom (1861) are behind his nickname 'The Liberator.' Ironically, he was assassinated by leftists.

ANDREYEV, Leonid Nikolayevich (1871–1919). Russian dramatist and prose writer.

ANTONOV-OVSEYENKO, Vladimir Aleksandrovich (1883–1938). Ukrainian Bolshevik. Despite the Treaty of Brest-Litovsk, he remained true to the Bolshevik Party and was instrumental in defeating forces hostile to it in Ukraine. A Soviet emissary to the Spanish Communists during the Spanish Civil War, he was recalled to Russia and executed.

AVKSENTYEV, Nikolai Dmitriyevich (1878–1943). Russian politician, member of the Russian Socialist Revolutionary Party. Arrested by Admiral Kolchak, he subsequently fled Russia for the West, living first in France and later in the United States, where he died.

BALMONT, Konstantin Dmitriyevich (1867–1942). Russian poet, translator of Whitman.

BENCÚR, Gyula Benczúr (1844–1920). Magyar painter of Slovak extraction. A typical naturalist (although his Narcissus is remarkable for its expressive use of expressive tenebristic effects).

BLACK-HUNDREDISTS. In Russian: *Chornaya sotnya*, the 'Black Hundred.' A radical monarchist-nationalist organisation in Tsarist Russia.

BRUSILOV, Alexei Alekseivich (1853–1926). Russian general. Despite his noble family background, he eventually went over to the Bolsheviks and was instrumental in the creation of the Red Army.

BRYUSOV, Valery Yakovlevich (1873–1924). Russian symbolist poet, translator of Verlaine and Poe.

ČERMÁK, Bohumil (1870–1921). Czech politician. President of the Union of Czechoslovak Associations in Russia, founder of the Čechoslovan and one of the founders of the Czechoslovak Legions. After the war, Czechoslovak ambassador to Romania.

ČERVINKA, Jaroslav (1848–1933). Czech legionary general; his son, also named Jaroslav (1885–1985) was a captain in the Legions and later general in the Czechoslovak Army.

CHICHERIN, Grigory Vasilyevich (1872–1936). Soviet commissar for foreign affairs; one of the architects of the Brest-Litovsk Treaty.

CZECHOSLOVAK LEGIONS. Military formations of Czechs and Slovaks fighting alongside Entente powers against the Austro-Hungarian Empire, in hopes that with its fall, their nation would regain its independence. Legions were formed in France and Italy as well as Russia; the Russian legions were mainly formed of Czech and Slovak prisoners of war, like Jesenský. Following the war, they became the core of the army of the newly established Czechoslovak Republic.

DÁVID, Joža (1884–1968). Czech legionnaire, elected later to the Czechoslovak National Assembly.

DAXNER, Igor (1893–1960). Jurist, judge, Czech legionnaire. Following the war, he served in courts in Bratislava and Brno; during the Communist years he continued in his profession, serving the Party.

DIMITRIEV, Radko (1859–1918). Bulgarian general, officer in the Russian Army during the First World War. Executed by the Bolsheviks in a slaughter of Tsarist officers.

DROBNÝ, Ján (1881–1948). Politician of the Slovak People's Party (HSĽS), first Regional President (Krajinský prezident) of the Slovak portions of the Czecho-Slovak Republic, between 1928 and 1929.

DUCHAJ, Ján (1869–1954). Slovak politician of the agrarian party; after the war, a representative in the Czechoslovak National Assembly.

DULA, Matúš (1846–1926). Slovak politician, later one of the signatories of the Martin Declaration (1918) which proclaimed the independence of the Slovak regions from the Hungarian Kingdom and the desire of the Slovaks to enter into a Czecho-Slovak Republic. Although he was the head of the Slovak National Council (an organisation aiming at Slovak autonomy), Dula suspended activities of the Council for the duration of the war — a gesture Jesenský seems to associate here with loyalism and timidity.

DÜRICH, Josef (1847–1927). Czech writer and politician, collaborator of Masaryk, but of a pro-Russian, monarchist orientation; one of the organisers of the Czechoslovak Legions.

DÝMA, Josef (1882–1933). Translator, dramatist, and Czech legionnaire.

FRAŠTÁK. A Trnava regionalism for Hlohovec, the German name of which is Freistadt an der Waag.

FÜLÖP, László (1869–1937). Magyar painter known for his portraits of European nobility, including Queen Elizabeth II (whom he painted when she was seven).

GAJDA, Radola (Rudolf Geidl, 1892–1948). Czechoslovak officer, of Montenegrin background. A Czech legionnaire, who also fought alongside Admiral Kolchak and the Whites in the Russian Civil War against the Red

Army. Following the First World War, he was a general of the Czechoslovak Army.

GALICIA. Polish: *Halicz*. A portion of the former Austrian partition of Poland. Although geographically associated with eastern Poland and the Ukraine, administratively it stretched west past Kraków.

GIRSA, Václav (1875–1954). Czech physician, member of the Union of Czechoslovak Associations in Russia, and one of the moving forces behind the Czechoslovak Legions. After the war, he served as Czechoslovak ambassador to Poland and Yugoslavia. He was a member of the Czech underground during the Nazi occupation of the Czech lands, and although arrested by the Gestapo, survived the war.

GORKY, Maxim (Alexei Maximovich Peshkov, 1868–1936). Soviet Marxist writer, the father of Socialist Realism.

GREGOR, Jozef Gregor Tajovský (Jozef Aloyz Gregor, 1874–1940). Slovak poet and dramatist.

GRISHIN-ALMAZOV, Alexei Nikolayevich (1880–??). Colonel of the Siberian Army during the Russian Civil War, later Military Governor of Odessa.

GUCHKOV, Alexander Ivanovich (1862–1936). Russian statesman, Minister of War in the Provisional Government (March–April 1917), later a proponent of the anti-Bolshevik Whites.

HAASE, Hugo (1863–1919). German socialist parliamentarian, pacifist, one of the architects of the postwar Weimar Republic.

HAŠEK, Jaroslav (1883–1923). Czech writer; most famous for his anti-Austrian humorous novel *Osudy dobrého vojáka Švejka za světové války* [The Adventures of the Brave Soldier Švejk During the World War, 1921–1923], which remained unfinished at this death. Although decorated for bravery by the Austrians, and having joined the Czechoslovak Legions following his capture by the Russians, he later went over to the Communists and served in the Red Army. He conducted propaganda for the Bolsheviks intended to convince Czechoslovak legionnaires to defect to the Soviets. A Czechoslovak military court court-martialled him *in absentia*, and plans were made to arrest him and bring him to justice. For a more detailed discussion of this period in the life of the great writer, along with a collection of his writings from this period, see: Jaroslav Hašek, *The Secret History of my Sojourn in Russia* (London: Glagoslav, 2017). It is more than possible that Jesenský's words concerning his difficulties in 'convincing' or 'counteracting' the activity of a 'Red commissar' refers to him.

'HEJ, SLOVÁCI' — Hey, Slovaks. Also 'Hej, Slované' [Hey, Slavs]. A song of Pan-Slavic tint written in 1834 by Samuel Tomášik, to the tune of 'Dąbrowski's Mazurek,' the Polish national anthem. It served as the national anthem of the Slovak state during its brief autonomy from the Bohemian-Moravian Protectorate under Nazi occupation between 1939 and 1945.

HERZENSTEIN, Mikhail Yakovlevich (1859–1906). Deputy to the Duma, assassinated by anti-Semites despite the fact that he was a convert to Christianity. The Russian Duma was a parliamentary organisation conceded by the Tsar under the pressure of the 1905 revolutions at home, and the devastating Russo-Japanese war abroad.

The Decembrists were unsuccessful Russian revolutionaries, mainly military men, in the early nineteenth century.

HODŽA, Milan (1878–1944). Slovak writer and politician, proponent of a federative republic of Central European States. He served as Prime Minister of Czechoslovakia from 1935 to 1938.

HOLLÓSY, Simon (1857–1916). Magyar realist painter, whose works bleed into a Monet type of impressionism (*Haystacks, After Harvest*); the 'school' spoken of is probably the Nagybánya Artists' Colony, although he also ran a private academy in Munich.

HORNÉ JASENO (z Horného Jasena). The noble title of the clan to which Jesenský's family belongs. There are three lines; Jesenský belonged to the Jesenský-Gašparé branch.

HOUDEK, Otomar (Otomár, 1882–1960). Brother of Fedor Houdek (1877–1953). Czechoslovak politician. His brother Zdenko (1893–1966) is also mentioned by Jesenský.

HUNČIK, Štefan (1873–1963). Slovak tinker and businessman; he founded the largest tin factory in the world. Imrich Krutošík was his partner.

HUSSITE and TABORITE. A reference to the followers of early fifteenth-century Church reformer Jan Hus (c. 1370–1415). Among other things, Hus called for a moral reform of the clergy and preaching in the language of the people (Czech); he was put to death as a heretic at the Council of Constance. The Hussite reform was widely adopted by the Czech people, and Hus became a national rallying point after his death. Military struggles developed against a religious and quasi-nationalistic background; the Hussite forces, most famously led by Jan Žižka (1360–1424), were known as Taborites from their christening of their camps after Mount Tabor. This period in Czech history came to a conclusive end at the Battle of Bílá Hora, near Prague, in 1620. The defeat of the Hussite Czechs by the Habsburg Catholics subsequently led to the Czech lands being subsumed by the Austrian Empire, in which they were to remain until the end of the First World War. For many, Hus and the Hussites are national heroes, and Masaryk frequently invoked them as rallying cries for his independence movement.

IZMAILOV, Alexander Alexeyevich (1873–1921). Poet and critic; his *Literary Olympus* is a collection of essays.

JACCHIA, Pierro (Piero). According to the University of Barcelona's International Brigade files, he was born in Trieste in 1883 and died at the rank of major of the Garibaldi Brigade (Brigada XII) in the Spanish Civil War in 1937. As profession, 'poet' is listed.

JANČEK, Ján (1881–1933). Slovak politician, for a while based in the U.S., a signatory of the Pittsburgh Accord.

JANÍK, Ján (1872–1951). Slovak politician. After the war, a senator in the Czechoslovak National Assembly.

JAROŠ. As Jesenský does not mention the first name of 'brother' Jaroš, this could refer to the lawyer Josef Jaroš (1879–1942) or the military officer Jiří Jaroš (1896–1943) both of whom were in Russia at the time.

JESENSKÝ, Fedor (1877–1958). Banker, politician, Slovak cultural activist. Technical translator. Brother of Janko Jesenský.

JESENSKÝ, Vladimír Milan Gustáv (1879–1960). Banker, politician, Slovak cultural activist. Brother of Janko Jesenský.

KADLEC, Eduard (1880–1961). Czechoslovak legionnaire; one of the most successful legionary officers during the Anabasis; wounded at the battle of Bakhmach. He ended his career in the Czechoslovak Army at the rank of general.

KÁROLYI, Mihály (1875–1955). Hungarian politician, Prime Minister and, later, President of the First Hungarian Republic (1918–1919).

'Kde domov môj,' in Czech: 'Kde domov můj' [Where is my homeland?]. The Czech national anthem (also the Czechoslovak National Anthem). Written in 1834 by Czech dramatist Josef Kajetán Tyl to music by František Škroup.

'Kdo za pravdu horí.' In Czech: 'Kdo za pravdu hoří' [Whoever Burns for the Truth]. A Protestant religious hymn in reference to Jan Hus; words by Karol Kuzmány (1848), set to music by Štefan Fajnor.

KERENSKY, Alexander Fyodorovich (1881–1970). President of the Russian Republic following the abdication of the Tsar. He held this position from 14 September 1917 until 7 November of the same year, when the Provisional Government was overthrown by Lenin and the

Bolsheviks, ushering in the seventy-odd year one-party rule of the Communists in Russia.

KHVOSTOV, Alexei Nikolayevich (1872–1918). Russian conservative politician, Minister of the Interior. He was executed by the Bolsheviks.

KISS, József (1843–1921). Magyar poet and journalist.

KOGAN, P.S. (died 1932). Russian writer; the book mentioned here is entitled *Literary Essays*.

KOLCHAK, Alexander Vasilyevich (1874–1920). Russian admiral, head of the Siberian government and Russian military forces fighting against the Red Army in the Russian Civil War. Handed over to the Russian Socialists by the Czechoslovak Legions, these in turn handed him over to the Bolsheviks. He was executed by firing squad.

KOLLÁR, Ján (1793–1852). Czechoslovak poet and writer of the early nineteenth century; one of the moving spirits behind both the 'national revival' of Slavonic culture in the Austro-Hungarian empire and the 'Czechoslavak' tendency. To such an extent this latter, that unlike other Slovaks (Štúr, Hollý), he proposed, not the separation of Czech and Slovak into two distinct languages, but the codification of both in one 'Czechoslovak' language. His most famous work is *Slávy dcera* [The Daughter of Sláva], a long sonnet cycle devoted to Pan-Slavism, in which his contemporary Slavs are judged according to their devotion to the Slavonic ideal.

KOLTSOV, Alexei Vasilyevich (1809–1842). Russian poet from Voronezh.

KORNILOV, Lavr Georgiyevich (1870–1918). Russian general, accused of attempting a *coup d'état* against Kerensky's Provisional Government, when actually he was trying to strengthen it. He later died in battle against the Bolsheviks during the Russian Civil War.

KOUTŇÁK, Josef (1890–1961). Czechoslovak legionnaire, later Brigadier General in the Czechoslovak Army.

KRÁL, Bartloměj (1882–1942). Czech politician; member of the National Assembly; murdered by the Germans in Auschwitz.

KRAMÁŘ, Karel (1860–1937). Lawyer, Czechoslovak politician. A proponent of a Slavic federation of nations, later president of the independent National Assembly.

KUDELA, Josef (1886–1942). Czech classicist and writer; supporter of Masaryk rather than Dürich during Russian captivity and the creation of the Czechoslovak Legions; he became head of the information and educational service of the Legions. A member of the Czech underground during the Nazi occupation of the country, he was arrested and transported to the German concentration camp Auschwitz, where he died.

KVAČALA, Ján Radomil (1862–1934). Slovak Protestant minister, Slavist, and pedagogue.

MAKOVICKÝ, Dušan, Jr. Son of Dušan Makovický Sr., (1866–1921), Slovak physician and translator of Tolstoy, whom he served as private physician between the years 1904 and 1910. His two volume *Jasnopoľanské zápisky* [Notes from Yasnaya Polyana, 1922–1923] document his years with the Russian writer.

MÁRK, Lajos (1867–1942). Magyar painter, a student of Hollósy's at Munich, and his paintings, which waver between the naturalism of his *Elegant Lady in a Jacobean Chair* and the more impressionistic, dream-like *Birthday*, testify to this fact. His paintings of women are often coquettish, but rarely daring; his models often pose with bared shoulders.

MARKOVIČ, Ivan (1888–1944). Slovak politician and journalist, and one of Masaryk's closest collaborators in the Czechoslovak idea in Russia.

MASARYK, Tomáš Garrigue (1850–1937). Czech philosopher and historian, professor, politician, architect of the independent Czechoslovak Republic, of which he served as first president from 1918 until his death in 1937.

MAXA, Prokop (1883–1961). Czechoslovak diplomat; collaborator of Masaryk's in Petrograd, one of the organisers of the Czechoslovak Legions. For his anti-Bolshevik attitude, he was imprisoned for a time by the Soviets.

MEDEK, Rudolf (1890–1940). Czechoslovak writer and legionnaire; editor of the *Československý voják* [Czechoslovak Warrior] newspaper in Russia.

MEREZHKOVSKY, Dmitry Sergeyevich (1866–1941). Russian poet and religious thinker.

MILYUKOV, Pavel Nikolayevich (1859–1943). Foreign Minister of the Russian Provisional Government for two months in the spring of 1917. He was opposed to Russia withdrawing from the war.

MIRBACH, Wilhelm von (1871–1918). German diplomat, ambassador to Russia, one of the architects of the Treaty of Brest-Litovsk. Assassinated in Moscow by Russian revolutionaries opposed to the separate peace.

MIŠKÓCI, Matej (1886–1952). Slovak educator, Czechoslovak legionnaire.

MURAVYOV, General Mikhail Artemyevich (1880–1918). Following the revolution, he was originally a Red Army officer, although he later switched sides to fight against the Bolsheviks. Captured by them, he was killed resisting arrest. In the context of the Czechoslovak anabasis, Muravyov fought against the Czechoslovak Legions as they pushed west to Vladivostok against the wishes of the Soviets.

NĚMEČEK, Zdeněk (1894–1957). Multilingual Czech dramatist and writer; following the First World War, a Czechoslovak diplomat (for example, in Spain); during the Second World War he fought in the Czech underground; following the Second World War he was a diplomat in Denmark, whence he emigrated to Canada after the Communist takeover of his homeland in 1948.

NEMIROVICH-DANCHENKO, Vladimir Ivanovich (1858–1943). Russian playwright and theatrical director, colleague of Stanislavsky.

NIKITIN, Ivan Savich (1824–1861). Russian poet, who spent his entire life in Voronezh.

ORÍŠEK, Martin (1887–1966). Slovak agrarian politician, elected to the National Assembly after the war; Czechoslovak legionnaire.

ORSZÁGOVCI. An old Slovak noble family.

PANKHURST, Emmeline (1858–1928). British political activist and leading light of the suffragette movement. Originally of liberal views, she travelled to Russia to encourage the Russian people and Provisional Government to remain in the fight against the Central Powers. Her time spent in Russia opened her eyes to the dangers of Communism, and she returned to Great Britain a conservative.

PATEJDL, Josef (1878–1940). Lawyer, Czechoslovak legionnaire, head of the Czechoslovak Legionnaire Association after the war, and a representative to the National Assembly. He was murdered in Dachau.

PAULÍNY. Perhaps a member of a rather prominent Slovak (and Magyar) family. However, Jesenský does not provide us with a first name.

PAVLŮ, Bohdan (1883–1938). Journalist, Czech legionnaire; following the establishment of the Czechoslovak Republic, he served as a diplomat in Bulgaria, Denmark, and the USSR.

PIETOR, Ambro (1843–1906). Slovak journalist and national activist. At one time he was imprisoned for his defence of Slovak cultural rights.

POLÁK, František (1889–1971). Czech legionnaire, lawyer, Communist, but anti-Soviet. Arrested twice (in 1939 and 1942) and imprisoned by the Soviets, after the Second World War he emigrated to the West. Author of several eyewitness accounts of forced labour and the Gulag.

PROTOPOPOV, Alexander Dmitriyevich (1866–1918). Minister of the Interior in the Provisional Government. He was executed by the Cheka.

PRZEMYŚL. The siege of the Galician city of Przemyśl (in eastern Poland) lasted for 133 days, from 16 September 1914, until the Austro-Hungarian garrison surrendered to the Russians on 22 March 1915 — making it the longest siege of the First World War.

RENNENKAMPF, Paul von (1854–1918). Baltic German officer, who served in the Tsarist Russian Cavalry, in both the Russo-Japanese and First World Wars. He was later executed by the Bolsheviks.

RUPPELT, Miloš (1881–1943). Slovak violinist, composer, orchestral director, and literary translator.

SEMYONOV, Grigory Mikhailovich (1890–1946). Ataman of the Baikal Cossacks. He fought against the Red Army during the Russian Civil War. Hunted down by the Russians in Manchuria after World War Two, he was executed by them.

SHCHERBACHEV, Dmitri Grigoryevich (1857–1832). Russian general. Later, he fought on the side of the Whites during the Russian Civil War.

ŠTEFÁNIK, Milan Rastislav (1880–1919). Slovak scientist, aviator, General of the French Army, collaborator with Masaryk in the organisation of the Czechoslovak National Council. Before his death, he served as Minister of War in Masaryk's government. He died in an air accident. Like Masaryk among the Czechs, he is venerated among the Slovaks as one of the prime architects of the independent Czechoslovak Republic.

ŠTÚR, Ľudovit (1815–1856). Slovak romantic poet and national activist; Pan-Slavist. A collection of his writings is available from Glagoslav.

STÜRMER, Boris Vladimirovich (1848–1917). Russian Prime Minister, Minister of Internal Affairs and Foreign Minister, all in 1916. He died in prison of uraemia.

ŠVIHOVSKÝ, Věnceslav (1875–1957). Owner of the Slovenská printery in Kiev, founder and publisher of the *Čechoslovan*, which appeared in Kiev as the only Czech-language paper in Russia since 1911.

SYROVÝ, Jan (1888–1970). Czech general during the legionary anabasis in Russia. He remained in the army following the war, and was part of the government during the Munich crisis. Persecuted by the Communists after the Second World War.

TABORITE. See Hussite.

TROTSKY, Lev Davidovich (Bronstein, 1879–1940). Ukrainian Communist and member of Lenin's inner circle. Exiled by Stalin following Lenin's death, he was eventually assassinated by an agent of Stalin's in Mexico City.

VAJANSKÝ, Svetozár Miloslav Hurban (pen name Vajanský, 1847–1916). Slovak writer, journalist and national activist. He travelled to Russia several times, where he sought a teaching position.

VONDRÁK, Václav (1859–1925). Czech Slavist, philologist and translator, specialising in Old Church Slavonic.

YOUNG SLOVAKS (*Mladoslováci*). As the name suggests, the term is used to indicate a group of Slovak writers of the generation younger than Ján Kollár and other proponents of a 'Czechoslovak' language, who strived for the codification of Slovak as a separate tongue. Ľudovít Štúr, Michal Hodža, and Josef Hurban, all born in the second decade of the nineteenth century, and all Protestants (which is significant, given the fact that the Czech language was used for centuries in Slovak Protestant worship), are sometimes thus referred to. your ills.

BIBLIOGRAPHY

SOURCE TEXTS:

JESENSKÝ, Janko. *Cestou k slobode, 1914–1918*. Turčiansky svätý Martin: Matica Slovenská, 1933.

JESENSKÝ, Janko. *Zo zajatia. Básne Janka Jesenského*. Pittsburgh: Slovenská Líga v Amerike, 1918.

SECONDARY SOURCES:

ANONYMOUS. 'Banská Štiavnica – Kalvária,' <https://kriz.epocha.sk/banska-stiavnica-kalvaria> [accessed 4 December 2021].

BABEJOVÁ, Eleonóra. *Fin-de-siècle Pressburg: Conflict and Cultural Coexistence in Bratislava 1897–1914*. New York: Columbia University Press, 2003.

DUNN, Seamus and FRASER, T.G. (Eds.). *Europe and Ethnicity: The First World War and Contemporary Ethnic Conflict*. London: Routledge, 2005.

FLORYAN, Władysław. (Ed.). *Dzieje Literatur Europejskich*, Vol. 3, Issue 1. Warsaw: PWN, 1989.

FROMKIN, David. *Europe's Last Summer: Who Started the Great War in 1917?* New York: Vintage, 2007.

GALANDAUER, Jan. *Chrám bez boha nad Prahou. Památník na Vítkově.* Prague: Havran, 2014.

GLOS, Blanka Ševčík and GLOS, George E. *Czechoslovak Troops in Russia and Siberia during the First World War.* New York: Vantage, 2000.

HAŠEK, Jaroslav. *The Secret History of my Sojourn in Russia.* London: Glagoslav, 2017.

HAŠEK, Jaroslav. *Osudy dobrého vojáka Švejka za světové války.* Prague: Baronet, 1996.

JOKEŠ, Petr. *Czesi: Przewodnik po historii narodu i państwa.* Kraków: Avalon, 2020.

KEEFE, Eugene K. et al. *Area Handbook for Czechoslovakia.* Washington: U.S. Government Printing Office, 1972.

KRASIŃSKI, Zygmunt. *Dramatic Works.* London: Glagoslav, 2019.

KRČMÉRY, Štefan. 'A Survey of Modern Slovak Literature,' *The Slavonic and East European Review*, Vol. 7, No. 19 (June 1928): 160–170.

LUPAȘ, Ioan. 'The Hungarian Policy of Magyarization,' *Bulletin of the Center for Transylvanian Studies*, Vol. 1, No. 1 (1992).

ODDO, Gilbert L. *Slovakia and its People.* New York: Robert Speller and Sons, 1960.

PIAHANAU, Aliaksandr. 'A Priest at the Front. Jozef Tiso Changing Social Identities in the First World War,' *Revue des études slaves*, Vol. 88, No. 4 (2017): 721–741.

PREISNER, Rio. *Až na konec Česka.* London: Rozmluvy, 1987.

PREISNER, Rio. *Básně.* Prague: Torst, 1997.

ŠPIESZ, Anton. *Ilustrované dejiny Slovenska: na ceste k sebauvedomiu.* Bratislava: Perfekt, 1992.

ŠTÚR, Ľudovít. *Diela.* ed. by Rudolf Chmel. Bratislava: Kalligram/Ústav Slovenskej Literatúry SAV, 2007.

ŠTÚR, Ľudovít. *Slavdom. A Selection of his Writings in Prose and Verse.* London: Glagoslav, 2021.

VALUCHEK, Andrew. '*Demokrati* by Janko Jesenský,' *Books Abroad*, Vol. 11, No. 4 (Autumn, 1937): 500.

VLČEK, Jaroslav. *Dejiny literatúry slovenskej.* Turčiansky sv. Martin: Matica slovenská, 1923.

VRAŽDA, Daniel. 'Z neznámeho vojaka urobili Migaš s Rusmi červenoarmejca,' *Denník N* (9 July 2015), <https://dennikn.sk/182872/z-neznameho-voja-ka-urobili-migas-s-rusmi-cervenoarmejca/> [accessed 4 December 2021].

ABOUT THE AUTHOR

Janko Jesenský (1874–1945). Poet, prose writer, translator and Slovak statesman. Jesenský was the scion of the noble Slovak family Jesenský z Horného Jasena. Like his father, Jen Baltazár Jesenský-Gasparé and brothers Fedor and Vladimír, he was active in the propagation of Slovak culture and language during the difficult years of the Habsburg Empire, when Slovakia was subjected to strong Magyarising pressure. Jesenský is well known as a poet, having published nine collections of verse, including *Zo zajatia* [From Captivity, 1918], which chronicle his four years as a Russian prisoner of war and member of the Czechoslovak Legions, two plays (unpublished in his lifetime) and eleven works in prose, including his memoirs *Cestou k slobode* [On the Road to Freedom, 1933], an important eyewitness account of the First World War, the establishment of the Czechoslovak Legions and the Czechoslovak National Council, the Russian Revolution and subsequent Russian Civil War. His translations from Russian include Alexander Pushkin's masterpiece *Eugene Onegin*. In the newly established First Czechoslovak Republic he served as county governor (*župan*) in Rimavská Sobota and Nitra, and later in the regional-national government in Bratislava, eventually becoming Vice President of the Regional Government for Slovakia. During the Second World War, at the breakup of Czechoslovakia and the establishment of the collaborationist Slovak Republic of Monsignor Tiso, he retired from public life but continued to compose anti-Fascist poetry, much of which was broadcast from the free Czechoslovak radio service in London.

ABOUT THE TRANSLATOR

Charles S. Kraszewski (born 1962) is a poet and translator, creative in both English and Polish. He is the author of three volumes of original verse in English (*Diet of Nails*; *Beast*; *Chanameed*), and two in Polish (*Hallo, Sztokholm*; *Skowycik*). He also authored a satirical novel *Accomplices, You Ask?* (San Francisco: Montag, 2021). He translates from Polish, Czech and Slovak into English, and from English and Spanish into Polish. He is a member of the Union of Polish Writers Abroad (London) and of the Association of Polish Writers (SPP, Kraków). In 2022 he was awarded the Gloria Artis medal (III Class) by the Ministry of Culture of the Republic of Poland. In 2023, he was awarded the ZAiKS prize for Translation into a Foreign Tongue by the Polish Author's Association (ZAiKS).

- *The Time of Women by Elena Chizhova*
- *Andrei Tarkovsky: A Life on the Cross by Lyudmila Boyadzhieva*
- *Sin by Zakhar Prilepin*
- *Hardly Ever Otherwise by Maria Matios*
- *Khatyn by Ales Adamovich*
- *The Lost Button by Irene Rozdobudko*
- *Christened with Crosses by Eduard Kochergin*
- *The Vital Needs of the Dead by Igor Sakhnovsky*
- *The Sarabande of Sara's Band by Larysa Denysenko*
- *A Poet and Bin Laden by Hamid Ismailov*
- *Zo Gaat Dat in Rusland (Dutch Edition) by Maria Konjoekova*
- *Kobzar by Taras Shevchenko*
- *The Stone Bridge by Alexander Terekhov*
- *Moryak by Lee Mandel*
- *King Stakh's Wild Hunt by Uladzimir Karatkevich*
- *The Hawks of Peace by Dmitry Rogozin*
- *Harlequin's Costume by Leonid Yuzefovich*
- *Depeche Mode by Serhii Zhadan*
- *Groot Slem en Andere Verhalen (Dutch Edition) by Leonid Andrejev*
- *METRO 2033 (Dutch Edition) by Dmitry Glukhovsky*
- *METRO 2034 (Dutch Edition) by Dmitry Glukhovsky*
- *A Russian Story by Eugenia Kononenko*
- *Herstories, An Anthology of New Ukrainian Women Prose Writers*
- *The Battle of the Sexes Russian Style by Nadezhda Ptushkina*
- *A Book Without Photographs by Sergey Shargunov*
- *Down Among The Fishes by Natalka Babina*
- *disUNITY by Anatoly Kudryavitsky*
- *Sankya by Zakhar Prilepin*
- *Wolf Messing by Tatiana Lungin*
- *Good Stalin by Victor Erofeyev*
- *Solar Plexus by Rustam Ibragimbekov*
- *Don't Call me a Victim! by Dina Yafasova*
- *Poetin (Dutch Edition) by Chris Hutchins and Alexander Korobko*

More to come . . .

GLAGOSLAV PUBLICATIONS
www.glagoslav.com